Love in a Time of Homeschooling

Love in a Time of Homeschooling

→>-<←

A Mother and Daughter's Uncommon Year

Laura Brodie

HARPER

An Imprint of HarperCollins*Publishers*
www.harpercollins.com

The author would like to thank the editors of *Brain, Child* magazine, where portions of this book first appeared, in slightly different form.

HarperCollins books may be purchased for educational, business, or sales promotional use. For information, please write: Special Markets Department, HarperCollins Publishers, 10 East 53rd Street, New York, NY 10022.

FIRST EDITION

Designed by Leah Carlson-Stanisic

Library of Congress Cataloging-in-Publication Data

Brodie, Laura Fairchild.
Love in a time of homeschooling : a mother and daughter's uncommon year / Laura Brodie. — 1st ed.
    p. cm.
ISBN 978-0-06-170646-2
1. Home schooling—United States—Case studies. 2. Brodie, Laura Fairchild. 3. Brodie, Laura Fairchild—Family. 4. Mothers and daughters—United States. I. Title.
LC40.B76 2010
371.04'20973—dc22

2009025331

---

10 11 12 13 14 ID/RRD 10 9 8 7 6 5 4 3 2 1

To all the parents who, when looking at their children's schooling, have sometimes thought that they could do it better themselves, if only for a little while

And as always, to Julia, with love

Love in a Time of Homeschooling

Prologue

O N A COLD OCTOBER MORNING MY TEN-YEAR-OLD daughter, Julia, sat at our kitchen table and contemplated the Earth's layers. She had been tasked with making a cross section of the planet's interior—core, mantle, and crust—part of the fifth-grade curriculum in Virginia. Now she needed to decide what materials to use for a three-dimensional model.

From my angle at the stove, I saw Julia's eyes wander out the window, across our country road, where the neighbors' horses grazed on a hillside beyond a wooden fence. Another minute and her mind would disappear over that hill, heading north through the Shenandoah Valley. Before that could happen I sat down beside her and called her thoughts back to the project at hand.

"Julia, what do you want to use? Play-Doh?" I imagined concentric rings of clay, balls within balls, cut in half to reveal the Earth's multicolored strata. "Or would you like to cut a Styrofoam ball in half? You could paint the Earth's layers onto the flat center."

Julia shook her head.

"Well, what *do* you want to use?"

"Fruit," she said.

"Fruit?"

Yes, fruit.

From the basket in the center of our kitchen table Julia lifted a kiwi, then took a steak knife and cut it in half. She held the green fruit up to my eyes, and there was a model of the Earth: the white core surrounded by the squishy green mantle, with black seeds like the rocks that float in the Earth's magma, and on the outside, the thin, dry crust, its fuzz like brittle, drought-ridden grass. I felt completely humbled, reminded that all life is connected in repeated patterns, as when one learns that the ratio of water to land on our planet is the same as the ratio of liquid to solid in the human body.

For five minutes Julia and I took turns cutting tectonic plates into the kiwi's surface, carving a drippy Ring of Fire. "Look," she said, "when the plates shift, the mountain ranges form." She squeezed the kiwi, and a ridge of lumpy green flesh emerged on the surface. I couldn't have been more proud if she had painted the *Mona Lisa*. My daughter could see the world within a slice of fruit.

If this had been a typical school project, Julia would have found a way to glue rings of kiwi onto poster board, adding labels and writing a brief report. The poster might have been soggy and smeared by the end, but she probably would have gotten an A. As it was, we peeled the mutilated fruit and ate it. Julia didn't need to carry her work into school; she didn't need to receive a grade, because for that day, that month, that entire year, I was her teacher and our home was her school.

Julia and I had decided that for her fifth-grade year she would take a break from her usual public school routine. We had chosen to stay at home and craft a curriculum that included not only Virginia's standardized essentials, but plenty of subjects her school never covered—like knitting, and speaking a foreign language, and playing the violin. I called this Julia's homeschooling sabbatical, because, as an English professor, I understand the need for intellectual rejuvenation. With five years of public education under her belt, and seven more looming in the future, Julia needed time to do her own research and writing, time to explore the world beyond an elementary school classroom, time to wander and travel and think in ways her school couldn't accommodate.

My friends found our version of homeschooling a strange curiosity. "Why are you doing it?" they asked, knowing that my motivations wouldn't fit the usual home-ed norms. I'm not an overtly religious person appalled by the lack of moral values in the public schools' secular swamp. Nor am I a radical bohemian opposed to the state's authoritarian, assembly-line approach to education. Those are the chief homeschooling stereotypes— caricatures of the two camps that spearheaded home education as a populist movement in the 1970s. These days, homeschooling has expanded beyond its traditional base, reaching into the lives of millions of American families, and appealing even to moderate Moms like me, who don't have the religious or philosophical compulsion to become full-time homeschoolers, but who want to give a special child one good year.

And so, when friends and family asked, "Why are you home-schooling?" my answers varied according to my mood.

"Julia was getting really burnt out in her school routine."

"We wanted to try something different for a year."

"Julia needs a boost before middle school, to renew her interest in learning, and to fill the gaps in her math and English skills."

"I've always thought the public schools are weak on writing, so Julia's going to do a year of writing across the curriculum."

All of these answers, however, were incomplete. To understand how Julia and I came to be home on a Tuesday morning carving tectonic plates into the skin of a kiwi, we must go back five months—back to a spring afternoon in southwest Virginia, when, for one nerve-wracking hour, Julia disappeared.

CHAPTER ONE

⇥Losing Julia⇤

Happiness and homework don't mix.

JULIA

IN APRIL OF 2005, I LOST MY DAUGHTER.

Not for long. Not the permanent loss of death or the nightmare disappearances that leave parents consigned to the third circle of hell. Mine was only one of those hour-long dislocations when a child is not where she is expected to be. Such moments happen every so often in a parent's life, but that does not soften the twist in one's stomach, the surge of unreasoning dread. In those minor disorientations, each parent previews the greater fear, a world in which the child is gone forever. For me, my human brain devolves into a dog mind that can't comprehend a different future, knowing only the present absence.

Children come into our lives so abruptly; nine months of pregnancy cannot prepare us for the startling reality of their presence. And so I sometimes fear that mine will disappear with the same abruptness, God's temporary gift taken back. But on that April afternoon, I should not have worried. Julia was nine years old and we were dawdling at home, and our home is not a threatening place. We live at the edge of a meadow in a rural corner of Virginia, five miles beyond the main street of a small college town. Our backyard rolls downhill to a wide, stony creek that flows past cows, and fields of Queen Anne's Lace, and a light-ning-warped tree that leans at a forty-five-degree angle over the water. A hundred yards beyond that hunchbacked maple, an old barn stands among cedar trees, a gray sentinel that precedes the first layer of foothills at the base of the Blue Ridge Mountains.

One mile west of those mountains stands our two-story farm-house, originally built in 1911 and revisited half a dozen times by half a dozen owners. One owner covered most of the rooms with Laura Ashley wallpaper, miniature flowers and mauve paisley and thin blue stripes, presumably to hide the cracks in the plas-ter. Another painted all the doors and chair rails and eight-inch floorboards with a white semi-gloss, to brighten a house filled with wood: oak floors, a walnut banister, knotty pine kitchen walls. Our family's contribution to this collaborative enterprise has been to demolish the one bathroom and expand it into two, and to sandwich the whole house between a pair of tiled porches, screened and unscreened, with white wicker furniture and carved white railings that brush against dwarf lilacs.

It's all very pretty, very safe. Not a place to worry about a child roaming free. And yet I have been trained to worry—first by the road that stands less than fifteen feet from the side of our house, where walkers glance into my kitchen window and wave at me in my bathrobe. On that country road, pickups race by at fifty miles an hour, accelerating down a straightaway before braking at the sharp left curve beyond our third acre. Four times in the past eighteen years that curve has triumphed over a driver, usually young people who miss the sharp turn and go airborne through our neighbor's wooden fence, sending the horses gal-loping. I once watched from my porch swing as a group of high-schoolers spun out at the curve and carved a half donut into the top of our yard, narrowly missing my husband, John, on his lawn tractor. Deep in headphoned oblivion, John didn't hear the Pontiac lurch to a halt behind him, the unlocked door flung open as a boy tumbled out. The kid jumped to his feet and scrambled back into the car, and John turned in time to see the vehicle screech down the street, and to contemplate the tire tracks clawed into the grass.

No humans have died at that curve in our twenty-year residence, but we have lost a cat and a dog, and when Julia was born, my mother-in-law insisted that we should build a fence, hundreds of white pickets to hold the world's dangers at bay. Or perhaps we should fence in a small area behind the house, furnish it with a swing set, a plastic slide, and a small round sandbox with a turtleback lid? That way Julia would be kept away from the road and the creek's deepest pools. But I liked the open yard and the accessibility of water, and I had no intention of leaving my child in an overgrown playpen that any intelligent four-year-old could easily escape. I intended to watch my daughter every minute of every hour, to keep her safe from the road, the creek, the precipice at the top of the stairs. From kitchen knives and bathroom cleansers and medicine cabinets and electric sockets. What is a mother's purpose except to serve as a pair of eyes, to observe and guide and occasionally swoop down and whisk a child away from a rocky ledge or a growling dog?

My mother-in-law, who raised six children, was right about one thing. A mother cannot always watch. Sometimes a woman has to pee. Sometimes she must help one child while another wanders out of reach. By 2001, I had three daughters—Julia, six; Rachel, four; and Kathryn, two—and my world was no longer within my control.

Going inside one afternoon to answer the telephone, I was confident that I could see my girls from the kitchen window. There they were, catching caterpillars. There they were, plucking grass. There they were, digging in the dirt with large kitchen spoons. And then, in less time than it takes to write a note on a calendar, they were gone. All that remained were the dirty spoons lying in the grass. I dropped the phone and ran outside, instinctively bolting for the road, and there they were, crouched in the ditch on the other side. Kathryn and Rachel, seeing my alarmed expression, stood up, extended their pudgy arms, and prepared to run back to me, oblivious to the car approaching from the right, coming fast, the driver blind to the little children in their lowered hiding place.

"Don't move!" I yelled to my girls. "STAY WHERE YOU ARE!"

Thank God for Rachel, my pragmatic middle child, who held her little sister back from the asphalt. They waited while the car sliced through the air between us, and when the danger had passed, I crossed the road and looked down at them. I wondered if they were crouched in this ditch to hide from me, or if they had paused there in awe at their accomplishment, fearful that they could never cross back.

"Why did you cross the road?" I asked, half expecting the old punch line: "To get to the other side."

Rachel pointed her finger. "Julia brought us."

I looked at my eldest daughter, with her wolfish blue eyes, her wavy brown hair in perpetual tangles, and I knew that I should expect no explanations, no logic or contrition. Here was a child who, sensing the one moment when she was not under observation, had instinctively done the thing that was most forbidden. She sought out the place of greatest danger and did not go alone, but took her little sisters with her.

"We crossed the road," she said, and I couldn't tell if there was triumph in her voice or bare matter-of-factness. Perhaps she meant to show me that it was all right. She could cross the road safely, and safely lead others. But I thought only of Hardy's *Jude the Obscure*, the inscrutable Father Time, a tragic, deadly child, *Done because we are too menny.*

"You must *never* come to the road without an adult," I said. "Not until you are much older. You all could have *died*." And then, trying to penetrate those six blue eyes—"*Remember the cat.*"

With that image of bloody warning impressed on their minds, I solemnly led my little brood across the street, into the house, up the stairs, and into the bedroom that all three of them shared. "You will stay here until dinner because I cannot trust you outside. I need to know that I can trust you." And I closed their door.

Some parents will find this punishment absurdly mild. Some parents would spank, smack, hit, whip, paddle, or swat—whatever the family euphemism for corporal punishment. My husband grew up in fear of his father's belt, and dreading wooden rulers in the clenched hands of aging nuns. But I was raised by a liberal mother who did not believe in spanking, who preferred the power of words, and who was blessed with mild-mannered, obedient children.

Julia has never been mild-mannered or obedient. Kind, yes, and sensitive and lovely and bright, but from her toddler years forward she was always the sort of child to run twenty yards ahead, toward intersections and escalators and cliff edges. I am the harried mother you've seen on the sidewalk, with a newborn in one arm and a toddler at her side, yelling, "No!" or "Stop!" or "Come back here *right now!*" to the gleeful third child who has wandered out of orbit, escaping the parent's gravitational pull. I am the mother with the edge of madness in her voice, and I have come to view the entire world as an elaborate deathtrap. Which explains why, on that April afternoon in 2005, when Julia went missing for one hour, I worried.

She had been sitting on the living room floor pressing tiny Legos into dragon bodies with colorful wings and tails. And so it was a surprise to call her name from the kitchen and get no reply. Inside the living room I found the four-inch dragons scattered across the carpet. I walked upstairs and called again, moving from room to room, checking beds and bathrooms. Rachel and Kathryn, immersed in a world of Polly Pockets, had not seen her. Outside, on our screened porch, I shouted Julia's name to the east and west. Sometimes when our neighbor's cows graze in a distant field, leaving the front meadow empty and inviting, Julia climbs between the barbed wire and follows the creek a hundred yards downstream, where a waterfall drops six feet into a wide, shallow pool. I stared into the field and tried to see a girl's head poking above the water-carved gulley, but nothing moved that afternoon except a pair of mallards and a great blue heron, tiptoeing in the grass.

Up at the road, I saw a car disappear behind the curve and I remembered Samantha Runnion, that beautiful five-year-old in California, who, with her long curly brown hair, looked a lot like Julia. One moment she was playing safely in her yard, and the next she had disappeared into a murderer's car. There could be murderers, I thought, driving on our road. They might be the ones responsible for the trash that I often find on the fringes of our property. People who throw beer cans from the windows of their cars might also be the type to open their doors and coax a child inside. But Julia had been trained to be suspicious of strangers, to avoid stopped cars, and to scream and bite and kick and claw if any unknown person were to take her arm.

I doubted that Julia had disappeared at the road. It was more likely that she was hidden somewhere along the creek, scooping crayfish and minnows with my kitchen strainers. Julia has always been a child of nature, the sort who prefers animals to human beings. As a preschooler, she liked to stand under pine trees and serenade the mockingbirds, or sing lullabies to the house wrens that built their summer nests in the nooks of our carport. She also liked to run among flocks of starlings in our grass, as if they were a dark puddle to be stomped, raising a cloud of splashing wings.

During those preschool years, I called Julia my feral child because of her resistance to clothing and hairbrushes. Once, when I arrived at her Montessori classroom and told her that she must put away her beadwork, finished or not, she growled at me—a low, menacing animal growl. I responded as any mother would: by growling back.

In the third grade a little friend suggested to Julia that she might have an easier time getting along with the other children if she did not so often crawl on the floor, pretending to be a cat. But even at age ten, hiking through the Rockies, she twice stopped to howl into the forest, and both times I hushed her, wondering what kindred beasts she might call down from the mountains.

Back in our yard, on that April afternoon, I checked the rocky alcove where the spring that provides our drinking water drains into a little marsh full of watercress and mint. There, Julia liked to sit on the concrete slab and scoop up tiny salamanders that wiggled across her palm and plopped back into the water, external gills flared like a dinosaur's frill. Finding that spot empty, I searched the deepest stretch of our creek, overgrown by a canopy of weed trees. Beneath those shadows, water slides down a mossy rock into a narrow miniature canyon before widening into a channel four feet deep, home to water snakes and the occasional muskrat.

Julia was not at the creek, nor was she walking the "shining path," a trail that bisects our one unmown acre. Ten years ago John and I decided that two acres were the limit of our mowing. We let our third acre grow wild in an arboreal experiment, filled with blackberry bushes and sumac trees and sheltered forts of cedar, where deer sleep on winter nights. Julia can point out the traces of their curled bodies.

On that April afternoon, she was not there. Back inside the house I telephoned our neighbors, a pair of elderly widows who live at the end of the shining path and who keep their door perpetually open to our girls. No, Julia had not stopped by for a visit. They would call if she appeared.

Having done all that I could, and with no real reason to believe she was in danger, I resigned myself to the fact that a fourth-grader is old enough to wander alone outside for a little while, and I lay down in my bedroom and tried to concentrate on a paperback novel. I would give Julia another fifteen minutes before I started to panic.

After ten I heard a small rustling in the closet. Probably a mouse, I thought. In the winter they occasionally scratch their noisy way through our walls and poke twitching heads from the heating vents. But the next sound was louder, heavy and shifting, too large to be a rodent. I opened the shuttered doors and found Julia hiding beneath the dresses and slacks.

Now, I understand the appeal of closets, their liminal nature and womblike darkness, the primitive call of the animal den, full of smells and secrecy and the promise of dress-up clothes. My grandmother's closets were otherworldly to my child-mind: large dark rooms lined in mahogany, with seersucker suits and lace dresses and light bulb cords too high to reach. Only the bravest hide-and-seek player would dare go inside and close the door.

My own closet, however, is not so intriguing. It has no whiff of Narnia, no fur coats. It is not one of these enormous affairs mandated in today's McMansions, carpeted havens with skylights and recessed bulbs, the size of a home office or a small bedroom, where a child could disappear for several placid hours, silent within a carousel of dresses.

My closet is a disgrace. Two feet deep and five feet wide, with wooden shuttered doors and a hard pine floor piled with old sneakers and broken sandals and wrinkled pumps untouched for a decade. Beneath the sedimentary layers of dirty laundry, one can excavate lost library books, old greeting cards, crayons, earplugs, and scraps of paper that once seemed worth keeping. Above the racks of sloppily hangered blouses, the sweaters are not folded tight on their rows of shelves, but lie sprawled in loose piles, sleeves dangling.

It is a closet fit for Sarah Sylvia Cynthia Stout. My yearly attempt to clean it feels like Hercules tackling the Augean stables, except that I never finish my task. Nevertheless, there, in that unsightly mess, Julia had chosen to sit for almost an hour, crouched silent on a pile of old shoeboxes.

"Didn't you hear me calling?" I asked.

Yes, she nodded.

"Why have you been hiding there?"

"I heard you say that it was time for me to do my homework."

Ah, yes. I should have remembered. Just before her disappearance I had said that Julia must finish her homework before dinner, and rather than taking out pencil and paper, she had crawled into this dark space and closed the door. That, to me, was a sign.

Every child has a misery quotient, the line at which mere whining turns into real unhappiness. Some children are born miserable, their glass always half empty; some are made miserable by the adult world. And there's nothing like homework to squash a child's joy. In Julia's mind, homework was the shadow haunting every day, the shapeless dread that grew larger with each passing year.

I don't recall having so much homework when I was a fourth grader. Today's public schools seem to have responded to the endless cry for "*achievement!*" by adding more worksheets to the homework pile. Math worksheets, grammar worksheets, bland spelling exercises. I wouldn't mind the work if it seemed more interesting—if Julia were asked to try a fun science experiment, or to walk outside and compose a poem about the sounds in her yard. What rankles is the monotony of colorless paper, the columns of equations and fill-in-the-blank history.

For Julia, homework had always been a monumental burden. Sometimes I could persuade her to complete the work by reiterating our house rules: she could not have her daily hour of screen time (TV, DVD, or computer) until her homework was finished and she had practiced her violin. But often I had to resort to cajoling and threats, nagging the poor creature all the way to the kitchen table, and hovering for the duration, saying, "That's good. Keep going." Without constant prodding Julia's mind tended to wander out the window, into the meadow, "away down the valley, a hundred miles or more." A twenty-minute math assignment could take two hours, with Julia staring into the boundless space between each fraction.

On that April afternoon Julia's homework was surprisingly minimal. Rather than her usual hour of assignments, which might have dragged on for twice that long, the day's task barely filled ten minutes. She had spent an hour of hiding to avoid ten minutes of schoolwork, and the thought of that warped equation broke my heart.

Many parents know the ache of raising a child who doesn't fit smoothly into a traditional school routine; all children learn in different ways, and for some, the rituals of education are a daily struggle. Although Julia's younger sisters could navigate social and academic waters with relative ease, for Julia, there were in-

dications even from her toddler years that she would not conform easily to a highly structured environment. At every stage
of development she had chafed, not only against her homework,
but also against the world of classrooms and desks so alien to
her nature. In retrospect, I see these moments of discomfort as
signposts on a road to homeschooling, a road traveled by many
families who have children with special needs, special gifts, special personalities—families who look at the mismatch between
school and child and ask themselves year after year: Can't we do
better than this?

There are countless reasons why parents homeschool—stories
of unhappy children or ambitious parents, bad schools or persis-
tent bullies, religious fundamentalists or nerdy academics—and
these narratives, with their varied characters, are as compelling
as the homeschooling itself. They reveal the vast complexities
of education in today's America. On that April day, however, I
wasn't thinking about all of that. I didn't assume that I was headed
toward homeschooling. I only knew that something about my
daughter's education was going wrong, and I must try to fix it. My
once-joyful child now felt so oppressed by her schoolwork that she
wanted to retreat into dark spaces. This couldn't continue.

Over the next few days I pondered Julia's education up until
that moment. Awake at night, staring into my bedroom's shadows, I recalled scenes from preschool, kindergarten, and third
grade. Some of the scenes were happy, but others were tinged
with conflict and stress. These memories struck me as symptoms that might yield a diagnosis. I told myself that if I could sift
through these glimpses from the past, I might be able to choose
the right direction for the future.

And so, in the days to come, I pieced together the narrative of
Julia's education, beginning at a little Montessori school beside a
rippling creek.

CHAPTER TWO

➤➤Julia and the Schools◀◀

*It's hard to focus when you look outside and see
that the branches of trees are forming eyelids.*

JULIA

J ULIA WAS TWO YEARS OLD WHEN SHE ENTERED WOODS
Creek Montessori—a sweet, small place situated in an old
brick house on a half-acre of land surrounded by a buffer of
trees. In front of the school ran a wide stream and jogging trail,
where the children took regular nature walks. A stroll to the left
led through a tunnel above shaded pools that housed one large
snapping turtle and several eight-inch fish. Beyond that, the trail
opened onto a wooded enclave behind student apartments, and
there, for two years, an anonymous undergraduate maintained
a small fairy house. A three-inch-high, round wooden door was
attached with hinges to the hollowed-out base of a tree, and when
the children kneeled to open it, they found a little statue inside,
sometimes a fairy, once a gnome, most often a red, round-bellied
Buddha. The children scribbled notes for the fairy/Buddha, and
left gifts of flowers, drawings, beads, and tiny plastic furniture.
The anonymous student responded with messages of gratitude
and friendship, until, one morning, the children found the door
ripped from its hinges and the occupant gone. A note explained

that some vicious human troll had taken everything, and the fairy had gone into hiding.

Fortunately another good spirit came to watch over the children, a reddish brown screech owl perched in a squirrel's nook, high in a tree that stood in the middle of the school's small parking lot. For over a year that sleepy bird faced the Montessori entrance, mostly drowsing, sometimes opening one eyelid at a time. The school's largely Quaker staff dubbed him "Friend Owl."

I never felt guilty about sending my firstborn away to that preschool. Some people imagine homeschooling moms as ultra-clingy zealots who refuse to relinquish control of their children, but that's not me. By the time Julia was two, I was eager to set her loose for a few hours each day. I had another baby to tend, six-month-old Rachel, and I did not plan to become a full-time stay-at-home mom. I was busy toting Rachel around the campus of the Virginia Military Institute, where John taught band, and where I was contracted to write a book about the college's transition to coeducation. Every day, I carried Rachel to meetings with generals, colonels, and captains, placing her on the floor in her car seat, which I rocked with the ball of my foot while I took notes at the table. I figured that if these military men were serious about making their culture female-friendly, they might as well get used to having a baby in the boardroom.

Meanwhile, Julia was in good hands at the Montessori school, because she had a brilliant teacher, aptly named Molly Wise. Molly was a dark-haired, tanned, Southern woman in her early fifties, an exuberant cross between an aging cowgirl and a priestess of Mother Earth. I once attended a ceremony over which she presided, with candles and flowers and eggs, to welcome the coming spring. A small group of friends formed a circle, cross-legged, on the floor of a carpeted living room, and Molly told us to envision an enclosure at our backs. If anyone needed to attend to children in the next room, we should cut a window into this imaginary barrier. That sounded kind of strange, and it got weird when I tried it. Julia cried out so often, I was constantly slicing a rectangle into the air, lifting my legs, and dipping my head to step through the fictive opening. With all my ducking and climbing I'm afraid I ruined the ritual's mystic ambience, transforming it into a third-rate mime act.

Some adults might sniff at the hint of Wicca, but the Montessori preschoolers adored Molly's earth-centered style. They loved her animal books and games, her songs about the sun and moon, and the New Age music full of waterfalls and ocean breezes that murmured in her classroom's background, alternating with Mozart or a little bluegrass. The effect was never flighty; Molly projected a wholly grounded strength, communicated in part by the width of her biceps. As John put it: "I would always do whatever Molly says. Otherwise she might kick my ass."

I was glad that John liked Molly, because he was a little skeptical about the whole Montessori concept. "We're going to spend four thousand dollars a year," he groaned, "so that our kid can learn how to share and hang up her coat?" Having been raised in conservative Catholic schools, John found the Montessori teachers a little too hippie, and he jokingly called their enclave "People's Republic School Number Three." Nevertheless, he soon became a fan of Molly's style.

In keeping with Montessori principles, Molly viewed herself more as a guide than a teacher, responsible for maintaining a clean, inviting space with beautiful materials, designed primarily by Montessori experts. She and her assistant, Dierdre, steered their eleven toddlers toward the pouring work, the beadwork, the sand work. No Disney toys, no Barbies, no TV or videos. No teacher-led arts and crafts—group work was a rarity. They adhered to the Montessori belief in two-hour sessions of undisturbed individual work—*work* was not yet an onerous word for the children—followed by *gather time*, when the toddlers sat in a circle and sang songs, shared life events, then traipsed off on a nature walk.

"I liked everything about that place," Julia would recall, years later. "The creek, the walks, the nice teachers, the sandbox where I first learned to make stories about the plastic animals that I buried and dug up." The flexibility in the Montessori method matched Julia's temperament. "But the best thing," she added, "was the lack of judgment. In regular school, everybody is judged all the time. You take tests constantly to see who's smart and who's not. Socially you get labeled as a nerd or a class clown. We didn't have that at Montessori, but maybe that's just preschool."

The only form of evaluation in the Woods Creek program came from each teacher's watchful gaze. Molly often stated that her ideal morning was one in which the class ran itself, when she could sit back and watch each child choose his or her work, carry it on its plastic tray to a table, then manipulate the materials for as long as desired, before returning it neatly to its place. I valued this minimization of adult intervention, although it sometimes mystified John: "When I was a kid, students were never treated as individuals. Nobody ever asked, 'How would you think to play with these blocks?' You were just expected to walk the line." But he and I wanted something better for Julia, and Molly fit the bill. Her hours of observation gave Molly a thorough understanding of each child, so that parent-teacher conferences were scenes of revelation. For those of us baffled by the tyranny of our first-borns, Molly served as a guiding light.

Molly was the first teacher to recognize that Julia was "different." At our initial parent-teacher conference, seated at a child's table in knee-high chairs, Molly explained to John and me that Julia had her own way of doing *everything*.

"Let me show you."

From a shelf at her right, Molly lifted a plastic tray and placed it on our table. It contained two white porcelain bowls, one with half a dozen large marbles the size of peach pits, in cloudy pastels. Beside the bowls lay a small pair of silver tongs.

"Here is the basic lesson I give on this work." Molly pinched the tongs, transferring each marble from one bowl to the other.

"It's a simple exercise, designed to help develop fine motor skills." Apparently tongs are a challenge for toddler fingers.

"But here," Molly went on, "is what Julia does."

She turned the second bowl upside down, revealing its flat bottom. With her fingers, she arranged a few marbles on the upturned bowl, put the tongs on top, and then smiled at us. "It's *wonderful*."

Most new parents grasp at straws of genius in their toddlers, but I looked upon that pile of marbles with deep skepticism. It was nice; it was original, but far from brilliant.

Nevertheless, Molly remained a fan. She welcomed "creative variations" on the classroom materials; so long as each child had mastered the concept behind each activity, she could experiment to her heart's delight. And several children did; Julia had no monopoly on creativity. What struck Molly was that Julia's variations were unusual; she maneuvered objects in unexpected ways.

I had noticed some of this "unexpected" behavior at home. Upon opening Julia's bedroom door one winter afternoon, I found the floor tiled in hardcover picture books, pieced together like a puzzle, spine to spine. It was beautiful and original, and a librarian's nightmare—a preschooler arranging books into a flooring to be trod upon.

"It's very pretty," I said to Julia. "But it's time for the books to go back on the shelf."

Two weeks later I stepped into my bathroom and was met by a

sudden onset of cobwebs. They hung from cabinet knob to knob, draped across the sink, stretching from the linen closet to the tub faucets. It took a few seconds for me to realize that this was not a spider's silk. My toddler had been spinning webs of minty dental floss, transforming the room into her private Halloween. It was strange and beautiful—a preschool version of installation art. I let the webs remain for twenty-four hours before taking them down. Dental floss, I showed Julia, is for your teeth.

Julia showed little interest in the proper use of household objects. Once, on a rainy afternoon, I tried to demonstrate the marvels of a plastic egg-slicer. See how the top lifts like the cover of a book? See, inside, this oval cradle, divided into eleven thin white strips? You place the peeled egg into the cradle, gently, very gently, and then pull down the top. Look! The metal wires cut the egg into eleven slices, and each slice has a yellow center! Would you like to eat one? Would you like some salt for that?

I gave Julia the slicer. Would you like to put an egg inside and cut it up? She took the white apparatus into her two-year-old fingers, opened its cover, and inspected the metal wires with their tiny shreds of egg still clinging. Then she reached forward and plucked the wires, emitting a twangy music with an Asian ring. The loose wires in the middle produced an indistinct, low thrumming pitch, but the tighter metal at the edges offered clear, high notes. She plucked a tune for a minute or two, then put the slicer down and walked away.

Imagine us a year later, alone on the carpeted floor of a friend's family room, surrounded by a city of blocks, the last remnants of a group playdate. The other children's impulses were clearly vertical: apartment buildings and skyscrapers, steeples and tall arches. I, too, was enamored with height, stacking one cube on to another until they fell in a heap. Meanwhile, Julia sat twelve feet away, at the opposite end of the room, with a set of colored blocks, spreading them flat on the floor, apparently incapable of building a tower.

"Look at this, Julia." I pointed to my narrow structure, twenty-one stories, teetering, collapsing. "Wouldn't you like to build a tower?"

She glanced at my pile of rubble and shook her head. Sighing, I stood up and walked across the room, determined to teach my daughter, now three years old, the art of balancing one block upon another. But when I reached her corner and looked at the floor, there before her knees lay a wooden dragon with a long red-and-green tail and triangular spikes arranged across its back, its feet, and its huge snout—the first of many dragons to come.

"Julia," I murmured, "I love it."

✦

"If I had a grant," Molly once stated, "I would spend a year observing Julia. She seems to learn in ways that I've never seen before."

But Julia's time with Molly was all too short. The next year, Julia moved upstairs to join the "big kids," ages three through six, in a space three times as large, with twenty-eight children, two teachers, and one assistant. The transition, to put it mildly, was not a success. Most children flew from Molly's nest with pride in their mature status, excited by the many shelves of materials in their new classroom and delighted by the expansive size of the upper playground. Julia, however, refused to take flight. She took one look at the upper classroom, with its crowd and noise and constant motion, and she balked. She wanted to go back downstairs and stay with the little ones.

"It's not a problem," Molly assured us. "Many children like to make a gradual transition. After a while she'll get tired of this, and the upstairs class will seem more appealing. In the meantime, she can come down here as much as she likes."

For two months Julia spent half the day, every day, in the toddler classroom, showing no signs of letting go. She didn't mind that the newcomers were half her age and still in diapers. She barely noticed them. She remained absorbed in her own work, her own marbles and tongs. Eventually the upstairs teachers became exasperated. With my guilty acquiescence, Julia was exiled from the toddler space—the first in the string of losses that we adults know as life.

This was my initial encounter with my daughter's aversion to change: the tears, the howling fury, the desire to go back, back, back. In coming years, the trait would appear over and over—most notably in dismay at home improvements. A simple change—a scratched brick fireplace newly covered with ceramic tile—would cause Julia to weep for twenty minutes. Once, when I hired a contractor to demolish our thin, crooked front porch and build a wider screened space, Julia complained for months. She mourned the holly bush that was cut down in the process, and the original porch columns, which were octagonal cement lampposts.

Many human beings, young and old, deplore change. What seemed unusual in a child less than ten years old was Julia's capacity for profound nostalgia. From her preschool years forward, she vocalized the belief that all human life, and her life in particular, was better in the past. Her yearnings for her toddler classroom were mirrored at age five, when she entered a public kindergarten, full of lamentations for her lost Montessori world. From first grade forward, she longed to return to kindergarten, with its blocks and Legos and dolls. At every stage, she became more convinced that life got harder—not more interesting—as she aged. Each new year brought new responsibilities, added homework, and the incremental loss of basic comforts. Soon, in her average school day, the toys would be gone, the carpet gone, the background music gone. By middle school, recess would be gone.

And all of these losses began at age three, when she never quite adjusted to her new Montessori classroom. Over the next two years Julia would often cry when John or I brought her to school.

"Just drop her off and drive away," advised the teachers, who met the line of cars at the preschool gate. "It's worse if you linger. You'd be surprised how quickly the kids dry their eyes and jump into their work as soon as the parents are gone."

One teacher added this bit of wisdom: "Don't worry if Julia doesn't want to go when you drop her off. The real question is whether she wants to stay when you come to pick her up."

Therein lay my comfort. Because, at twelve-thirty, whenever I came to retrieve my daughter, she was never eager to leave. At pickup time, when parents parked their cars and went inside the classroom, I would inevitably find Julia absorbed in a puzzle, a painting, a collection of tiny barnyard animals. I welcomed her absorption as a sign of contentment, but her concentration was often so complete it was hard to drag her away. Other children might complain when it was time to go; they might beg for a few more minutes, maybe whine and drag their heels, but eventually they would finish their work and follow along. Julia, however, often refused to budge. She remained oblivious to time and to the needs of her waiting sisters. Oblivious to me, with my string of errands to complete.

If I could have given my daughter any gift in the world, I would have given her endless bundles of time, hours and years and centuries. Time to explore every caterpillar on the playground, to cover every inch of a canvas with intricate detail, to finish every game, every puzzle, every book. To me, Julia's imagination was a constant source of wonder, but she was often painstakingly slow at her tasks, sometimes because of her wandering mind, sometimes because of her meticulous attention. She maintained a separate schedule that never fit the group, and at the end of the school day, I sometimes had to resort to lifting her up and carrying her out scratching and screaming, while the other mothers watched. "Yes," I felt like saying, "my daughter is a wild animal."

"Transitions are hard," the teachers would say. "Go to your car, and we will bring her to you." (Like most children, Julia would obey a teacher more readily than a parent—one of the big challenges behind homeschooling.) Meanwhile, they recommended books to read, such as *Raising Your Spirited Child*. But I suspected that Julia's behavior was something different from mere willfulness. Both her creativity and her resistance to transitions (from one grade to the next, one hour to the next) seemed to stem from a deep inwardness, an engagement with her own imaginative universe, which often cut her off from the customs and schedules of the world around her.

This trait had already manifested itself in her social life. By age three it was clear that Julia was not engaging readily with her peers. In the classroom, she rarely spoke to other children, unless they spoke first. On the playground, she would dig or climb or run, but usually alone. If other children joined her, she welcomed them, but she seldom looked for companions. "The other children seem comfortable with her," the teachers assured me. "And she seems fine with them. She doesn't seem to be shy; she just prefers to be alone." Then the teachers would tell me about the benefits of independence, and the problems of children who were never happy alone. "To be content with oneself is a gift," they said. "Our society places too much emphasis on social life."

I knew all about that. I knew that genius often springs from solitude, and that Albert Einstein avoided other children. (Mothers with unusual children always point to Albert Einstein.) Little Albert was right to prefer solitude, since the boys of his day spent so much time playing soldier in an ominous prelude to their eventual goose-stepping.

I had been somewhat solitary as a child, happy with the silence of books and puzzles. But I had always enjoyed two or three good friends with whom I could play whenever the desire struck. And because of my social delicacy, I knew firsthand that people who are happy alone can also yearn for companionship; they can feel their separateness like a deficiency in the bones.

John, meanwhile, had no sphere of reference for fathoming Julia's lone-wolf nature. He had been a social child, and was now a happily extroverted adult—the sort who could stretch a five-minute grocery store errand into an hour-long social event. To him, Julia's preference for solitude was a strange anomaly, but no great cause for concern.

"Given a choice between a box of Legos and a pair of kids, Julia will choose the Legos. Maybe that's antisocial, or maybe she just knows what she wants. What can you do?"

I, for one, was determined to do *something*. Over the next few years I planned playdates and sleepovers and elaborate birthday parties. I took Julia to dance classes and art workshops—any place she might feel encouraged to be social.

"Isn't this too much?" John asked. "Ice hockey was my only scheduled activity when I was a kid; other than that, I just played outside."

"But you lived in a neighborhood full of children," I explained. "If Julia wants to see kids her age, I have to bring them out here, or take her to events in town. And she seems to like these activities. At least, that's what she says."

My efforts bore fruit in playdates and birthday party invitations. Still, Julia never became easygoing in a group. Left in a room with one child, she might start a conversation. Left with three or more, she would usually walk away.

Meanwhile, preschool ended and she was destined for the public schools. Our small Montessori program was not offering kindergarten the following fall, something they had done in the past and would resume in the future. Instead, Julia's teachers said farewell with cautionary phrases.

"I hope Julia is assigned teachers who will appreciate her unique nature"—the parting words of Carmen, Julia's upstairs teacher.

"She would be an ideal candidate for a Montessori elementary program," Molly added. "Her style of learning is different from the public school routine." But the nearest Montessori program was an hour away, and I was not willing to face the drive, or the steep tuition. Besides, our town's small elementary school seemed charming—far superior to anything John or I had experienced as a child.

I had attended the public schools in Raleigh, North Carolina, during the early years of desegregation. Grade school in those days was most notable for lessons in water fountain bigotry, taught by a few authoritative white children, who claimed that if you drank from a fountain after a black person, the water would taste bad. I tried it a few times and imagined that, yes, I could taste a slight difference. Not enough to make me go thirsty, or to stand around and wait for some white kid's lips to purify the water, but just enough to make me think.

The adults at my elementary school taught their own disturbing lessons, mostly in the form of thick wooden paddles. My second-grade teacher handled the paddling for the entire grade, and I can still recall her dragging a limp, screaming boy across our classroom's linoleum and stuffing his crumpled body into the tiny, pine-walled bathroom in the corner. For the next few minutes our class listened to the smacks and howls, until eventually Mrs. Strand emerged alone and continued the history lesson, while gasping sobs and whimpers filtered through the pine door.

As for John, his elementary years were spent on the receiving end of the paddling. He was the sort of high-energy boy who today would be dosed with Ritalin, but in the 1960s was treated with multiple visits to the principal's office. John never minded the paddling—he was used to that at home—but he did object to the soap that Sister Mary Catherine stuffed into his mouth. Once, she forgot about his bar of Irish Spring until the foam started running down his throat, and the child next to John announced, "You have bubbles coming out of your ears!"

I suspect that many homeschooling parents were driven by dismal grade-school memories. Considering our dreary experiences, one might ask why John and I didn't homeschool all of our daughters from day one. The answer lies in the promise of a small school system located in a college town where education takes center stage. To our jaded eyes, the tiny school district of Lexington, Virginia (which consists of one elementary school and one middle school), seemed naïvely endearing.

In Lexington, there are no paddles, no soap-stuffed mouths, and no serious drugs or alcohol until ninth grade, when the city merges with the county to form a larger, consolidated senior high. The school that Julia planned to enter in the fall looked like something Mr. Rogers would have endorsed. Waddell Elementary's dignified brick structure stands in a tree-filled neighborhood where hundred-year-old houses sell for half a million dollars. (My elementary school neighborhood consisted of middle-class ranch houses most memorable for the guy who liked to perform naked calisthenics in front of his picture window every morning while hordes of squealing girls spied through his boxwood hedges.)

Julia's school seemed to be a secure haven surrounded by natural beauty. Woods Creek, which skirted her Montessori preschool, flowed behind Waddell Elementary as well, and although a tall fence kept children away from danger at the water's edge, at recess they could see ducks paddling and hear water cascading over a small dam.

Between the creek and the elementary school's back wall, a large garden beckoned, with sunflowers and rosy arbors. It was the brainchild of a gracious retired couple, who had conceived, created, and maintained the "Roots and Shoots Garden" with the help of children and community members. Each elementary grade tended a separate space: the kindergartners nurtured a "sunflower farm" while the first graders maintained the Peter Rabbit Garden, where a small jacket, shirt, and shoes hung on a scarecrow's empty cross. The largest space was assigned to second-graders, who helped to seed and weed several raised vegetable beds, growing enough golden spuds for an annual potato bake. Meanwhile, the third-graders maintained an alphabet garden: *A* is for aster, *B* is for black-eyed Susan, *C* is for coneflower. From there, a blooming arch led to the fourth-graders' herb garden, overgrown with basil, lemon balm, sorrel, and catmint; and beside that stood the fifth-graders' butterfly garden. This lovely outdoor classroom also held tiny Edens in little corners not assigned to any grade. Julia's favorite was the fairy garden, a five-by-five space where three-inch gnomes and winged ceramic creatures kneeled on mossy rocks, mingling among painted toadstools at the edge of a tiny pond. To the left of the garden were a baseball diamond, a basketball blacktop, swings beneath shady trees, and a vast wooden playscape with slides and wobbly bridges and miniature climbing walls.

The garden made me hopeful for Julia's education. It seemed a living testament that here were people who cared about nature, community, and children. Decades from now, Julia might look back on her elementary school years with a fondness for that patch of ground.

And inside the school? There, the class size averaged around sixteen students, led by teachers who were very bright and kind—people the children knew from the local grocery stores, or swimming pool, or churches. As for the families, since our town's two chief employers were a pair of colleges, Washington and Lee University, and the Virginia Military Institute, most of the parents had a deep commitment to education.

Nothing about Waddell's environment would have steered me toward homeschooling. In fact, John and I felt lucky to have such a pleasant school in our town. Many American families are less fortunate, facing overcrowded classrooms, dangerous disciplinary problems, and exhausted or unmotivated teachers. But Waddell Elementary wasn't like that. In Lexington's ideal environment, where natural beauty and small-town values combined with the intellect of a college crowd, I thought that Julia might enjoy her school. She might learn in a loving environment, making friends and nurturing her spirit. Everything might be okay.

Or not. Despite all of the promising signs, Julia's early days at Waddell were awash in tears. Every afternoon, when I picked her up, she climbed into her car seat and sobbed—"Kindergarten is so haaaard." She didn't mean the classwork, which consisted mainly of coloring and cutting and pasting. What she resented was the lack of freedom: sitting at an assigned desk for long stretches of time, filling out the same worksheet as every other child, speaking only when called upon, and having to ask to go to the bathroom. Lack of choice, lack of movement, lack of soothing background music. She had entered a fallen world from which she could not escape.

The trouble, some parents might say, was her Montessori background. Julia had become accustomed to independent work, allowed to concentrate on one task for as long as she desired and to visit the bathroom whenever she chose. If she had been enrolled in a more structured daycare center, she might have gotten used to following the crowd.

Highly structured preschool programs might benefit some children, but in Julia's case such a preschool would only have inaugurated the misery three years earlier. And misery it was. Each day, when I retrieved my unhappy child, I remembered the Montessori teachers' ominous words: "Don't worry about tears at drop-off time. Was your child crying when you picked her up?" Yes, mine was weeping.

In part, Julia's tears were a sign of exhaustion. After attending preschool until 12:30 each day, it was hard for her to sit through kindergarten from 8:30 to 3:00. John and I had both attended half-day kindergartens, and we were skeptical about the full-day routine. Six and a half hours of school activities seemed like a lot to ask of a five-year-old.

"Your child will be tired and cranky," several mothers had warned. "She'll need a snack right away." But all the grapes and cheese squares in the world could not quell Julia's feeling that school was a dreadful burden.

"She'll get used to it," John said. "You can't expect her to actually *like* school."

In fact, there were plenty of kids who seemed to like it. I asked other mothers what their children thought of kindergarten, and soon got sick of hearing "She loves it!" or "He's having a blast!" I knew there must be other moms with tearful children who loathed school, but in our cheery little town, Julia and I appeared to be members of a brooding minority.

Nevertheless, Julia stuck it out, and after a few weeks the tears dwindled. She became attached to her teacher, Mrs. Larson, an older woman who kneeled down to her five-year-olds' eye level whenever she first met new students. I valued that small gesture, and the challenge it presented to the woman's aging knees. An eye-level greeting meant a lot to a five-year-old—the assurance of having an older face smiling into one's own, and warm, older hands cupping one's palms.

Julia would admire Mrs. Larson for years to come, returning to her classroom to share birthday cupcakes. In fact, Julia was fond of most of her teachers, in and out of school. Once, in the middle of an afternoon "creative movement" class, when her dance teacher began gesticulating with lovely floating fingers, Julia walked over, took hold of one of the fluttering hands, and kissed it.

"Thank you, Julia." The teacher patted her hair, and then continued with her instructions for the group. I looked at my five-year-old daughter and saw that she was not listening to anything the teacher said. She was only watching those floating hands, only wanting to kiss them. Meanwhile, in kindergarten, Mrs. Larson began to have a problem that would often recur in the coming years. She began to lose Julia.

"I lose her on the playground," she sighed. "When it's time to go inside and the children line up, Julia isn't there." Each time, an adult would be sent to perform a playground search. Was Julia sitting in the shaded nooks beneath the wooden walkways? Had she wandered to the trees at the farthest acre of the baseball field?

Julia was not a "runner," a term I learned from a college friend who had become a first-grade teacher. Runners, she explained, are children who exit the building and hit the road. They might walk home or wander the neighborhood, but either way, they are a teacher's worst nightmare.

Julia never ran away from elementary school; she just didn't stick with the group. On the way to the cafeteria she would lag behind in the hallway, stopping to examine bulletin boards or wandering into the library to read a book, so that her class arrived at lunch with Julia nowhere in sight.

"I was never hiding," she would declare years later. "They might lose me, but I was never trying to lose them. On the playground I just liked to stand behind the trees near the garden and arrange stones and bark and twigs in the trunks' nooks and crannies. But the other kids would take them, so then I crawled under the playscape, where there were pieces of broken asphalt that looked like moonstones—all white with gray and black. I liked to gather them up and bury them, so no one would find them."

Julia's instinctive avoidance of the group created big problems on her first-grade field trip. Three classes were visiting the Natural Bridge, a vast stone arch 215 feet tall, carved by a meandering stream fifteen miles south of our town. The Bridge is hailed as one of Virginia's natural wonders, surveyed by George Washington and Thomas Jefferson, and owned today by a corporation that sells expensive admission tickets in a massive gift shop.

Earlier in the day, the first-graders had toured the nearby underground caverns, and after lunch they had visited the bridge. They were unpacking snacks at a cluster of outdoor tables when the teachers noticed that Julia was missing. Parent chaperones were dispersed to track her down, a worrisome prospect when surrounded by miles of woods traversed by a wide, deep stream. After twenty minutes of rising panic, Julia's teacher decided to call the police. But first the adults walked all of the children back to the buses, and there, lo and behold, sat Julia, waiting patiently.

"In all my years of teaching," Julia's teacher complained when she called me and John in for a mandatory conference, "I've never had this happen." (This from a woman who had taught for more than three decades.) John and I were thoroughly apologetic. We would "have it out" with Julia.

"What happened?" we asked her that evening.

"I was staring into the stream," she said. "There were fish swimming on the bottom, and I was watching them for a long time. And when I looked up, everyone was gone. So I went back to the bus to wait."

I had to admire my six-year-old's calm logic. Although I lectured her on the need to stick with her class, in retrospect I would have placed more blame on the supervising adults. If a child could be left behind so easily, how simple would it be for a stranger to lead a first-grader away from the group?

I looked down at Julia with my most serious expression: "Thank God this didn't happen when you were in the caverns. Imagine how scary that would have been, to be alone in those miles of darkness." My mind was filled with images of Tom Sawyer and Becky Thatcher lost in McDougal's cave.

The next year, John and I were informed that Julia could not attend the second-grade scavenger hunt (located in wooded hills surrounding a deep lake) unless a parent came along to watch her; John dutifully complied. Later, during the fourth-grade trip to Monticello, Julia's teacher held her hand for the entire visit.

"It's lucky she's such a delightful child to have at your side," the teacher said.

"Do you still lose her in the school building?" I asked her.

"Oh yes," she said, nodding.

Apart from physically losing Julia, the teachers also lost her attention. Back in the first grade, the teacher who had lamented Julia's disappearance at the Natural Bridge also worried about our daughter's lack of focus in the classroom. Julia seemed to be tuning out the class for hours at a time.

"She's in her own world," explained Mrs. Hennis, "and it's a *wonderful* world. But she needs to spend more time in *our* world."

John and I knew all about that. At dinner, I would sometimes nudge John and say, "Look at Julia." And there she would be sitting, frozen in mid-chew, her fork at her mouth and her mind miles away. Her behavior reminded me of the words of the English poet William Wordsworth, in his "Ode: Intimations of Immortality." Wordsworth suggests that humans enjoy a state of consciousness before birth, a connection to the spiritual world that lingers in the minds of young children until their earthly experiences fully sever the connection. As Wordsworth puts it, "Trailing clouds of glory do we come from God."

Julia seemed to be tuned to a different frequency, a reality preferable to our own, and I would have liked for her to enjoy her alternate world for as long as possible. But success in the public schools demanded that she march in step, and especially with our firstborns, we parents crave success.

Back at our parent-teacher conference, Mrs. Hennis compared Julia to her own son, a unique and creative boy who had struggled through elementary and middle school. Fortunately, by high school this young man had found his niche, and had succeeded, academically and socially, from that point forward. Nevertheless, when Mrs. Hennis considered her son and our daughter, she shook her head and uttered one prophetic statement: "The public schools aren't for everyone."

Those are mighty depressing words to hear at a first-grade parent-teacher conference when eleven years of public education loom in the future. In our small town, there are few alternatives to the public system. The only private school in Lexington, Virginia, is a tiny Christian academy; all other options require hours of driving up and down the local interstate—a truck-ridden hazard. For most families in our area, "private" education means homeschooling, something I was not yet ready to consider. But in the coming years, whenever Julia struggled with her classroom routine, I would recall Mrs. Hennis's words: "The public schools aren't for everyone."

Meanwhile, we tried to carve out strategies to help Julia function in a traditional classroom. Mrs. Hennis taped an index card to Julia's desk, reminding her of tasks that were automatic for other children. *Hang up your coat and backpack. Put your lunch away. Write your name on all work. Listen to the teacher.* I posted a similar checklist at home. *Have you finished your homework? Is it packed in your backpack? Do you know where your shoes are?*

I also decided to have Julia's hearing checked, since children with poor hearing often tune out the group and withdraw into themselves. I visited our small-town doctor's office, which boasted the only physician within a thirty-mile radius with a background in pediatrics, and I spoke privately with this man before bringing Julia in to see him.

"She seems to inhabit her own world," I explained to the doctor. "She's wonderfully creative and artistic, and has a special love of visual patterns. She's always arranging objects into symmetrical designs. She's also got an almost obsessive power of concentration on subjects that interest her, but she tunes out her first-grade classroom for hours at a time and shows little interest in other children."

The doctor spoke the words that I had been avoiding for months. "Do you think she might be autistic?"

Yes, the idea had crossed my mind. Not autistic in a disabling sense, but in its mildest variety. On an autism spectrum of one to ten, Julia might fall somewhere around two.

The doctor called her into the room and tested her hearing,

which seemed normal. Then he gave her a brief checkup and spoke to her for several minutes about her interests, her artwork, and her ideas.

When she left, the doctor turned to me and smiled. "She's not autistic. She's just doing her own thing."

Since then, I've often wondered if that answer was too simple. Years later, when reading *Songs of the Gorilla Nation*, by Dawn Prince-Hughes, I marveled at the small similarities between Julia and this author who struggled with Asperger's syndrome. It was as if Prince-Hughes was a distant cousin, twice removed. Julia has never demonstrated the more debilitating symptoms of Asperger's: exaggerated tactile sensitivity, avoidance of eye contact, responding to stress by locking her muscles into repeated gestures. But Julia did share Prince-Hughes's obsessive love of symmetry, the tendency to connect with animals more readily than humans, a constant disregard for hair brushing and table manners, and an odd verbal habit of occasionally repeating one syllable of a word several times, as if she had her own built-in echo. Above all, Prince-Hughes's hatred of change sounded like an intense version of Julia's feelings:

> *I would feel like I was dying—my heart would pound, my ears would ring, and my whole consciousness would go hollow—if something changed. I remember instances of buildings being torn down, trees being cut, new roads going in, and two building fires happening along my routes. It took weeks for me to recover from these things. I would cry and yell and announce my convictions regarding the basic evil of mankind. I hated the changers and the changed. To me, change was nothing less than murder.*

"I think Julia might have a touch of Asperger's syndrome," I told a cousin who works as an English professor at an ultra-liberal college.

He shrugged. "I think half of my colleagues have Asperger's. If you want to talk about highly intelligent and creative people who are socially inept, that covers most of our faculty."

I also wondered if Julia's behavior might be categorized as attention deficit disorder. I never took her to be diagnosed, because her problems weren't severe, but recent studies have shown that in girls, ADD often manifests itself in "space cadet" behavior, characterized by a wandering mind and lack of organizational skills. That seemed to describe Julia, and it matched John's childhood memories. "I never could pay attention in school," he explained. "I sat at my desk with a toy hidden in my lap, and my mind constantly wandered."

His mother gave me the full story one afternoon, when I spoke to her about my concerns for Julia. "When John was little, I had a regular weekly conference with the nuns. Every Friday, I was required to go in and hear them complain about how immature John was, and how badly he was doing. Each year they wanted to hold him back. . . . But look how well he turned out!"

Somehow these revelations weren't reassuring. On the one hand, it was good to know that despite his inauspicious start, my husband had gone on to earn a Ph.D. in music education. John had great talents in music and art, aptitudes that Julia shared, along with his blue eyes, dark hair, and fair skin. But at the same time, John's repeated insistence on what a "moron" he used to be, and how he made Ds and Fs throughout his early school years, sometimes made me doubt the wisdom of having had three children with this man. There's nothing like parenthood to bring out all the skeletons in one's childhood closet, and in the coming years John took pleasure in regaling me with a host of colorful confessions, joking that I would have to help Julia overcome her Brodie genes. Of course I had my own share of childhood vices, but none were academic, and I sometimes found it hard to grasp what could be so difficult about elementary school.

Julia's teachers explained that although she was obviously very bright, her work didn't always show it. Her spelling was poor, her handwriting resembled a caveman's scrawl, and she could get the right answers in math only if given lots of extra time. I was almost resigned to the idea that Julia's intellect would never shine in a regular classroom when, at the end of the second grade, I received a letter stating that the school was considering her for its gifted program. Apparently she had scored in the ninety-ninth percentile on something called the Naglieri test.

"What is this?" I asked Mrs. Patrick, the school's coordinator of the gifted program.

"It's a nonverbal test," Mrs. Patrick explained. "The children are shown black-and-white images, and they have to recognize patterns or differences, or guess what comes next."

That made sense; Julia's brain had a knack for processing visual information. Once, at the end of a little boy's birthday party, the hostess remarked that Julia had won their party game. Apparently this mom had stood before the children with a cookie sheet full of small objects—toys and kitchen gadgets and knick-knacks—and she'd given the kids a brief moment to survey it all. Then she had put the cookie sheet away and asked the children to write down every object they could remember. (A pretty boring game for a bunch of eight-year-olds, if you ask me.) Anyway, Julia won hands down. After a short glance, she could recall almost every object on the sheet.

Clearly, Julia had a unique intelligence churning inside her head, and so Waddell tried her out in its third-grade gifted program. The experience didn't amount to much: twice a week Julia spent a little time outside the regular classroom, doing special activities in math and English. She didn't last long in the advanced math group, but the Junior Great Books Club seemed right up her alley. There, the children discussed and wrote about stories they read together. "I love having Julia in the group," Mrs. Patrick said, beaming. "She's so creative. She always has something unusual to say."

Unusual was the operative word, a word that sometimes made me sigh. How many mothers of unusual children have occasionally prayed for a little normalcy—just enough to ease their child's passage through the world of averages that constitutes America's public schools? Nevertheless, I was pleased that Julia had been recognized as a bright kid. This gifted program might give her a boost, especially since the regular curriculum was getting very dull.

In Virginia, third grade marks the onset of annual standardized tests, something all states employ, but some are more zealous than others when it comes to dictating the schools' test-driven curriculum. In the 1990s, Virginia instituted a new curriculum called the Standards of Learning, or SOLs—an appropriate acronym, since most parents and teachers I've met seem to feel that when it comes to the SOLs, we are all "shit out of luck." As one high-school teacher put it, "The SOLs are the monster that is devouring our schools."

If Julia's wandering mind had been our only challenge—if her school curriculum had been full of exciting materials, taught with creative approaches—I never would have opted for homeschooling. But Virginia's ardent embrace of our nationwide test-prep culture pushed me over the edge. I kept looking at the bland content in Julia's worksheets and tests, and thinking, "Oh, c'mon. *I* could do much better than this."

Most of Julia's teachers felt the same way. During her early years at Waddell, they consistently lamented the effect of the SOL tests on their program. "We *always* had standards," one veteran teacher sighed, but now the standards were being dictated by strangers in Richmond, and there was little time left in the day for teachers to use their own imaginations. "More than eighty percent of our curriculum is mandated by the state," another teacher explained. "And don't let anyone tell you that we don't teach to the test. We *absolutely* teach to the test."

To make time for extra test preparation, Waddell had abandoned many of the teachers' favorite units. "We used to do a first-grade unit on dinosaurs," one teacher recalled. "The children loved it." But since dinosaurs weren't part of the first-grade standards, they had become extinct in the classroom. "I used to do more creative writing," a fourth-grade teacher noted. "But now with all the testing, we don't have time for it." The Roots and Shoots Garden was another SOL casualty, incorporated less and less into the children's schedule. By Rachel's fifth-grade year, she would complain that they never visited the garden at all.

John, who had started his career as a K–12 music teacher, felt a personal loathing for the tests. "When I taught in the public schools we didn't have these strict standards. If a teacher had a passion for chemistry or politics, he could share that. Teachers could play to their strengths." John acknowledged that some teachers and schools were weak, and needed state standards to hold them accountable. But for most conscientious educators, the testing requirements had gone way too far: "Now you don't have the time to elaborate on the finer or more interesting points of a subject. All you want the kids to do is spit out that the symbol for salt is NaCL."

"In the end," one local principal explained, "the SOLs make great teachers good and good teachers bad."

None of Julia's teachers seemed to mind Virginia's math and English requirements. Math and English were the bread and butter of elementary school; it was fine for the state to insist that grade-school teachers hammer home the basics of arithmetic and reading comprehension. The problems stemmed from the state's increasingly specific mandates in science and social studies, which covered everything from elementary economics to Virginia state history. When I told a friend about Virginia's fourth-grade test on state history, this veteran public school principal threw back her head and laughed. "My teachers would revolt if we instituted a standardized test on Pennsylvania history. The whole concept behind *standards* is to cover basic knowledge that is essential for everyone—not to memorize facts that are specific to one region." Unfortunately, with each successive year, Julia seemed to spend more and more time on rote memorization for multiple-choice exams, preparing for what one teacher called "these horrible trivia tests."

To me, multiple choice is the greatest sign of the failure of American education—a form of testing developed for the convenience of grading machines, that has little to do with real learning. Genuine education involves writing, making connections, and drawing conclusions, but at Julia's school, as at many schools nationwide, writing played second fiddle to "fill in the bubble."

Waddell was such a promising place, it was sad to see the teachers dragging around their state-mandated ball and chain. But our little school was a good foot soldier in Virginia's SOL crusade, which meant that Julia and I, along with all the other families and teachers, kept marching in step.

That march became especially dreary at the end of the third grade, as Julia prepared for her first standardized test in social studies. School districts throughout Virginia were issuing flash cards from a private company that gave its package the silly title

"Race for the Governor's Mansion." Trying to be a dutiful parent, I quizzed Julia on the cards and was dismayed by their poor quality.

Life, liberty, and the pursuit of happiness are _____ *that all Americans enjoy*, one flash card read. "Inalienable rights," Julia responded, repeating Jefferson's words from the Declaration of Independence. I flipped the card over. *Privileges*, it read. How ridiculous, I thought, to have the children memorize an arbitrary word pulled out of a hat.

In fact, the flash cards would get worse in upcoming years, containing numerous errors. "What ancient cities farmed on hillsides?" *Greece and Rome.* "What country was home to several great empires?" *Africa.*

Julia didn't mind all the flash cards and multiple choice as much as her homework assignments. By the fourth grade, she had become so bored that homework was a daily struggle. Every day, I tried to allow her time to play outside for a few hours after school, but by five thirty I was usually telling her to start her homework. I offered a little television or computer time as an incentive, but often these weren't enough inspiration. By seven, I'd be unpacking her books myself, insisting that she sit down at the table and concentrate. By eight, when she had finished only a fraction of her work and was complaining about how her sisters were watching *SpongeBob* without her, I could feel my jaw tighten. At nine, when Rachel and Kathryn were in bed and Julia wasn't finished with her math, I usually launched into some lecture about time management and the need to concentrate. By ten o'clock, when my fourth-grader finally went to bed, she and I were both angry and exhausted. I began to dread every single afternoon.

Had I known then what I know now: that in the elementary grades, studies show that the link between homework and academic achievement is minimal at best—its impact grows in middle and high school—I might have staged my own little homework rebellion. I could have written a letter to Julia's teacher explaining that homework had become counterproductive for my daughter; the tension it produced negated any potential benefits. For the rest of the fourth grade, I would see that Julia devoted forty minutes each school day to homework—the old ten-minutes-per-grade rule. Beyond that, she had my permission to skip the rest.

Julia's teacher, a thoughtful and intelligent woman, would probably have worked with us had she known that Julia's homework was taking so much time, dragging down our family routine. She might have given Julia shorter assignments—ten math problems instead of twenty. And if this woman had not been willing to compromise—so what? So, Julia would get a minus on the "completes homework" line on her report card. What did it matter?

Homework has not always been accepted as a valuable part of education. These days there are plenty of books that argue against America's homework overload: *The Homework Myth, The Case Against Homework, The End of Homework*. Most of the authors stress that our country's attitude toward homework has fluctuated over time, according to political and social trends. The 1930s and 1940s witnessed a growing movement for the abolition of homework, as doctors and educators emphasized the need for healthy, joyful children who spent plenty of time playing outside. This move for health and happiness mirrored labor advocates' calls for more recreation and no unpaid overtime. But the anti-homework trend ended in 1957, with the Soviet launch of *Sputnik*. In recent years, the desire to produce citizens who can compete in the global economy has produced a spike in homework for American children.

I didn't know any of this back in 2005. Still suffering the residual intimidation from my own public school days, I assumed that Julia should complete all of the teacher's assignments, even if it meant that I must push and prod. Waddell seemed to assume that parents would do some prodding. Every week we were asked to administer practice vocabulary tests, time math quizzes, call out flashcards, and sign forms verifying that our child had completed her reading, her spelling, her arithmetic.

To John, this level of parent involvement was perplexing. His mom and dad had never paid attention to his homework: "I was the fourth of six kids, so their attitude was, 'Hey, you're on your own.' Their only job was to go to the teachers at the end of each year and say, 'Pleeease let John go on to the next grade.'"

Given John's laissez-faire attitude, I wondered if I was too wrapped up in Julia's homework. Maybe the problem was me, not my daughter. Maybe I was joining the ranks of helicopter parents—overly ambitious and intrusive.

In her book *Perfect Madness: Motherhood in the Age of Anxiety*, Judith Warner describes how today's mothers have become a generation of control freaks, frantically prepping children to get their piece of a shrinking American pie, rather than taking political action to ensure that there is enough pie for everyone. The result is stressed-out women and kids, all suffering from an existential crisis that Warner calls "the mess."

Although Lexington's small-town culture is shielded from the worst extremes of "the mess" (there are no private schools that families compete to enter, no exclusive afterschool lessons, no excess of choices), around me I saw plenty of moms heavily invested in their children's schoolwork and extracurriculars: monitoring homework, helping with projects, driving to dance and lacrosse and Girl Scouts, volunteering in the classroom, and sometimes arguing with teachers. Most of this involvement seemed appropriate and loving, but some of it was over the top, and I wondered what category I fell under: helpful, concerned parent or stressed-out Uber-Mom?

"Should we let Julia fail?" I sometimes asked John. Should we let her skip her homework and school projects until she had the maturity and desire to complete them without my prodding? At this, John shrugged and offered another confession: "You know, I never did any of my homework until about the fifth grade. That's one of the reasons I was failing."

I wondered if Julia would benefit from seeing the consequences of failure; maybe a bad report card would ruffle her complacency. And yet, whenever I did step back from the process and allowed my daughter to miss project deadlines or receive zeros on homework, or sometimes go for days without brushing her hair, it never bothered Julia as much as it bothered me. She displayed little interest in whether her papers were marked with As or Fs, and on one level, her utter lack of concern seemed healthy. When I was a child, I had been too intent on pleasing other people—making my teachers and parents happy, wanting to fit in at school. That mind-set can produce good grades, but it can also have dangerous consequences for young girls: trying to please peers who are passing out drugs, wanting to please boys who try to go too far.

Julia's independence would serve her well on future occasions, but for now I couldn't wrap my head around the idea of a smart child doing poorly in school, and neither could Julia's teachers. Whenever I mentioned the thought of stepping back and letting Julia's school fortunes rise or fall as they might, her teachers objected strongly. They cared about Julia's success, and I'm sure they also cared about their school's accreditation. In the era of No Child Left Behind, Waddell needed bright kids like Julia to "perform," and they encouraged me to serve as her homework coach. Some children needed a helper, they explained—someone who could sit at the kitchen table and keep the child focused.

But serving as a homework coach is an exhausting job, and Julia and I butted heads every time she dragged her feet. I didn't enjoy ushering the clouds into so many of her afternoons, bringing out the books and pencils and calling her in from the creek. I feared that her hatred of homework would soon morph into a hatred of me. And then came the closet incident, which threw me into days of worried reflection. We had reached the breaking point, and something had to change.

CHAPTER THREE

⇥Making a Plan⇤

School is all about copying the teacher.
I mean, I've been saying the pledge of allegiance
for six years, and I only learned what
"pledge" meant one year ago.

JULIA

T HAT'S WHEN THE HOMESCHOOLING BUG FIRST FLARED within me. After puzzling over the trajectory of my daughter's education, I knew we had to try something different.

I had always thought of homeschooling as a drastic measure. Homeschooling was for Mormons, for Bible-thumping Baptists, for children with disabilities, mental or physical, and for families who live off the grid, with solar heat and composting toilets. Homeschooling was a little bit weird. But in the chameleonic world of modern parenthood, we mothers must constantly change colors to meet our children's needs. We become accomplished fund-raisers when our preschools need a fruit sale chair; we take up the violin when the Suzuki method calls for parent-child lessons. And when my daughter decided that she would rather hide in a closet than complete her homework, I knew that it was time for me to become a schoolteacher, if only for a little while.

On one level, my motives were entirely selfish. Sure, I wanted to help my child, but I also wanted to save myself from the tortures of our evening homework routine. After dinner, whenever I longed to relax and read or watch a movie, I was stuck at the kitchen table encouraging Julia to make a map of Virginia out of lentils and pinto beans. Homeschooling looked heavenly by comparison. If Julia were homeschooled, I could be off duty by three o'clock.

There was also the matter of my intellectual standards. If I was going to be spending a couple of hours each day on my daughter's schoolwork—supervising, cheering, and prodding—at least let it be on assignments I valued. Not this spelling busywork, this fill-in-the-blank history. Not this state-mandated world of multiple choice. If Julia were homeschooled, she could be writing essays, gathering evidence, forming conclusions, and reading constantly.

As I sat there at our dining room table night after night watching my daughter slog through another column of multiplication, I recalled the first time I had ever heard of homeschooling. It was way back in August of 1983, when I was up late watching *The Tonight Show*, with Johnny Carson. Johnny had a special guest from California, a young man who was going off to Harvard in the fall without ever having completed a year of school. His story caught my attention because I was a Harvard student as well, preparing for my sophomore year.

The incoming freshman was named Grant Colfax, and he had grown up on a remote forty-acre homestead in Northern California. Much of his education had been hands-on, helping his parents to clear land and build a farm. He had learned biology while raising animals, geometry while constructing a house, and his discovery of Indian ruins on the family property had inspired him to study North American archaeology.

Years later, Grant Colfax's name would become legendary in the homeschooling world when his parents, David and Micki, wrote a book called *Homeschooling for Excellence*. By the time of the book's publication, the Colfaxes had three sons at Harvard, and their brief manifesto provided inspiration to tens of thousands of Americans who believed that if they, too, took their children's educations in hand, their kids might end up in the Ivy League.

Back in 1983, the first thing that struck me about the televised Grant Colfax was his handsome face. (I was nineteen, after all.) My second impression was that he seemed so *normal*—articulate and easy-going. Grant and I would eventually wind up living in the same house at Harvard—"house" meaning a cluster of brick buildings that housed and fed more than four hundred students. We never had a conversation; I would pass him on the Radcliffe Quad, nod hello, and think to myself, "There's that guy who never went to school." Each time, I felt the same emotion that I had experienced watching him on *The Tonight Show*: a mixture of curiosity and envy.

College had opened my eyes to enormous vistas of learning, and I was appalled at how much time had been wasted in my public school years doodling in the margins of dull workbooks. Grant Colfax, I told myself, didn't spend a semester in Consumer Education, learning to balance a checkbook. He didn't suffer through Sex Education and Drug Education and the moronic swamp of multiple choice.

In truth, I knew nothing, then or now, of the real Grant Colfax, but I liked to imagine his education as an Emersonian experiment: immersed by day in the "discipline of nature" and surrounded at night by a pile of books. Ralph Waldo Emerson, in his 1837 Phi Beta Kappa address, *The American Scholar*, said that the ideal student should concentrate on three things: nature, to learn of God's present creation; books, to understand the past and human history; and activity, the sort that the Colfax boys enjoyed on a daily basis (building sheds, tending sheep, fixing plumbing and electrical wiring).

Twenty-two years later, as I called Julia away from her pleasure reading to do yet another science worksheet, I thought of Grant Colfax and how he never had homework. Instead, he had a life in which he learned by doing. I also thought of my childhood and how the most important part of my education had not come from the public schools. It had come from my mother, an educator in the finest sense.

Born in New York City in the 1930s, my mom was a child of German immigrants too poor to treat their children to much more than books from the public library and free opera performances in Central Park. Four years at Manhattan's Hunter High had led her to Hunter College and advanced degrees from Yale and the University of Washington. Married at age thirty, she had three children in four years, and raised us while working on her Ph.D. When her study group met in our dining room, we children sat under the table maneuvering our toys around the graduate students' feet.

My mother filled our house with classical music, and insisted that all her children play instruments. Because she and my father loved the outdoors, we spent more family vacations in tents than hotels. When my father died at forty-two, my mom (by then a full-time political science professor) continued our education on weekends, taking us to museums, parks, and tennis lessons. She included us on trips to Europe with groups of college students, and when I showed an interest in creative writing, she introduced me to poetry readings: Gwendolyn Brooks and Czeslaw Milosz.

As I thought back on my mom, it occurred to me that all good parents are homeschoolers. Homeschooling is what happens when families turn off their TVs, cell phones, and iPods. It occurs in long, thoughtful conversations at the dinner table, as well as at baseball games and ballet recitals, and in the planting of a vegetable garden. Parents who enrich their children's lives with art and sports and multiple trips to the library provide the backbone of American education. Unfortunately, in our busy lives, parents and children have less and less time for hours of thoughtful interaction, which is one reason why homeschooling has been on the rise. Homeschooling provides families with the quality time that used to occur after school.

Now I began to look at the homeschooling moms around me with a new respect. Maybe they weren't so strange after all. Maybe they weren't overly religious, overly liberal, or overly mothering. Maybe they knew something that I didn't know.

My work as a part-time English professor at Washington and Lee had always left me free to accept or decline courses in any given semester, so I started to consider how I might fit some homeschooling into my schedule. For one year, I told myself, I could teach a minimal load. For one year I could concentrate on fifth-grade mathematics instead of Jane Austen. I could give Julia a break from her homework burnout; a year of intensive writing and one-on-one math tutorials might provide her with a leg up before the sixth grade. Our local middle school was supposed to be very good, and the change in scenery and schedule would hopefully motivate Julia once she reached that school. But for the fifth grade, she might enjoy something totally different.

The idea of taking a one-year hiatus appealed to my academic mind, steeped as I was in the culture of sabbaticals. Julia was approaching her sixth year at Waddell—the sabbatical year at most colleges. Why shouldn't she take time off to try her own line of study? Why shouldn't kids have sabbaticals, too?

Many committed homeschoolers will cringe at the idea of a

one-year experiment. Studies show that the academic benefits of homeschooling (higher test scores and college admission rates) emerge only after several years of work. And the emotional benefits that many homeschoolers cite—enthusiasm for lifetime learning, strengthened family ties—develop slowly over many years.

Still, long-term homeschooling held no allure for me. I wanted plenty of time for my own teaching and writing and solitude. One year was the limit of my excitement.

At the time, a year of homeschooling seemed like an original, even radical idea. How many mothers took their children out of school for one grade to give them an individually tailored education?

As it turns out, plenty. The more I looked into it, the more I discovered that short-term homeschooling is a growing trend in America, for a vast array of reasons. Some parents have academic motives: they want to expose their kids to ideas and experiences beyond the usual curriculum, but they don't have the time or desire to pull their children from traditional schools permanently. Other families fall into temporary homeschooling unexpectedly, as the result of sudden crises; Hurricane Katrina made homeschoolers out of many reluctant moms and dads. Severe bullying can also drive parents to homeschool for the short term. In our town, I met one mother who withdrew her daughter midyear from the seventh grade when the preteen nastiness of the middle-school girls became too painful. "She was up at midnight crying," the woman explained. One semester sufficed to steer that child past the social tempest, and she was a happy eighth-grader the following year. Another mom explained that she removed her daughter from middle school in South Carolina when the girl came home with choking marks on her neck. That child was scheduled to return to the public system once ninth grade began, with hopes that her high school would be better policed.

When parents become teachers in response to short-term crises, *Home Education Magazine* calls it "emergency homeschooling." For Julia and me, however, there was no emergency. Julia's stint in the closet was a wake-up call, not a crisis. It was the proverbial straw that broke my back, providing just enough of a jolt to force me into action.

A few weeks after the incident, I presented Julia with the words that had been running through my mind.

"Would you like to try a year of homeschooling?"

She looked up from her copy of *Dragons of Deltora*. "What does that mean?"

"It means you wouldn't go to Waddell for the fifth grade. I'd be your teacher." Julia crinkled her nose. Apparently the vision of Mom as her teacher was not a strong selling point. "You'd get to study things that interest you," I added, "not just the usual school stuff. And we could plan lots of field trips, to Washington and Williamsburg, and all around town."

"I dunno." Julia shrugged and returned to her book.

I stood there mutely embarrassed, amazed at her lack of enthusiasm. I had thought she would jump at the chance, embracing me as the best mom ever. In my eyes, Julia was a caged bird, and I was opening the door, offering her the sky, the clouds, the freedom to let her mind soar. But like so many imprisoned creatures, when the cage door opened, Julia remained perched in the back, wary and bored.

"Don't you think homeschooling might be fun?" I prodded.

She sighed. "How is it any better than what I've got right now?"

"You wouldn't have the usual homework. The only homework I'd require is that you read for an hour every day and write one page in a journal."

"Write about what?" I had caught my daughter's attention, and I could sense her inching toward the door of her cage.

"Whatever you want."

Those were the magic words. "I like that." Julia smiled. "That sounds good."

"Think about it for a while," I said. "It's a serious decision. Think about what you'd miss at school, and what you'd gain at home. We don't have to make any commitment yet." Nevertheless, it was clear from that point forward that Julia and I were harboring a special secret. We were contemplating playing hooky for a year.

A few days later, standing at the edge of the Waddell playground, watching children slide and climb and swing in the last few minutes before the final bell, I approached my friend Ruth. Ruth is a woman of sturdy good sense, with children roughly the same age as mine.

When she asked, "What's up with you?" I replied, "I'm thinking about homeschooling Julia for the fifth grade."

She didn't express surprise or ask a single question. Instead, she looked me straight in the eye and said, "You're crazy."

Ruth is famous for being blunt, but "crazy" seemed harsh. While I spluttered some self-defensive nonsense, she shrugged in a "choose your own poison" gesture. "No way I'd ever do that."

No way Ruth ever could, since she works as a full-time lawyer. But she wasn't talking about her job; she was referring to her temperament. Ruth is a high-energy, career-oriented, contemporary woman. Staying home with a child day after day, reviewing multiplication tables and rules of grammar, would be her idea of hell. Or at least Purgatory. Obviously, she was not the best audience for trying out my fledgling idea.

Smoothing my slightly ruffled feathers, I collected my girls and drove home, hoping for a better response from John. His co-operation would be crucial in the coming year, not only for moral support, but because I wanted him to teach Julia flute lessons and French on the two afternoons each week when I would be busy at Washington and Lee.

That evening I waited until he was relaxed and well fed, lounging at the computer, before I mentioned the idea casually from my armchair across the room.

"I think I'd like to homeschool Julia next year."

John was barely listening, his mouse moving in crooked circles. "What was that?"

"About Julia," I said. "I'd like to take her out of school next year and try some homeschooling."

The mouse came to a halt and John turned to face me. "You can't be serious."

"Why not?"

"You two fight all the time."

"We fight over her homework," I replied. "We fight because I have to force her to do schoolwork she hates. If she were homeschooled she would only have to read and write after three o'clock. She wouldn't mind that."

"You fight over her violin," he pointed out, and he was right. Julia had been taking violin lessons for three years and showed real talent, but getting her to practice was an ugly ordeal.

"If she were homeschooled, her violin practice could be part of the school day," I replied. "She wouldn't object so much if it took place before three o'clock. She just resents spending seven hours at school, then coming home and having more lessons."

"You also argue about the mess she makes."

There again, John was right. (I was beginning to sense he had a list.) Julia tends to leave her clothes and toys scattered throughout the house in serpentine trails, as if she were Gretel dropping crumbs to find her way home. In response I gradually progress from patient tolerance ("Pick up your toys please, Julia") to teeth-gritting tolerance ("Please pick up your toys *now*, Julia") to raging frustration ("What the &*%^$ are all these toys still doing in the hall!"). The length of my fuse depends on the stress of my day and the sharpness of the object I've just stepped on.

John could see from my tightened jaw that this homeschooling idea wasn't merely a casual impulse. He sighed. "Why do you even ask me when you've already made up your mind?"

"I wasn't asking. I was telling."

Actually, I didn't say those words aloud, but that's pretty much what ran through my head. In our household, most child-rearing decisions fall under my authority; with three daughters, so many questions relate to ballet and Barbies and training bras that John gratefully allows me free rein. This decision, however, involved an important, gender-neutral subject, and he wasn't going to acquiesce with his usual "Yes, dear. Just tell me what to do."

"Look," he began, "you've got to remember that I started out as a public school teacher, and the first time I heard about homeschooling, about twenty years ago, my instant reaction was 'Oh *hell* no!' That's like a slap in the face, to say that a parent with no training can do my job. I know homeschooling has come a long way since then, but I think it's going to be a lot harder than you imagine."

"I know it will be hard," I said, "but I think Julia needs it."

"You're thinking about what's good for Julia," he replied, "but I'm worried about what's good for you. Teaching kids is exhausting. A few months at home with Julia and you're going to be miserable."

I sighed. "Her school situation already makes me miserable.

She hates the routine; I hate the boring SOLs. We can't do any worse."

At which point he turned back to the computer. "You're the one with the Harvard degree."

John only mentions Harvard when he thinks I'm doing something stupid. Whenever I let the oil in my car run dangerously low, or when I'm careless with the laundry and all our underwear turns pink, John's response remains the same: "What school did you go to?"

But after nineteen years of marriage, he knew it was useless to argue. Of late he had embraced the motto "Happy wife, happy life."

"By the way," I said as he clicked through some YouTube clips. "I'll need your help with Julia two afternoons each week, when I'm teaching."

He didn't even reply.

Wow, I thought as I lay in bed that night. This was not going well. I had expected to encounter some skepticism, some questions and curiosity, but not the direct, in-your-face, "you're a naïve idiot" variety. I decided to lie low for a while and shield my fragile vision from any other potential naysayers.

Julia, however, had no inhibitions. She raised the subject at our local dance studio while her fellow modern dancers were donning leotards and kneepads.

"Mom's going to homeschool me," she announced to her instructor, Ms. Sellers, who turned to me with eyebrows raised.

"Only for a year," I added, feeling defensive and apologetic.

Ms. Sellers's face broke into a broad smile. "That's fabulous. Julia is the perfect child for homeschooling."

God bless Nina Sellers, our town's creative diva. She's a fiery woman with red hair halfway down her back, who stood last

August at our community festival under the shade of a Japanese parasol ("A prop from our last recital," she said, laughing) wearing a batik skirt rustling above Greek sandals, trailed by an entourage of adoring children and equally adoring fiftysomething bachelors.

Now, as the modern dancers began to congregate in her studio, she smiled at me. "You know, I homeschooled my two daughters."

"Really?"

She nodded. "I took them out halfway through middle school, and let them study on their own until college."

"Why did you do it?"

She frowned and issued a guttural noise of disgust: "I can't stand our country's industrialized form of education; these assembly-line schools that just ruin childhood." Then she laughed, as if the cloud of public education had lifted from her thoughts. "I'm not the best model for homeschooling. With my oldest daughter, I just left her alone to read anything she wanted. And she read *everything*. Novels, history, biographies, newspapers. When she got to the verbal part of her SATs, she scored off the charts, almost one hundred percent. But I never made her study math, so her math scores were pretty low."

I couldn't imagine Nina teaching algebra. She's an artsy spirit, the sort who often lets modern dance students choreograph their own recital numbers, sometimes to the parents' chagrin. Whenever John sees Julia rolling across the floor at an end-of-the-year performance, he turns to me and whispers, "How much did we pay for this?"

Reassured to find a hidden homeschooler among my acquaintance, I resolved to mention my plans to other homeschooling moms, beginning with Julia's violin teacher, Esther Vine. Esther is a Mormon homeschooler with seven children—facts that, in my mind, would normally conjure an image of a repressed housewife and religious extremist. In fact, Esther is one very cool Latter Day Saint. In addition to raising her large family, she performs in orchestras and chamber groups and teaches college students and children. She serves as the perfect poster woman for her faith.

Esther is a very calm home educator. Just that fall, when her seventh child asked to attend fourth grade at the county school, she packed his lunch and sent him off on the bus, no problem. But by January, when he'd had enough, she confessed to being relieved. "He had so much homework every day," she told me, "it really cut into our family time. I don't know how all the other families can stand it."

When I told Esther that I might try a year of homeschooling, her eyes lit up. "Wait a moment. I've got something for you." She left the room and came back a few minutes later with a fat, glossy hardcover book: *The Well-Trained Mind: A Guide to Classical Education at Home.*

"This is what I use," she said, smiling. "Or try to use. It's a lot more than I could ever manage, but if you're thinking about homeschooling, there's no better place to start."

That evening, after settling in bed, I lifted the heavy book and plopped it onto my covers. Turning first to the final chapter, I glanced at the last page number—810, Lord help us. More of a reference book than a bedtime story. Next, I contemplated the jacket photos of the smiling authors, a mother-daughter team, Jessie Wise and Susan Wise Bauer. Their names immediately appealed. After my fortunate experience with Montessori's Molly Wise, I had an instinctive respect for Wise women.

Apparently Jessie had taught Susan and her brother back in the 1970s, when homeschooling was a new and somewhat bizarre phenomenon. Susan had become a professor of literature and writing at the College of William and Mary, but as I flipped through the book, I was surprised that they didn't mention the brother much. I wondered what he thought of his homeschooling years.

Within these 810 pages, mother and daughter advocated a classical education in which global history served as the guiding principle, with literary masterpieces and scientific discoveries taught in a historical chronology. The first through twelfth grades were divided into three repetitions of a four-year pattern: the ancients (5000 BC–AD 400), medieval through early Renaissance (400–1600), late Renaissance through early modern times (1600–1850), and modern times (1850–present). Grade-school children were supposed to study each time period at a simple level; fifth- through eighth-graders delved into the same subjects with increasing complexity, and by high school, students should be reading original sources in translation.

It was all very impressive, and reminded me of another illuminating book that provided a backdrop for my homeschooling. Many secular homeschoolers point to John Holt's *Teach Your Own* as their inspiration, but my own thoughts hearken back to John Stuart Mill's *Autobiography*. Mill was one of the greatest intellectuals of the nineteenth century, and it all began with his extraordinary home education. Starting at age three, his father gave him lessons in Greek and arithmetic, the latter being "a most disagreeable process." In his autobiography, Mill doesn't mention any lessons in reading English—a feat he probably mastered in utero. At an age when most American children would be first encountering phonics, Mill was lisping Greek vocables. Meanwhile, his father took long walks every morning before breakfast, and from ages four through eight, little John Stuart accompanied him, giving his dad daily accounts of all he had read the day before, assisted by notes that he wrote on slips of paper.

No *Cat in the Hat* for this four-year-old; in his kindergarten years, Mill read the great histories of the world: Hume, Gibbon, Herodotus, Plutarch. This little boy absorbed the lessons of Rome and Greece, England and Napoleonic France, the Netherlands fighting Spain, the knights of Malta fighting the Turks. At age seven he "felt a lively interest in Frederic of Prussia," and when it came to "the American War," he supported what he called in retrospect "the wrong side" (i.e., the English). Because Mill's father was a historian, the family possessed a huge historical library. Fiction, however, received short shrift, although Mill did read *The Arabian Nights* and *Don Quixote* before age eight. At that point he commenced Latin lessons, which he was required to repeat to his younger sister, and from there, Mill began to teach all of his little siblings, which compelled him to learn his subjects more thoroughly than ever.

In other words, by age fourteen John Stuart Mill had read and taught more than most Harvard professors. Mill is to classical education what Mozart is to music.

Unfortunately his education strengthened his mind more than his soul. In his early twenties, Mill suffered a mental breakdown, falling into a deep depression that lasted a few years. Some readers point to this crisis in Mill's life with almost ghoulish glee, as if the genius's breakdown provides license for the rest of us to wallow in mediocrity. But I remain fascinated with Mill's education. Although I never wanted to inflict Greek on my toddlers, his experience offers a reminder of how much potential resides in children's minds.

The Well-Trained Mind seemed to outline a modest version of Mill's superhuman education. Here was the classical trivium presented for the intellectual mortals among us. These authors allowed eighteen years instead of eight for a child to learn the classics (and in *translation*, moreover). Nevertheless, their ambitious agenda left me daunted. Fingering through that book, I fell asleep each night thinking how, in our imperfect worlds, we mothers constantly fall short. In my brief homeschooling experiment, the best I could hope for Julia was that, by year's end, she would have read some children's versions of the *Iliad* and *Odyssey*.

Jessie Wise and her daughter did write something that gave me hope; they explained that fifth grade is an ideal year to homeschool. In the earlier years, children are busy learning the nuts and bolts of reading and math, memorizing facts in science and history without gathering them into a coherent picture. By fifth grade, most kids are eager to discuss the world. They are curious and inquisitive, ready to exercise all the skills accumulated in previous years, and they are primed to benefit from one-on-one tutoring. It seemed that Julia and I would be stepping into homeschooling at the perfect moment, and I felt grateful to the public school teachers who had laid the foundation before me.

One other thing struck me about *The Well-Trained Mind*, an issue destined to come up frequently as I surveyed homeschooling books. In this case it emerged in the opening sentences:

> *If you're fortunate, you live near an elementary school filled with excellent teachers who are dedicated to developing your child's skills in reading, writing, arithmetic, history, and science. These teachers have small classes—no more than ten students—and can give each student plenty of attention.*

Whoa. I sat up in bed. *No more than ten students?* That pie-in-the-sky number appeared like an arrogant wave of a queen's hand, abruptly dismissing all the lowly public schools in America, and most private ones as well. Admittedly, the overcrowding in America's public schools is unconscionable. Elementary classes with thirty or more children are a national disgrace, and any administrators or statisticians who claim that class size doesn't substantially affect performance have obviously had their brains addled by test-score fever. Sure, one hundred children can recite in unison that Columbus sailed the ocean blue in fourteen hundred ninety-two. But small class size is crucial for the one-on-one attention needed to teach writing, which is why many American schools fail miserably in that area. I thought our local elementary school was doing an admirable job holding classroom maximums at around seventeen.

In the coming weeks I found that *The Well-Trained Mind*'s dismissive tone toward the public schools was mild compared to other homeschooling books, where attitudes toward government-sponsored education could get openly nasty. Take *Homeschooling for Excellence*, by David and Micki Colfax. I sought that book out next because I was curious to read a homeschooling manifesto penned by the parents of a college acquaintance. *Homeschooling for Excellence* was blessedly short: an easy 150 pages, a home educator's beach read. Stretched in our backyard hammock with book in hand, I found myself very impressed with the Colfaxes' unique lifestyle. Their California homestead had no television and no close neighbors, and their sons' daily physical labor was essential to maintaining the farm. Under those circumstances, reading was a delightful recreation for the children—a break from work, not work itself. The same was true for math equations; they were puzzles, not problems.

With so much to admire in the Colfaxes' book, I regretted every time the tone got highhanded. Take the book's full title: *Homeschooling for Excellence: How to Take Charge of Your Child's Education and Why You Absolutely Must*. Who are these presumptuous strangers, I wondered, to tell other parents what we *must* do? And as for their assessment of public education: "an abysmal performance by an institution rife with mediocrity, ineptitude, and political corruption." Ouch.

Over the coming weeks, as I surveyed more books, I often found battle lines drawn between home educators and the public schools. It seemed that in the year ahead I would have to tread carefully in the no-man's-land between the two camps.

The Colfaxes had some standing for criticizing public education, because Micki Colfax had been a public school teacher. So, too, for Jessie Wise, who had worked as a teacher and principal before turning to homeschooling. In fact, many Titans of today's homeschooling movement, John Holt among them, started out as disaffected public school teachers. The most eloquent homeschooling book I encountered was written by one such veteran: David Guterson. These days Guterson is known for having written the highly acclaimed novel *Snow Falling on Cedars*, but before penning that story, he taught high school in Seattle, growing so disillusioned that when it came time for his eldest son to enter kindergarten, he and his wife walked their boy to the school bus stop, waited until the bus arrived and opened its door, then couldn't bear to let him go. They turned back and began a new life as committed homeschoolers.

Guterson wanted a community-based education for his sons; he wanted them to learn from real-life encounters. His book *Family Matters: Why Homeschooling Makes Sense* offers lyrical descriptions of how he nurtured his sons' curiosity about salmon: "Feeding the salmon fry, weekly, at a nearby holding pond, and measuring their growth and development, graphing changes in water temperature and flow, examining eggs, weighing out feed." Not to mention the days they spent "visiting the Elwha River hatchery, the fish ladders at the Rocky Reach dam, the Science Center Display on the Nootka people."

Family Matters presents a gorgeous vision of education, made even more beautiful by its Pacific Northwest setting. Here are long, rapturous field trips and even longer, more rapturous conversations. Daily kitchen-table practice with math and grammar is followed by excursions to the Fish Market and Space Needle. Homeschooling Guterson-style sounds like paradise.

Only one thing bothered me as I read that book, and it was a problem I also had with the others. None of these authors described the daily struggles of homeschooling. They mulled over curricula and philosophies and all the flaws of traditional schools, but they didn't discuss the power struggles and irrational moments of fury that emerge in any family, however loving.

Maybe they wanted to protect their children's privacy. Maybe they didn't want to reveal their families' dark sides. Or perhaps their families don't have dark sides. Perhaps they all enjoy perfect parent-child relationships, with minimal arguing, whining, and teeth-gnashing.

Julia and I aren't like that. Raising Julia has always been a struggle as well as a joy. She cried so much as a baby that John and I let her keep a pacifier until age four. Once the pacifier was removed, out of her mouth flowed a stream of objections: objections to shoes, hairbrushes, and toothpaste; objections to leaving the house, leaving the store, leaving the creek. I prefer an argumentative child to a sheepish one, but parenthood is especially challenging when every request becomes a battle. Getting Julia out of bed can be a Sisyphean task.

Among the millions of homeschoolers in America, there must be plenty who have stormy encounters with their children, and who sometimes doubt the efficacy of their teaching. Those people, however, don't seem to write books. In the homeschooling volumes I encountered, expressions of serious frustration seemed taboo. One afternoon, when browsing through our library's reference section, I picked up *The Homeschooling Alma-*

nac, 2000–2001, and began scanning through the "Frequently Asked Questions." Only one query approached my concerns:

Q: "What if I can't stand to be with my kids all day?"

Admittedly, the question was ill-phrased. I might have put it this way: "What if my daughter and I are both strong-willed females who might drive each other crazy if we spend all day together?" Regardless of semantics, the authors' reply left me dumbfounded:

> *A: People don't ask this question often, but when they do, we are always shocked and saddened. We believe parents who cannot stand to be with their children don't really know them. And if they don't like their children, they are probably seeing a child who isn't "real" but is a creation of marketing, school peer pressure, fear, low self-esteem, and alienation.*

Oh pllllease, I thought. The question didn't say, "What if I don't like my children?" or "What if I can't stand to be with my kids?" The questioner was expressing anxiety about being with one's kids *all day*, which struck me as a reasonable concern. Moms need downtime; they need silence and solitude and some occasional peace. Most stay-at-home-moms can recall the blessed joy on the first day when their toddler was old enough to attend preschool for a few mornings each week. Oh, the pleasure of those hours—the napping, the reading, the shopping that gets done without a child in tow. "But a homeschooled child can help you with the shopping," some authors might interject. Yes, but it's not the same. There should be a special punishment (a day in the stocks?) for writers who call it "shocking" and "saddening" when a parent confesses that she might go nuts if she spent all day with her kids.

Nevertheless, I kept reading homeschooling books, setting

aside ones with chapter headings such as "Homeschooling God's Way." In the process, I discovered the queens of homeschooling how-to guides, Linda Dobson and Rebecca Rupp, and I made a mental note to return to them later.

As I perused these books, one question kept coming up: Why should I focus exclusively on one child? If homeschooling had so many benefits, shouldn't I teach all three of my daughters, and make it a family affair? That's how most homeschoolers operate; the siblings form a social unit, and learn from one another as the years progress. One-on-one homeschooling seemed like a lonely proposition for Julia.

And yet, when I looked at the largest homeschooling families in our town, with three or four children still under the parents' wings, I wondered if a few of those kids might not thrive in a good public school classroom. Realistically, homeschooling could not work equally well for all members of a family.

My daughters provided a clear example. It took me less than sixty seconds to decide that Rachel, my middle child, would hate homeschooling. For Rachel, maternal instruction equals maternal criticism. When it comes to most school projects, Rachel prefers to keep me at arm's length, and I bless her for it. On those rare occasions when she solicits aid, the results can be volatile, because Rachel is a perfectionist with a fiery temper. As a preschooler, she used to spend fifteen minutes every morning putting on her socks, taking them off, and putting them on again, raging at the intransigence of cotton as she tried to get the line of stitching at the end of each sock to fall evenly, like a white rainbow, over the tips of her toes. While I fretted over Julia's loner instincts and rocky start in the public schools, my mother in-law just shook her head.

"Julia is not the one you need to worry about." She nodded toward Rachel. "That's the one to keep an eye on. She's wound way too tightly around the axle."

I never did worry very much about Rachel, largely because of her intellectual gifts. At age three, she read comfortably; at age seven, voraciously. She hit the public schools running and delighted in making As on almost every assignment. Report cards cannot measure a child's well-being, but Rachel also seemed to enjoy the social life of school. When I asked if she would want to be homeschooled, she didn't hesitate: "I'd miss my friends too much."

Hanging out with her sister would provide no substitute for Rachel's friends. Far from it. Only eighteen months apart in age, Julia and Rachel mix like baking soda and vinegar. Every day I play referee in their verbal, and sometimes physical, battles, sending them to their separate corners of the house. If Julia, Rachel, and I were to stay home for a year, the results would be worse than a three ring circus—more like the Bermuda triangle.

And what about Kathryn, my youngest daughter? Kathryn could be very happy as a homeschooler, or very happy in the public schools, because Kathryn is naturally cheerful. Perhaps the public schools would thwart that happiness; perhaps the test-prep culture would sap her joy. I couldn't say, because she had yet to enter kindergarten. In the fall, Kathryn was scheduled to try her first taste of public education. Most of her preschool friends would be attending Waddell, and I wanted to let her take the plunge at their side. If the experience turned out badly, maybe Kathryn could try some homeschooling in the future. For now, she needed time away from Mom, since she tended to be overly, sometimes ferociously, attached to me.

Waddell seemed sufficient for Rachel and Kathryn; only Julia needed a break from school. The coming year would be a special one-on-one experience with my eldest daughter—an educational odyssey scripted to meet her unique needs.

"You're really going through with this homeschooling idea?" John asked one night as we sat up reading in bed.

"Sure looks like it," I answered, holding up my latest home-schooling volume.

"I know that the one-on-one tutoring would be great for Julia," John said, his position apparently softening. "But what about her socialization?"

I sighed. "She's not really connected to the social world at school. Most of her social life takes place afterward. And besides, this is just for one year. She's going to have twelve years of public education." I didn't add that the "socialization" offered at most public and private schools contains an equal proportion of benefits and dangers, and that social skills can be learned in many places, far from classrooms and cafeterias and gymnasiums.

"I guess you've got a point," John said, "if it's just for one year."

Feeling totally committed (crazy or not), I found my questions coming in an avalanche. Was I legally allowed to homeschool Julia? Would she still be required to take Virginia's fifth-grade Standards of Learning tests? Could she be forced to repeat the fifth grade if I did a lousy job?

"Questions? Call Claire!" said the homeschool bulletin board at our public library, and as fate would have it, I already knew Claire. She was another ex-schoolteacher who hadn't wanted to entrust her two sons to the public system. Too many aspects of the schools conflicted with her Christian background and her pedagogical ideals. "It's sad," she said, "to get all that training and then have your hands tied." With her own boys, she wanted to be free of state mandates and employ her teaching degree in the manner she saw fit.

When I asked about legal requirements, she directed me to the website for the Home School Legal Defense Association. HSLDA offers advice and legal services for homeschoolers facing problems from local or state officials, and when I opened their website and typed in "legal requirements," I encountered a map of America, with states colored green, yellow, orange, and red. In the green states, homeschoolers enjoy a complete green light; they don't even have to notify the local schools of their intent to abstain. Ten states fall under this category, and I wasn't surprised to see Texas among them. But New Jersey and Connecticut? There, too, parents could do anything with their kids' education, no questions asked.

Virginia appeared bright orange, having what the HSLDA considers to be "moderate regulation." I would substitute the word *minimal* for *moderate*. It seemed that, in Virginia, you needed a high school diploma in order to homeschool, or else you had to hire a tutor for your kids. Virginians also needed to inform the local school superintendent of their intention to homeschool, and had to describe their curricular plans. "Curricular plans," however, could be as concise as one sentence: "I plan to use the Calvert Curriculum," or "I plan to follow Virginia's SOLs."

At the end of the year, most homeschooled children in Virginia must take some sort of standardized test, the only requirement that made me a little queasy. But Claire explained that if I sent twenty-five dollars to an Internet company, they would mail the fifth-grade California Achievement Tests to my home. I could administer the exams myself, then send Julia's answer sheet back to the company's PO Box. In a couple of weeks I would receive a copy of the results, to be forwarded to our school superintendent. So long as Julia scored above the lowest twenty-fifth percentile, she could advance to the next grade.

Overall, Virginia's homeschooling regulations struck me as very lax. There were no attendance or recordkeeping requirements, no specific subjects that I needed to teach. In fact, parents in Virginia can ignore all of the regulations if they file for a religious exemption.

I had assumed that most states would require homeschooling parents to have a college degree, but as I clicked on all the states that had earned HSLDA's red light, North Dakota was the only one that asked for a BA. Even there, parents who had never finished college could still homeschool, as long as they passed the state teacher's examination.

I respected stodgy old North Dakota, with its mild attempt at holding homeschoolers accountable. The thought that in forty-nine states any parent who'd scraped through high school with a D average could then teach high school to their own children struck me as setting the bar very low. In my case, however, the lack of regulation was highly convenient. To homeschool Julia, I needed only to produce a curriculum, and although HSLDA advises against telling local school districts much of anything about one's plans—the less you reveal, the less they can challenge—I felt compelled to justify my decision to homeschool by assembling an impressive program.

I began by examining Virginia's fifth-grade Standards of Learning, available on the Internet, to see what Julia's peers would be taught. The English requirements were basic—all the grammar and spelling and reading comprehension that most kids can absorb through constant reading and writing—but they did inspire me to add one line to my to-do list: "Buy the *Schoolhouse Rock* DVD." After thirty years, "Conjunction Junction" still has no rival.

Next came math, the nemesis of my own school days. Virginia's fifth-grade requirements include decimals and fractions, geometry and probability, measurement and a tiny smattering of statistics. I supposed I was going to need a refresher course in dividing with decimals. Otherwise, the nice thing about homeschooling in the elementary grades is that the math still falls within most parents' comfort zones. By high school, many homeschoolers hire private tutors, or enroll their kids in college classes, but the early years are a different story. Even when it came to math, I felt that I was as smart as a fifth-grader.

One notable absence from Virginia's fifth-grade requirements was Roman numerals. In our school district, Roman numerals had become the exclusive knowledge of Latin students, but I still had a fondness for all those capital letters—those *V*s and *X*s and *L*s that almost made numbers into words.

"Hey, Julia," I asked, "did you ever talk about Roman numerals at school?"

"I don't think so," she responded.

"Would you like to learn them?"

"Sure," she said, shrugging, and I added them to our list.

I was also surprised that Julia couldn't guess where Arabic numerals came from. "*Arab-ic*," I said to her. "*ARAB-ic?*" She had no clue. (Actually, they originated in India, but the Arabs brought them to Europe's attention.) Neither did Julia (nor I) know much about the history of zero. Why didn't the Romans use it? Before embarking on Virginia's math essentials, I thought we should back up and learn about the history of mathematics: where numbers came from and why.

Math was the sole subject where I planned to buy a textbook; generally I avoid them. There's nothing like a heavy, dull text to drain the pleasure from literature or history. Most of my home-schooling friends recommended the Saxon math method, and the *Saxon 65* book seemed well organized and clear. In one area, however, the book couldn't help me.

Julia had not been learning her multiplication tables in the same manner I remembered as a child. I had learned my twos and threes and fours sequentially, in times tables, but Julia's instruction had hopped around, starting with easy numbers, such as two, five, and ten. This approach didn't seem to have worked for her, because her retention was entirely piecemeal. She needed to back up and relearn her math facts one number at a time: first two, then three, then four. I thought that we might spend a month (or less, as needed) on the number three—multiplying and dividing by 33.33, computing the area and perimeter of rectangles three inches long, cutting pies into thirds, then ninths, then twelfths. Whatever the mathematical concept at hand, we could practice it while saturated in our number of the week. This meant that I would have to write out a lot of math worksheets separate from the Saxon supply—but so be it. A weekly schedule for math was taking shape in my head.

When it came to social studies, Virginia's fifth-graders focused entirely on American history, from pre-Columbian times through the Civil War. Neither Julia nor I was impressed with that plan.

"Do you want to study American history next year?" I asked her. She replied by sticking her finger in the back of her throat and pretending to vomit.

Julia had been studying American history ever since kindergarten, in Virginia's "spiral method," where students return again and again to the same material at a slightly higher level, year after year. American history had dominated her elementary curriculum, and in middle school, Julia would face two more years of American history and government, followed by two more years in the second half of high school. Forget about the Renaissance or the Enlightenment. Forget about most foreign cultures; they could be crammed into a few years of world geography and history. In Virginia's model, America was the only country that merited in-depth study, which meant in-depth boredom for the children.

"Okay." I hastened to stop Julia's simulated barfing. "We'll race through American history in the last four months of the year. We can visit the new Museum of Native American History in Washington when we study Indians, and for the Colonial period, we can spend three days in the spring exploring Williamsburg and Yorktown." Since we reside in a town where Robert E. Lee and Stonewall Jackson lived and are buried, Julia already knew plenty about the "War of Northern Aggression."

"So what should we study instead of America?" I asked Julia. "Are there any ancient cultures you'd like to know more about?" I thought she would choose the Egyptians, or maybe Greece or Rome, but one of Julia's greatest strengths is that she never does what one expects.

"The Maya," she said. Fair enough. I had always wanted to learn more about the Incas, so I persuaded Julia that they would complement the Maya well, and we threw in the Aztecs to complete the trio. Her school had touched upon Montezuma's world in the past, but they hadn't gone into detail.

"And what about science?" Virginia's SOLs seemed haphazard on that score. Fifth-graders were supposed to study the oceans, and sound and light, and loads of other topics. But what did it matter whether a ten-year-old focused on the sea or sky? Who cared whether she studied weather in the third grade or the fourth? Julia's interests were clear: "I want to study dinosaurs."

I hesitated to spend a lot of time on dinosaurs, since they were the one subject Julia knew inside and out. She had read every children's dinosaur book at our local public library, and we had taken her to see fossil collections at museums of natural history in New York, London, Philadelphia, and Washington. The first rule of homeschooling, however, is to encourage the child's interests.

"Sure, we'll do a whole unit on dinosaurs," I promised.

"And what else?"

"Dragons," she answered.

"Anything that does not involve a scaly beast?"

Julia thought for a while. "Maybe flight, since dragons can fly."

"And we can study flying dinosaurs, like pterodactyls?" I suggested.

Julia sighed. "How many times do I have to tell you that pterosaurs aren't dinosaurs."

Later that week, she and I visited the local library, looking for children's books that could form our reading list for the coming year. I discovered a wonderful cartoon book full of stocky little Romans counting vases with *L*s and *X*s and *I*s, and Julia handed me a bright maroon book with a roaring T. rex on the cover: *The Beginning*, by Peter Ackroyd. Inside were marvelous photographs and drawings, surveying not only dinosaurs, but the whole development of life on Earth, from the Big Bang through *Homo erectus*. The book was colorful, well written, and ideal for Julia, who liked not only dinosaurs but also all the bizarre fishes and mammals that came before and after. This, I told her, could be the guiding source for our first semester. In August and early September we could study atoms and tectonic plates and volcanoes (all SOL subjects) as we read about the formation of the planet. Then we could spend a few weeks learning about the oceans as we studied how life developed from them. Most of October could be devoted to dinosaurs; November, to early mammals; and December, to a brief survey of primates and cavemen. In January we could skip forward to the Maya, and use the ancient cultures of the Americas as a segue into pre-Columbian Native Americans. We'd reach 1492 by the end of February.

"That's ambitious," one homeschooling mom laughed when I told her our plan. In other words: "That's too much." The trouble with trying to balance a public curriculum with private interests is that you can fall into a game of "Anything you can do, I can do better." If the public school fifth-graders are adding and subtracting fractions, then your child should be multiplying and dividing them. If their history lessons begin in the sixteenth century, then yours should go back to the medieval age. This is not as difficult as it sounds, since the public school day includes a fair amount of repetition and wasted time, but still, you wind up with an agenda that leaves little room for relaxation.

"What the heck," I told myself. It was a rookie's prerogative to be ambitious, and Julia and I were getting excited about our big plans.

Even John was starting to get in the spirit. Never wanting to be left out of a family project, he agreed to my request to give Julia lessons in French and the flute on two afternoons each week. "It would be great to spend more time with Julia," he explained. "You just have to remember that I have a job." Fortunately, many of John's musical duties took place at evening rehearsals or weekend sports events, so the afternoons seemed like a good chance for father-daughter learning.

As a final step in drafting a curriculum, I decided to consult with Julia's current teacher, Mrs. Gonzalez. Thus far I had hesitated to mention my ideas to anyone at Julia's school; I had a childish fear that if word got around, I'd be in trouble with the principal. I also felt that telling Mrs. Gonzalez about our homeschooling schemes was sort of like informing your boyfriend that you've decided to live with a woman. I didn't want Mrs. G to think that she had driven us to it.

Nevertheless, I valued her opinion. She knew Julia; she knew the public system; her husband taught at the middle school that Julia would enter the following year, so she was well acquainted with the expectations for sixth-graders. She was an intelligent woman with decades of experience teaching and raising a daughter. I thought she might lend a sympathetic ear.

The two of us sat down after school one day in early May, and I explained that Julia and I would be taking a one-year break from the public schools. We were fine with the teachers at Waddell, I assured her, but Julia was exhausted, and I had a long-term predilection toward homeschooling, dating back to my own miserable public school days.

Mrs. Gonzalez nodded, completely unsurprised. "I think a year of homeschooling could be a really good thing for Julia."

"So," I continued, "I've started to put together a curriculum, and I've been wondering: If you were free from the SOLs, and could teach whatever you pleased, what would you spend your time on?"

She thought for a moment. "Well, I wouldn't worry about Virginia's history and science guidelines if I were you. Just read what you like in those areas. But if I had the choice, I'd do more author studies. I'd like to have the children read three or four books by one author at a time, learn about that person's life, and do class presentations. There are so many great writers that we never get to." She recommended Avi, Susan Cooper, and Natalie Babbitt. "And creative writing," she added. "We used to do much more writing in the fourth grade."

I had often heard this lament from Waddell's veteran teachers, as if there had been a paradisal state before the fall. "Just make sure that Julia doesn't lag behind in math," Mrs. Gonzalez added. "She has a gift for math."

I raised my eyebrows. "Math is her worst subject. She hasn't even learned all of her multiplication tables."

"There's a difference between arithmetic and mathematics," Mrs. G. explained. "Julia struggles with arithmetic. So did my daughter. It took her years to learn her times tables. But once Julia gets those math facts down, she'll have a great mind for math."

With many thanks to Mrs. G., I continued in the next few weeks to ask other teachers the same question: "What would you teach in your classroom if you were entirely free from the SOLs?"

"More science experiments," said one. "Children love them. Right now we don't get enough time to teach the scientific method."

"More hours in the garden," another said. "The children learn best from hands-on work."

"Typing," said Mrs. Patrick, the coordinator of Waddell's gifted program. "Students who can type have a real advantage in middle school."

With each conversation, I felt more convinced that Julia and I were lucky to have the freedom to take a year off. Here, in the public schools, all of these bright women and men, with years of experience and training, were constricted by bureaucratic guidelines, never teaching what they really wanted, never fully playing to their strengths, never left alone. What a gift it was for a parent and child to study whatever they valued most.

For some parents, an ideal curriculum might include carpentry or auto mechanics, geology or etymology, film study or Bible study—all of it is possible in homeschooling. All I knew was that the best education comes from sharing one's passions. My passions lay in literature and music, while Julia loved dinosaurs and art, so those four subjects would get center stage in the coming year.

Now I felt prepared to write a "letter of intent" to our school superintendent, Dr. Lane, but I wanted to phrase it delicately. Notifying a school system of your intention to homeschool resembles the break-up of a long-term love affair. You've been involved in a close daily relationship for years, but somehow it hasn't met your needs. You have to tell your significant other that you want out. For permanent homeschoolers, the process can resemble a divorce, complete with verbal nastiness and legal battles over custody of the kids. In my case, I basically wanted to say, "I'd like to date other people for a year, but at the end, I want you to take me back, okay?"

Our school system was not obliged to take Julia back. We are county residents who pay tuition (currently one thousand dollars a year per child) to have our kids attend the Lexington city schools. Each year, we must reapply for admission and put down a deposit. Normally the city schools gladly welcome rural children and their dollars, since Lexington's population is increasingly geriatric. But what if Dr. Lane didn't like homeschoolers? Would he bump Julia out to the county middle school?

Dr. Lane was a little unpredictable when it came to homeschooling. When another mom had told him about her plans to homeschool her son from eighth grade forward, he tried to talk her out of it. High school was crucial for college preparation, so he insisted. Homeschooling might hurt her son's chances of admission. That mom wound up being a one-year homeschooler like me, although not because of the superintendent's concerns.

In the end, I wrote a groveling letter that essentially translated as "It's not you, it's me." The local school system was fine, I explained to Dr. Lane (swallowing my impulse to write a ten-page critique of the excessive test preparations). My other two daughters would still attend, but Julia needed something different.

The superintendent offered no objections. Perhaps because I was talking about only the fifth grade, or perhaps because this man had once taken a turn searching for Julia in the Waddell halls, he was perfectly open to my homeschooling plans. "You've obviously thought this through," he wrote back; he hoped the experience "would renew Julia's love of learning." Dr. Lane foresaw no problems with Julia entering the sixth grade the following year, and although he wasn't obliged to do so, he returned our deposit for the fall.

That letter of blessing, with its assumption that middle school waited for Julia in another year, regardless of how well or badly we managed at home, felt like the wave of a starting flag. With my plans officially on record, I now shared them with all of my acquaintances and relatives. Most seemed to think it was a good idea, or at least that's what they said to my face. What they thought behind those indulgent smiles, I'll never know.

Now came one of the most fun aspects of homeschooling: the shopping. Some homeschoolers buy stacks of textbooks and worksheets; I bought toys and games and rockets, puzzles of human anatomy and world geography, and science kits for crystals and electric circuits. I bought card games that ranged from The Scrambled States of America to Fraction Jugglers, and I purchased season tickets to the American Shakespeare Theater, which performed in a small nearby city that boasted a reproduction of Shakespeare's Blackfriars Playhouse.

My favorite store for homeschooling supplies turned out to be the children's shop at the National Gallery in Washington. After all, why settle for Barbie coloring books when you could be coloring Van Gogh? And instead of painting kittens by number, how about mandalas? I purchased a card game that was a cross between gin rummy and Go Fish, where each card featured an impressionist painting; Julia would collect groups of masterpieces by Monet, Manet, Degas, and Berthe Morisot.

Thus our homeschooling began not with the first school day in August, but with all of our summer preparations. In June, I told Julia that she must choose a few authors to study in the coming fall. Would she please read one book by each of the writers on our list and decide which ones she'd like to examine further?

And would she try out this puzzle of the United States and let me know if it was any good? And what about this Quantum Leap geography game? Julia's learning was well under way as she sampled all our new products.

I also became much more diligent about including Julia in any cultural event that might be educational. In early August, when my sister asked if I'd like to join her and a friend at *Madama Butterfly*, performed outdoors at James Monroe's historic mansion, Ash Lawn–Highland, I asked, "Can Julia come along?" My ten-year-old proved to be a good opera companion, able to follow the story and appreciate the arias, although what she enjoyed most was the skunk that kept wandering in and out of the boxwoods, making the audience twitter.

"The skunk comes out whenever the soprano sings," Julia whispered.

By mid-August, as the first day of the new school year approached, I was feeling quite confident, thinking that Julia and I could handle this homeschooling thing, no problem. Of course there would be ups and downs, but how bad could they be?

Then came an ominous note of warning.

I was eating lunch at a local café when I ran into my friend Todd, a professor of history.

"You're going to homeschool?" he said when I told him about my plans. "I tried that once." He shook his head and sighed. Apparently the memories weren't very good.

"What happened?" I asked.

"When my son was in high school he got into a terrible bike accident and was out of school for six weeks, so I homeschooled him. I was a single parent at the time. My wife and I were in a commuting marriage, and she was only home on weekends, so I was on my own. Anyway, I knew what my son was capable of, so

I was demanding. But as I pushed, he resisted, and the result was very unpleasant."

From the expression on his face, I could tell that "unpleasant" was an understatement.

"The level of frustration was so painful"—Todd hesitated—"our relationship was deteriorating. It's not the academics that are the problem, you know. When my son went back to school and took his tests, he got the best grades he had all year. But those grades did not mean as much to me as our relationship."

"There is a natural role for the parent as teacher," Todd continued. "But that is primarily for the teaching of values. When it comes to teaching math and English, I'd rather let a third party do the pushing."

Seeing my slightly crestfallen expression, Todd tried to be kind: "If there's anyone I would trust as homeschoolers, it would be you and John. You two have the knowledge and the socialization skills to pass along to your daughter. But for me, it was a disaster."

Todd's words were especially sobering because he expressed with blunt honesty the fears that had been lingering in the back of my mind. I knew that I could handle the academic side of homeschooling; what mattered was how I tackled the emotional turmoil of a parent and child bound in close contact. At stake was nothing less than a mother and daughter's love.

With three days before the start of school, Todd's final word hovered above my head like an angel's sword: *disaster*.

CHAPTER FOUR

➤➤Day One◄◄

*I was a little nervous about starting
homeschooling. I mean, it's kind of like riding
on a roller coaster—you don't know what's going
to happen, and you're really scared before
you take the first plunge.*

JULIA

SCHOOL BEGAN ON A WARM MORNING IN THE THIRD WEEK OF August, as my three daughters climbed into the backseat of our car. Rachel and Kathryn lugged backpacks and lunchboxes stuffed with peanut butter and jelly sandwiches, apples and string cheese and chocolate chip cookies. Beneath their napkins lay cartoons that John inserts on special occasions: bug-eyed caricatures of the two of us saying, "Hope your day is going great!" Julia carried nothing but a five-by-eight notebook and a pencil.

When we reached Waddell and pulled up in the drop-off line, my younger girls hopped out, with Rachel pausing to blow me a kiss before taking Kathryn's hand. The day before, I had walked Kathryn inside the building for "Meet the Teacher," leading her to a classroom just beyond the front door. There we had found her name at a cluster of four desks: "Look! Kelly is sitting across from you!" Kathryn had arranged her notebooks and pencils, donated her glue and tissues to the class supply, and listened shyly while the teacher showed her where to put her lunch bag, backpack, and coat each morning. Between the brightly painted walls and the teacher's friendly smile, Kathryn felt comfortable enough so that now, on her first day of kindergarten, she didn't need me to hold her hand. Her big sister was sufficient, and much more cool. Meanwhile, a teacher stood outside at our open car door and waited.

"Aren't you coming, Julia?"

"No," Julia announced, glad to be asked. "I'm being home-schooled!"

The teacher glanced at me with surprise, and I nodded confirmation. Julia would not be coming to school this day or the next. Children within hearing distance turned to stare, and Julia waved, grinning out the back window as we pulled away.

She and I had agreed that if her sisters were going to attend school from 8:30 to 3:00 every day, she should follow a similar routine. No sleeping until ten—a luxury some homeschoolers enjoy. No finishing school by noon, even though much of our academic work could be compressed into less than four hours. For the sake of sibling equality, we would find activities to fill six and a half hours each day.

This didn't mean that Julia needed to ride in the car every morning. On most days she could linger in bed for an extra hour while Rachel and Kathryn dressed and ate. According to our agreement, by 8:45, when I got back from depositing her sisters, Julia had to be sitting at the kitchen table, dressed, fed, and ready to learn.

But this first morning was special. Julia had good reason to ride along in the car, apart from her desire to gloat at her school-bound peers. It was a Wednesday, and on Wednesday mornings the Lexington Coffee Shop opens its back room to any bluegrass musicians who feel inclined. The players range from intermediate to advanced; some perform in weekend bands, some play every blue moon. Some have names like Rooster and Burr, others answer to Steve and Joe. A few arrive in professional clothes: the upscale real estate agent in his crisp shirt and silk tie who picks at a guitar for an hour before opening his office at ten; the campus minister whose frizzy gray ponytail hangs down the back of a tweed blazer. Most wear denim and flannel.

They trickle in between 8:15 and 8:45, lugging black instrument cases and pouring free cups of the house blend before negotiating a short, narrow hallway into the back room. There they join tunes in progress, with the group growing from duet to trio, quartet to quintet. When Julia and I stepped into the shop at 8:30 we could hear strains of "Old Joe Clark."

Visitors to Lexington often ask for the nearest Starbucks, but they never seem disappointed by our home-grown alternative. The Lexington Coffee Shop, situated in a 150-year-old stretch of brick-front stores, has wood floors, a white ceiling molded like a frosted wedding cake, and peachy-salmon walls spattered antique-style that provide a gallery for local painters and photographers. Regular customers hang mugs on hooks near the counter, beside the muffins, pound cake, and scones made by a nearby baker. High on the walls behind the counter, chalkboards list flavors that range from the local (Blue Ridge Blend, Lexington Blend, Mrs. Hennis's Blend, named after Julia's beloved first-grade teacher) to the international (Ethiopia Harrar, Sumatra Mandheling, Tanzania Teaberry). Most are made from beans ground in a small warehouse outside of town, next to the drive-in theater.

For years, I had wanted to bring Julia to the coffee shop for a little bluegrass—to share with her the delight of starting the day with hot drinks and warm music. Julia had a wonderful ear for all types of music, but on Wednesday mornings she was usually at school, or sleeping late in the summer. Homeschooling was our chance to sample the local pleasures together.

On that first morning, Julia ordered hot chocolate, I bought an orange juice, and in a back room barely twenty feet by twenty feet, we edged our drinks past a half-dozen musicians and settled at a small table near the elbow of Jay Mills, a man in his late thirties with auburn hair and a broad moustache. Jay leaned over a small round table and opened the clasps on what looked to be a leather briefcase. Inside lay more than a dozen harmonicas tucked into two columns of crushed velvet.

"Look, Julia." I pointed. "Did you know that harmonicas come in different keys?"

Jay lifted one and it disappeared within his palms, cupped at his lips as if he were blowing on his fingers to warm them. Out came a chord like a train whistle, Jay's fingers flapping in a sideways wave goodbye.

"What instruments do you recognize?"

Julia noted the stand-up bass, the guitars, the harmonica, the violin (a fiddle in this context, I explained).

"But what is that round, twangy one?" she asked.

"That's a banjo."

"And what is that small instrument hunched in the man's arms?"

"A mandolin."

In Julia's mind these two words blurred, so that, over the next few weeks, she would sometimes say, "Look at the guy playing on his manjo."

"Banjo," I always replied, not mentioning that *manjo* sounded like an obscene Austin Powers euphemism.

On that first morning the group played "Rocky Top," and Julia did what comes naturally to her: she sang along. No words, just a harmony of ooooos and aahhhs.

A few eyes glanced our way, and I did what comes naturally to me: I shushed my daughter.

"Sing quietly, Julia. Not so loud."

My daughters are all spontaneous singers, as if life were one big musical, and I welcome their songs as expressions of joy—so long as they limit them to our car, our house, our walks in the woods. In public places I am a coward, determined not to disturb the peace. I tend to care about other people's opinions—although that inclination fades with age—and Rachel and Kathryn share my instincts, confining their melodies to private spaces. But in Julia's early years she was blessedly free of inhibitions. Throughout elementary school she was prone to sing and dance at public concerts, whether the music was classical, bluegrass, or jazz. As a young mother, I learned to take her to loud performances in venues with dark corners where she could dance to her heart's content, for Julia didn't dance with an adult's reserve. She spun, she jumped, she shook with exuberance, like a God-struck devotee at a tent revival. Rock concerts would have suited her well, but our small-town fare leaned toward string quartets and college musicals and John's band performances. Often, we listened to concerts from outside auditorium doors while Julia danced in the lobby.

At the coffee shop there was no room to dance. Listeners filled every table and barstool, some lined the wall, and Julia's singing dwindled as she dipped her lips into her whipped cream and chocolate flakes, emerging with a speckled moustache.

"Oops," she murmured, spying the hot chocolate that had dribbled onto her shirt. She wiped at her lips and shirt with her palm.

"Use a *napkin*," I said. Table manners would have to be added to the top of our curriculum.

In the meantime, I took out a small notebook.

"We spent two-fifty on your hot chocolate, one-twenty-five on my juice, and two dollars on that cranberry-walnut muffin. Can you calculate how much we spent?"

I passed the pencil and notebook to Julia, and she dutifully did the math.

"Now, tax is eight percent. Do you know how to translate eight percent into a decimal number?"

8.00? she wrote, and pushed the notebook back to me.

"Good guess, try again."

.8?

"No. Think about the word *percent*, how it has the word *cents* in there. How do you write eight cents as a decimal?"

.08?

"Right."

Eight percent tax, I explained, means that you have to pay eight pennies to the government for every dollar you spend.

"So how much tax did we just pay for our drinks and muffin?" I asked. Julia multiplied the bill by .08.

"That's right, good job," I nodded. Julia added the result into the total charge, and I showed her that it matched the number on the receipt.

On that first day I had elaborate visions of practical math lessons that could take place throughout our town. At the grocery store, Julia could carry a pocket notebook and pencil and estimate how much money we were spending. She could weigh fruit and vegetables to fulfill Virginia's SOL measurement requirements, and practice multiplication: If we buy three pounds of bananas at fifty-nine cents per pound, what's the total price?

I hoped to show her that our everyday lives are filled with arithmetic. If regular gas costs $2.92 per gallon, and we buy 15 gallons, how much will we pay? How much more will it cost if we buy the premium gas for $3.12? (We never do.)

Home improvements could provide lessons in geometry: "If we want to cover this *L*-shaped porch in green tile, how do we calculate the area of the space? And how many pieces of six-by-six tile will we need?" Menus might be more interesting than math worksheets: "Julia, how much will both of our lunches cost? If we tip the waitress eighteen percent, what does that come to? And what about the tax? Why do you think the tax at a restaurant is more than the tax at a grocery store?"

Oh, how naïve I was on that inaugural morning. I thought that Julia would appreciate these calculations, that they might be a kind of game, as well as a useful lesson in how quickly the daily expenses of life add up. But our first math lesson at the coffee shop offered a sign of things to come. Although Julia was willing to calculate our total for that day, when I gave her another problem, with hypothetical numbers ("What if we had ordered two coffees and a blueberry scone?"), she rolled her eyes.

"Can't I just enjoy the music, Mom?"

Good for her, you might say. Here was a child who knew what she wanted: to learn through sensory experience, to see and smell and touch and taste the world, and not be asked to add decimals when she could be watching a fiddler's bow. Which is all well and good, but it doesn't get you far when it comes to mastering long division. Practical math would require that Julia calculate more than one problem in an hour. Julia, however, clearly felt that the coffee shop was not a setting for math. As she put it: "Nothing ruins a good time like math equations."

Part of our challenge lay in the matter of de-schooling. Children from public schools are often locked into the belief that "education" happens at a desk, slumped over a textbook. It can take months of deprogramming for new homeschoolers to break their institutionalized habits—to open their minds to all the math and science and history lessons unfolding in the community around them, and be willing to spend time doing "schoolwork" outside a classroom setting.

Had I been more clever, I might have presented practical math to Julia in the form of a written contract: no math lessons at home on Wednesdays and Fridays so long as you agree to do a dozen math problems during our errands outside the house. Julia, a child enamored with making deals, who has a strong belief in justice and the sanctity of promises, would probably have signed on the dotted line. Then I could have waved the contract whenever she balked at calculating the fines on our overdue library books. Perhaps this would have worked, perhaps not. Homeschooling is a matter of constant experimentation.

When I saw that Julia resisted doing math problems at the coffee shop, I changed tack.

"Want to play cards?" Gin rummy could offer a brief lesson in arithmetic.

While Jay sang "Mustang Sally," taking a break from the bluegrass mode, Julia added up trios of kings and queens, threes and sevens, multiplying by fives and tens. Thus began a ritual that she and I would maintain on most Wednesday mornings for the rest of the year: listening to live music while playing cards, checkers, backgammon, dominoes, or mancala, all provided on the coffee shop's game table. Occasionally Julia would calculate three or four math equations. More often, I settled for the logic lessons that come from playing chess. As the weeks went by and Julia learned some basic French, we would also begin to converse in tiny foreign fragments:

"Tu as soif?"
"Oui, Maman."
"Qu'est-ce que tu veux boire?"

On that first morning, we left the coffee shop after forty-five minutes and drove less than a mile to the Virginia Military Institute. A drive through VMI's Post (what we civilians would call a "campus") provides an education in itself. Founded in 1837 as a kind of Southern West Point, VMI was the last all-male military college in the United States up until 1997, when it admitted women grudgingly in obedience to a Supreme Court ruling. VMI argued that women weren't suited to the school's "adversative method" for training freshmen, a system that was on display as Julia and I drove by. Cadets were clustered on the parade ground, sophomore cadre members in black T-shirts, camouflage pants, and army boots, barking into the faces of freshman "rats" with shaved heads. (Cadre members sometimes get so close that the rats' faces are showered with spit.) Graduates explain that VMI's program instills discipline and camaraderie, but in John's darkest moments he just shrugs and says, "VMI— where fun goes to die."

The military world, with its uniforms and guns and strict hierarchy, is more John's cup of tea than mine. Years ago, after his stint as a public school teacher, John shipped off to Marine Corps boot camp to preface four years of trumpet playing with the Marine Drum and Bugle Corps in Washington. So these days he feels comfortable with students who salute and call him Colonel Brodie, and he's completely at ease wearing camouflage to a parent-teacher conference. As for me, I feel a little apologetic every time I arrive at VMI, like I'm an agnostic visiting someone else's church.

Nevertheless, Julia and I proceeded down VMI's maple-lined avenue and she pointed to a statue across the parade ground. "There's George Marshall," she said, acknowledging the college's most famous alumnus. Julia once wrote a poem for Martin Luther King, Jr.'s birthday that contained these lines: "There are warriors for Peace / King, Gandhi, Marshall / These are their swords, / Life, light, and hope."

"Why did you put George Marshall next to King and Gandhi?" I asked.

"Because he's the only soldier to have won the Nobel Peace

prize." She had learned this on a school field trip to VMI's Marshall Museum, which now stood one hundred yards to our left.

Clever answer, I thought, but a little odd. Only in Lexington, Virginia, would a child group George Marshall alongside Gandhi.

That morning, we parked in front of VMI's Preston Library, stepped out of the car, and surveyed the buildings around us. VMI employs a similar architecture to its more famous counterpoint on the Hudson: tan stucco walls molded into castle façades, complete with parapets and cut-glass windows. However, the resemblance to West Point ends at the northern end of the parade ground, where an imposing statue of Stonewall Jackson assesses the field. He stands erect in his Confederate uniform, from angled hat to thigh-high boots, binoculars in one hand, sword in the other, an imaginary wind blowing open the flaps of his coat. Jackson taught at VMI before the Civil War began, and the school's rats are required to salute his statue every time they exit the barracks, a gesture that makes me flinch, though most of the cadets don't seem to mind.

Lexington treats Jackson as a kind of patron saint. Julia was born in Stonewall Jackson Hospital, and if she chooses to spend her entire life in this small town, she might live on Jackson Avenue or Stonewall Street. She might purchase a burial plot in the local cemetery, which radiates outward from a statue of the general that marks his grave. In fact, "Julia" was the name of Jackson's daughter, but we didn't know it at the time of our child's birth. We named her after John Lennon's song from the *White Album*.

That morning, Julia and I turned away from Jackson and entered Preston Library, where we walked upstairs through a room filled with solemn portraits of Confederate officers, mostly VMI alumni. A sign by a sofa contained the circled word *SUPINE* with a backslash through it.

"What does *supine* mean?" Julia asked.

"Lying down," I replied. "The cadets are sleepy all the time because they stay up late studying, and they wake at dawn for breakfast. They can't take afternoon naps because they have to roll up their mattresses in the morning and lean their bed frames against the wall, since they live four or five to a room, and there's no space for them to have their beds and desks out at the same time. The rats, in particular, are always exhausted, and the librarians don't want them coming here and sleeping on the couches."

Julia and I walked to the entrance of an enclosed room at the far end of the library, where a sign beside the door read "Timmins Music Room." We opened the door and entered a small oasis in VMI's Spartan world: comfortable armchairs, multiple CD players and headphones, and filing cabinets filled with classical music CDs. In the middle of the room stood a thin black sculpture of Orpheus, pitched forward in a balletic leap, toes pointed, a lyre held on his shoulder, shaped in a *V*. For "Victory"? For "VMI"? The sculpture's stone base read, "John W. Timmins, '49 / Killed in Action, Korea, 1950."

How sad, I thought. He died one year out of college.

"He's a pea brain," Julia remarked.

She was contemplating the sculpture's head, and she was right. Although Orpheus's body was a tapestry of muscles, anatomically well proportioned, his head was little bigger than his fist. All brawn and no brain.

"Maybe he's angry because the sculptor gave him a pea brain," Julia mused, staring at Orpheus's contemptuous sneer.

"Maybe he's angry," I said, "because his wife died shortly after they were married, and although he had a chance to get her out of the underworld, he blew it." I briefly recounted the story of Orpheus and Eurydice, thinking how homeschooling, just like parenthood, could inspire all sorts of impromptu lessons. I hadn't planned on talking about mythology that day, but there we stood, inspired by a statue I had never bothered to examine closely. This year's improvisations were bound to make me more attentive to the world around me, seeing it from Julia's perspective.

Julia eyed the statue critically. "So now he's going to be torn apart by wild women," she said, imagining the maenads. "That sucks."

"Stinks, not sucks," I murmured as I opened a filing cabinet full of CDs.

On that first day of homeschooling, I had the noble idea that each week I would introduce Julia to a famous piece of classical music, teaching her about various composers and musical genres. She had already been exposed to more music than most children, but up to that point she had never studied it in any systematic way. She liked Disney's *Fantasia*, versions one and two, but she couldn't name more than one of the composers featured in those films. Homeschooling, so I hoped, might give Julia a chance to become acquainted with a small repertoire of famous pieces. We could play them in the car—there would be lots of driving in our daily routine: fifteen-minute trips to town for violin lessons, tennis lessons, library visits, and shopping errands. In my rookie enthusiasm, I intended to pack those minutes with Brahms and Beethoven; God forbid that there be any unproductive gaps in our school day. (It would take me a couple of months to realize that unproductive gaps can produce wonderful, spontaneous lessons.)

In the mauve-walled Timmins Room, I flipped through the filing cabinets thinking, "Let us begin with something memorable for a child," maybe something used in the old *Bugs Bunny* cartoons. One reason that Warner Bros.' Looney Tunes cartoons still outclass today's Japanese imports—despite Julia's love of *anime*—is because the creators had good taste in music. *Peer*

Gynt accompanied each animated sunrise; Rossini's *William Tell Overture* sped every foot race; Bugs Bunny donned bullfighting gear to strains of *Carmen.*

I pulled out Richard Strauss's *Also Sprach Zarathustra*, a piece baby boomers know from *2001: A Space Odyssey.* It's a favorite musical selection for television advertisements and videotaped moon shots. The title, I explained to Julia, means "Thus Spoke Zarathustra," and it was taken from a book by a German philosopher, Friedrich Nietzsche. The main character in Nietzsche's book (are you listening, Julia?) was a deep-thinking, strong-willed man named after a prophet from Persia (now Iran) who lived thousands of years before the birth of Christ. The Persian Zarathustra was called Zoroaster, and he was one of the first men to preach a monotheistic religion, with a clear idea of heaven. (Pay attention, Julia, this is important.) Judaism and Christianity are thought to have taken many of their beliefs from Zoroastrianism. But Nietzsche didn't believe in heaven. His Zarathustra hails the coming of a Superman, an Ubermensch who transcends traditional morality.

By now Julia's eyes were focused out the window, watching cars drive by. Children, like most adults, cannot absorb abstractions that have no connection to their daily lives.

"You don't need to remember any of that," I said. "When you listen to the music, just try to imagine a solitary prophet walking through the Persian desert, and think about how his ideas inspired a German philosopher to write about a superman."

She nodded vaguely. Mom was still speaking in riddles.

I knew I sounded like the Professor on *Gilligan's Island*, but that was okay. I didn't mind if Julia couldn't grasp everything I was saying, because it was valuable for her just to hear an adult's vocabulary. I've never felt that children need to fully comprehend all that they hear and see. Better to let them absorb a little more with each new conversation and each new book—to sense that the world is full of knowledge yet to be learned, and mysteries still to be fathomed.

That afternoon I also pulled out Tchaikovsky's *Swan Lake*. Julia already knew the tunes from *The Swan Princess* movie, just as she knew the melodies from the *Nutcracker Suite* and the central theme in Disney's *Sleeping Beauty*. She didn't know, however, that all of these pieces were taken from ballets written by the same Russian composer.

We went downstairs and checked out the CDs at the circulation desk, then walked back to the car, where I put the key in the ignition and turned on Strauss.

"Let's listen to the opening before we drive home."

Outside our windows, cadets jogged by in narrow columns, singing their usual jodies: "I don't know but I've been told / Army wings are made of gold. / I don't know but it's been said / Navy wings are made of lead." Inside our car, the music started quietly. First the trumpets, playing three slow, ascending notes gradually getting louder, with the third note held to the limit of the trumpeter's breath, until the whole orchestra entered with two descending tones, one short, one long, holding the long note with a steady crescendo, cut off with a ringing aftertone. Then came a seesaw pounding of tympani, slowing steadily until the trumpets began the pattern again.

"Do you like it, Julia?" I asked at the end of the prelude.

"Yes," she said.

"What does it make you think of?"

She hesitated. "A bird, learning to fly. And it takes three tries."

We played the piece again, and Julia's fingers fluttered across the dashboard, lifting and falling. "On the third try," she said, as the music blossomed into major chords, "his wings open into beautiful colors and the bird flies up toward heaven."

We listened to the rest of the music as we drove out of town and into the countryside, the subdivisions giving way to fields peppered with cattle. We passed a friend's pasture where a group of two dozen deer regularly graze. Julia counted seventeen that morning; brass chords floated out our window toward the does' pricked ears, and I hoped that Julia would appreciate the beauty of it. In just looking out a car window, she might feel freed from the sadness of classrooms that had weighted her down over the past several years.

"Windows are the only thing that rivet me to this world," she once remarked. On that day, when I asked what she saw outside a window, she looked out from our living room at the trees and answered, "Everything that is really there that *you* can't see. Camels and a guinea pig and a kangaroo head."

"So you find trees to be just as evocative as clouds?"

"Oh, *clouds*," she said dismissively. "Clouds are so obvious."

✦

The best homeschooling lesson I ever taught would come a few months later, on that stretch of road where Julia counted the seventeen deer. All three of my girls were in the backseat that day, bickering, poking, whining—their habitual state—when I turned on Rimsky-Korsakov's *Scheherazade*.

"Have you ever heard of Scheherazade?" I asked over their noise, and they quieted enough to mutter a negative.

"There was once a sultan of Arabia," I began, "with a beautiful wife whom he loved very much, but she betrayed him."

"You mean she had s-e-x with another man?" Nine-year-old Rachel had an unlimited, disgusted fascination with s-e-x.

"Yes," I said, "she had *s-e-x* with several other men. As a result, the sultan was convinced that all women were unfaithful and should be killed. So each night he married another young woman, and every morning he ordered her to be strangled, until all his people were terrorized, fearing for their daughters' lives."

By now my girls were silent. Any story that contains both murder and sex can hold their attention. I told them the whole gist of the *Arabian Nights*, and how Disney got the ideas for Sinbad and Aladdin from Scheherazade. Then I turned on Rimsky-Korsakov, and the music began with loud brasses playing a few forceful notes.

"That sounds like the angry sultan," I suggested.

Next came the solo violin, sweetly melodic, with a harp in the background, playing a winding, twisting tune—the voice of Scheherazade weaving her stories. Rimsky-Korsakov titled his first number "The Sea and Sinbad's Ship," and when the full orchestra launched into its rhythm of rolling waves, Julia nodded: "It sounds like the ocean." And so it continued, with Sinbad's ship cresting wave after wave after wave. (Rimsky-Korsakov can be maddeningly repetitive.) Every so often the orchestra stepped back and the solo violin intervened with its lovely song, reminding us that Scheherazade was still there, narrating this sea story.

My girls were hooked. They asked to hear *Scheherazade* every day for two weeks, before school, after school, driving to errands. I checked out an illustrated version of the *Arabian Nights* from our local library, and we read some of the stories at bedtime. Once we took out the globe and located Saudi Arabia. And where is Iraq, they asked, home to the Thief of Baghdad? And why are our soldiers in Baghdad now?

This is homeschooling at its best—a constant segue from music history, to literature, to geography, to contemporary politics. It can take place anywhere, at almost any time, even with a carload of children driving home from their regular school. The key, when it comes to all music, is to choose pieces that tell a story. It doesn't matter whether the music is classical, jazz, salsa, or Broadway. The style is less important than the quality, and the ability of a piece to spark a child's imagination. In our case, I wanted to emphasize classical music, so in the upcoming year I thought that Julia and I might listen to Gustav Holst's *The Planets* when we studied the solar system. Aaron Copland's music could provide a good accompaniment for American history—*Billy the Kid* and "Hoedown" when studying the Old West; "Fanfare for the Common Man" for lessons on democracy. Johann Strauss's "Blue Danube Waltz" and Smetana's *Die Moldau* might inspire some interest in European geography.

"If I were a principal," I said to Julia on our first day, as we reached the last half-mile of our journey home, "I would pipe soothing classical music into the hallways, something for the children to contemplate when standing in line or visiting their lockers. Or maybe a little quiet Mozart in the cafeteria?"

By now we'd reached our house, and after a short break I asked Julia to take out paper and pencil. Writing was our top priority, so we might as well get down to it.

Many students arrive at today's universities with their AP ducks all in a row, but unable to write a thoughtful paragraph. Writing is the act of contemplation borne to life on a page, and too many high school students have minimal practice with quiet contemplation; they struggle to form their own ideas and support them with a coherent sequence of evidence.

"Write a page," I said to Julia, "about what we did this morning."

This was something new for her. At Waddell, writing assignments tend to be highly formulaic exercises. Bulletin boards in the second-grade hallway display dozens of student paragraphs, all beginning with the same sentence, followed by information that varies only minimally in content. "My favorite color is _____. It smells like_____. It looks like_____. It tastes like _____. This color makes me feel _____." Fill-in-the blank is one way to get children started as early writers, and Waddell's older children are encouraged to vary their sentence patterns, but even in the highest grades, their writing assignments usually dictate the content of every paragraph.

To be given a broad topic, without specific instructions for each stage, was a new challenge for Julia. After twenty minutes she handed me her sheet of paper.

Wensday

Today I went to the cofee shop. That day there was a blue grass band playing. The blue grass band played some songs with there insturments.

The musician's insturments were the banjos, mandalins, gitars and a bass.

There was only one girl who was playing a banjo.

We listened to the music and played two games of gin-rummy. I won both the games (but when we played war I lost.) We also had drinks. Mrs. Brodie had juice and I had hot chocolate.

After that we drove to the VMI libary and walked to the Timmins room. We got a C.D. by Richard Strauss it was called Also Sprach Zarathustra.

I read Julia's meager sentences with mixed emotions. On one hand, they were endearing; I was now "Mrs. Brodie" instead of Mom. But they were also somewhat pitiful. I knew that Julia's spelling and grammar were rough, but even for a ten-year-old, this writing struck me as primitive. Her teachers had often claimed that Julia was ahead of her peers when it came to writing skills, a possibility that now made me cringe. Staring at those words, I wondered: Where to begin?

The best teachers always begin with praise—that's one of the tenets of Shinichi Suzuki, the famous violin teacher. A friend of mine once saw Suzuki in practice, leading a master class where a little girl gave an incredibly bad performance. Her music was out of tune; the rhythm, imprecise; her bow grip, hand position, and stance, all wrong. What could the master possibly praise?

"Well," Suzuki said, smiling into the child's mournful face as she lowered her instrument. "You finished that whole piece!"

And so I smiled at Julia: "I'm impressed you noticed that only one of the bluegrass musicians was female. I hadn't paid attention to that. Why do you think there were so few women?"

She shrugged. "The women are all out working."

"You mean the men have time to fool around with music while the women are busy doing the work?"

Julia nodded.

"What kind of work are the women doing?" I expected her to say that the women were home taking care of children.

"They're teaching at the colleges," she stated matter-of-factly.

"Fair enough." I laughed. "Okay, let's work on your spelling."

Spelling, I'm convinced, is a genetic trait, in no way indicative of intelligence. F. Scott Fitzgerald, who penned *The Great Gatsby*, was a narrative genius but a spelling moron. He was humiliated on the one occasion when an editor published a piece of his writing without correcting all of the spelling and grammatical errors. Similarly, Zachary Taylor, America's twelfth president, was known (according to Julia's cartoon guide to U.S. government) for being a "turrible speller."

So, too, for my husband. It took the first three years of our marriage for me to convince John that *congratulations* was not spelled with a *d*. Julia, very much a daddy's girl, inherited her father's spelling genes along with his bright eyes. After learning basic phonics in kindergarten, she clung to them tenaciously throughout grade school, constantly frustrated by the inconsistencies of the English language: "*I* before *e* except after *c*, and except when the verb sounds like long *a* (*weight, neigh, sleigh*), and don't forget about *seize*, and *sleight*," et cetera et cetera.

I often tell my students that the only way to master spelling is to read, read, read, and pray that your brain absorbs the spelling of words seen again and again. Today, most students rely desperately on computer spell-check programs, which continually fail them. I once had an undergraduate explain that he didn't need to master spelling or grammar—his secretary would correct that for him. When I mentioned this to John over dinner, his response was blunt: "Tell the kid he's not going to have a secretary when he's working at Jiffy Lube."

Julia has never expected someone else to correct her spelling, but neither does she have much luck fixing it herself. From kindergarten through fourth grade most of her spelling instruction didn't sink in. She could memorize words for a weekly test (on those days when she bothered to study), but she rarely applied the test-drilled spelling to her sentences. She would ace a test one morning, then misspell the same words that afternoon.

"Okay, let's start a spelling journal," I said. "We'll keep a list of the words you misspell in your writing, and those will be the words you need to learn each week."

Julia took out a black marble notebook and wrote *Spelling J* at the top.

"How do you spell *journal*?" she asked.

"J-o-u-r-n-a-l."

Our first job, I explained, was to determine if she couldn't spell a word or if she was just being careless.

"How do you spell *library*?" I pronounced the *r* with deliberate emphasis, and she spelled the word correctly. "What about *instrument*?" Again I emphasized the *r*, and Julia fixed her spelling.

"What about 'guitar'?" Julia never guessed at the silent *u*, so we put that word at the top of her slate. "And how do you spell *coffee*? One *f* or two?" She couldn't say, so the word went on the agenda. Five minutes more and we had her first spelling list: *Wednesday*, *guitar*, *coffee*, *mandolin*, and the difference between *there*, *their*, and *they're*.

The fact that my ten-year-old could not spell *Wednesday* bothered me. It's a difficult word, full of silent letters, but it seemed a commentary on the spelling instruction at her school, where emphasis is placed on learning patterns—prefixes and suffixes, *mega-* and *-tion*—rather than learning practical, common nouns. As a result, Julia could spell *macroeconomics*, but she had never encountered *Wednesday* on an elementary school spelling test.

"How do you spell *February*?" I asked. As I suspected, she missed the *r*.

I sometimes recommend spelling journals for my college students. Personalized lists are useful because everyone makes different mistakes, and each person's vocabulary is unique. Carpenters, plumbers, and mathematicians all deal in different words. A ballet instructor should learn how to spell *plié*; a house painter should know *soffit*. Ten-year-old Julia needed to learn *Wednesday* and *February*. If, by Friday, she had mastered those two words, I would consider the week a success.

"It's okay to be a rotten speller," I told Julia, "so long as you are a very good proofreader. Whenever you write something, you need to get into the habit of checking all words that don't look right."

In upcoming weeks, whenever Julia finished a piece of writing, I would ask her to underline every word where she wasn't confident about the spelling. Unfortunately, she tended to underline half of her words, leaving me to ask, "Do you really think you've misspelled *they*?" Once she had shortened her list, she had to look the words up.

"What should you do," I asked her on our first morning, "if you've written something but you're not sure about your spelling?"

She shrugged.

"What can you use to find out whether you've spelled a word correctly?"

"A computer?"

"Yes, but what if there's no computer around?"

"A dictionary?"

"Right. Of course your spelling has to be close enough so that you can find what you're looking for. If you're trying to spell *knight*—the kind with a sword and horse—you'll never find it if you're looking in the *n*'s. But most of the time a dictionary can help."

We pulled our big *Merriam-Webster* down from the shelf.

"Have you used dictionaries at your school?"

"Once or twice," Julia replied.

It occurred to me that most children don't know how to read a dictionary entry. What do *n.*, *adv.*, and *adj.* stand for? What about *s.* and *pl.*? What are all these quotes, and this foreign derivation?

Here, I thought, is another small benefit of homeschooling. I could acquaint my child with a dictionary. To my surprise, I found that Julia had a lot of trouble searching for a word alphabetically. When looking up *guitar*, she opened the dictionary to *H*, then moved forward through the pages.

"Say the alphabet in your head," I suggested. "Where does the letter *g* come, compared to the page you're on now?" After thinking for a moment, Julia started to flip backward through the pages, heading in the right direction. Eventually she located the correct entry and squinted at its small print, clearly intimidated by this heavy, boring book, with its small text and minimal pictures. Never before had I thought to buy a children's dictionary, but now it seemed like common sense.

And so our morning continued, with me learning more than Julia. After lunch she played her violin for forty-five minutes, the only stressful time of our day, since an out-of-tune violin scrapes like sandpaper across my brain. "Look at the key signature," I said to Julia. "It's Bach, not Bartók."

"Bar talk?" Julia shrugged, and continued to scrape away.

Then on to the blessed silence of geography, with Julia spreading a jigsaw puzzle of the world across the glass table on our screened porch. While she pieced together the countries of Africa, a squirrel cackled in a maple tree, berating our cat, who watched it from the grass. Down at the creek, a pair of bathing mallards dipped and bobbed, shivering their feathers dry. A breeze lifted and lowered Julia's hair, and I thought: this has been a good day.

A half hour later, when we retrieved Julia's sisters from school, Kathryn beamed.

"How was your first day?" I asked.

"Great!" she said, smiling.

"What did you do?"

"We colored, and we sat in a circle while the teacher read to us."

How nice, to have a kindergartner who wasn't weeping after the first day, who seemed perfectly content to attend school with everyone else. Rachel was also comfortable with her school routine, although, for her, the social life was the chief draw; the work was way too easy.

"What did you do on your first day, Rachel?"

"Not much. We went over the classroom rules and labeled all of our notebooks. And we did a few worksheets."

"Did you write anything?"

"Not yet." Her first writing assignment would not come for another week.

Back at home, I reminded Julia that she must write one page in her journal, so she took out her misty blue five-by-seven notebook, with its Thomas Kinkade cover—snapdragons and wild roses and wisps of smoke rising from a stone cottage. Opening to the first page, she wrote in enormous letters and double-spaced lines, filling the space with as few sentences as possible:

August 24, 2005

Dear Diary,

Today we started school. I have begun homeschooling while Rachel and Kathryn have begun regular school. I'm realy happy about every thing exept for music. I just can't get violin to work so that it sonds good. But mom can make anything sound good. Well. Today is Wensday and next person I'm seeing is my friend Matt.

Sincerely,

Julia

When Julia showed me her entry I thanked her, while inwardly sighing: "Wensday." Always "Wensday."

CHAPTER FIVE

⇥Autumn Field Trips⇤

*The best thing about homeschooling is the
freedom—freedom from homework, freedom from
the sameness of school, and the freedom to take
field trips. That was my favorite.*

JULIA

I WISH I COULD SAY THAT OUR HOMESCHOOLING HONEYMOON
lasted for several months—that Julia and I spent the entire
fall basking, trouble-free, in our intellectual liberty. In truth,
the first conflict occurred on day two.

We were studying Fahrenheit and Celsius—a Virginia SOL
topic—but where the state presented it solely as a matter of measurement, I wanted to introduce a human, historical element. So
after Julia checked our front porch thermometer and recorded
the temperature on a coordinate line graph, I asked:

"Where did these words come from, *Fahrenheit* and *Celsius*?"
She shrugged. No clue.

"Why don't we look them up on the Internet?" I suggested.
There, Julia learned about Daniel Gabriel Fahrenheit and An-
ders Celsius, a German and a Dutchman living in the early 1700s,
who never met, but who shared an interest in meteorology, each
developing his own method for measuring temperatures. These
days, I explained to Julia, most countries prefer Celsius's prag-

matic scale, with the freezing point set at zero and boiling at one hundred. We stubborn Americans, however, have stuck with the old English model, which is why the word *Fahrenheit* now graces rock bands and movie titles and novel jackets, but few Americans know the temperature for boiling point (212°).

"This can be your first essay," I told Julia. "You can write a paragraph about each scientist, and how his method of measurement works. Then include a paragraph on how to convert from Fahrenheit to Celsius, and vice versa."

Poor child, what a boring topic. Homeschooling experts will shake their heads and say: "Shape the assignments around the child's interests!" But I figured that life is full of work not tailor-made to suit us.

Julia dutifully printed a few pages from two Internet sites, quickly discovering that Fahrenheit and Celsius were passé. Today's scientists prefer the more precise scales of Kelvin and Rankine, two guys I'd never heard of. Wonderful, I thought. This was precisely the benefit of homeschooling: the chance to discover and delve into unexpected knowledge.

I tried to show Julia how to highlight important facts with a yellow marker. She highlighted almost every sentence. While I hovered, saying things like "How do you spell *tem-per-a-ture?*" Julia wrote an introductory paragraph:

Temperatures measure how cold or hot it is. Without temperatures, people wouldn't know what to wear. But who invented methods for measuring? What kinds of temperatures are there? And how low do they get?

"Great start," I said. "Now keep on writing while I go upstairs and get dressed." Standing in the shower, I congratulated myself on how well things were going. On day two, instead of still labeling notebooks and arranging pencils, Julia was already doing research and writing, expanding a topic beyond the bare minimum required by the state. This homeschooling stuff was a breeze.

Twenty minutes later I went downstairs to the living room, where I had left Julia writing on the couch.

Rubbing my wet hair in a towel, I said, "Show me what you've got."

She handed me her sheet of paper. There, in a messy scrawl:

Well, the two most famos scientists in the field are Celsius and Fahrenheit. They were the two scientists who invented the mesurement of heat, Celsius and Fahrenheit.

"Two sentences?" I stared at Julia. "It took you twenty minutes to write two sentences?" And not very good ones.

Julia lowered her head in shame as my eyes turned to the television set.

"Have you been watching TV!"

"No!" she said.

"Are you sure?"

"I haven't been watching TV, Mom."

"What *have* you been doing?"

Julia glanced toward the far end of the couch. Walking over, I lifted a pillow and found a paperback novel about—what else? Dragons. I felt a brief twinge of pride; left alone in a room, my daughter had chosen a book over television. But that pride was quickly squelched by frustration. There I stood, just like Julia's other elementary school teachers, giving instructions while the child let her thoughts linger on her dragon book, ready to sneak-read at the first opportunity.

In that moment I foresaw the failure of our homeschooling. I saw how every time I left the room the curriculum would leave with me. Julia would enter middle school well versed in nothing but dragons, and the teachers would shake their heads at one more overzealous parent who thought that she could master their profession.

"You can't do this!" I said. "This homeschooling isn't going to work unless you do the assignments!"

Julia hung her head like a flinching Labrador.

I had been counting on the idea that she would be an independent learner—that after a brief daily math lesson she would concentrate on thirty minutes of practice problems while I graded my college students' papers. Julia would draft book reports while I wrote my novel, and our house would be unusually clean because of my extra time at home folding laundry, scrubbing pots, and occasionally answering questions.

Now I glimpsed the truth—if I was not nearby to constantly prod, push, and cheer, Julia would get nothing done. My annoyance grew as my visions of freedom ebbed away.

"I'm glad that you're a reader," I began, my voice crescendoing slightly, "but you also need to write, and do math problems, and science, whether or not I'm in the room. If you don't do the work, this year will be a disaster, and you won't be prepared for middle school. And you can't get by in middle school just reading dragon books; your teachers will fail you. Do you want to *fail?*"

Which was, admittedly, a stupid and mean thing to say. I think I was worried more about my failure than hers. One of the problems with short-term homeschooling is that you never escape the shadow of traditional schools, and remain perpetually concerned with whether your child is keeping up. I should have realized from day one that I was responsible only to Julia, not to any teachers she might encounter in the future, but in homeschooling it is hard to escape the sense of communal responsibility, and communal judgment.

Parenthood always involves an awareness of judgment; when children misbehave or don't do their schoolwork, all eyes fall upon the parents, especially the mother. And if that mother is a homeschooler, she is doubly accountable for her children's success or failure. As John would jokingly say in the coming months, "If Julia grows up to be a serial killer, you'll only have yourself to blame, because you took her out for the fifth grade." (Thanks, dear.)

In those early days, I was determined to negate the serial-killer possibility. I felt a strong obligation to meet some vague societal measure of success, if only to legitimate my decision to home-school. Petty as that might sound, I think other homeschoolers sometimes feel the same way—so many authors trumpet their children's high SAT scores, spelling bee trophies, or admission to elite colleges, as if they want to show the world that homeschooling isn't crazy.

All of these concerns about the world's judgmental eyes might be small-minded, but they are also inescapably human. To deny that I felt them would be dishonest. So there I was on day two, already laying my ridiculous fears squarely on Julia's birdlike shoulders, positing middle-school report cards as a guillotine poised to fall upon her should she blow off her fifth-grade schoolwork.

She shook her head as she stared into her hands. "This is terrible for my self-esteem."

I almost laughed, because on many levels Julia was wiser than me. It was stupid to lose my cool so early in the process; a good teacher should encourage, not harangue. But I am not a believer in empty self-esteem. Our culture seems to have developed the habit of offering major tributes for our children's most minor accomplishments; fifth-grade graduations now have the pomp and circumstance once reserved for high school. Self-esteem, I ·

should have told Julia, does not come from vacuous praise; self-esteem comes from a job well done. Neither Julia nor I was doing her job well that morning.

The rest of the day progressed through math and music and history with little tension, but also little joy.

"How did it go today?" John asked when he came home for dinner at six.

"Less than an hour into it, I was already yelling at Julia."

He nodded. "So it begins."

*

Nevertheless, each morning offered the hope of a new start, and our next day was better, as were many of the days to come, largely because the weather was beautiful and I was determined that we would get out of the house as much as possible.

There's good reason why children often compare school to prison, spending so much time confined to a building, a room, and a desk, with lunchtime and recess limited to less than thirty minutes. For a child like Julia, who didn't always finish her classwork, recess could be even shorter. Some of her elementary school teachers denied children chunks of outdoor time if they failed to complete assignments.

For Julia's year of homeschooling, I planned to use the outdoor world as a pedagogical tool, something to be incorporated into daily assignments. During English, she could write about sights in our yard. For science, she could keep a leaf journal, wandering through college campuses with a field guide to trees, writing paragraphs, taking photographs, and doing leaf rubbings. Many history lessons could be conducted on long walks; Julia and I might get some exercise while discussing books that she had read about the Maya and the Aztecs, just as John Stuart Mill's education had unfolded on walks with his father. I envisioned Socrates strolling through the Greek Acropolis while questioning his disciples.

I was also inspired by Richard Louv's *Last Child in the Woods*. According to Dr. Louv, today's children are suffering from "nature-deficit disorder," spending more time indoors than any previous generation. He suggests that the rise of ADHD diagnoses might be tied to American children's lack of interaction with nature. Nature has been proven to have a calming effect, so Louv argues; not to mention the healthy benefits of outdoor exercise. When Louv was a child, he and his friends devoted hours to roaming cornfields and woods, free to play outside until suppertime. Now many of those cornfields and woods have been replaced with strip malls and subdivisions. At the same time, more children face tightly scheduled afterschool activities, more homework, and more fearful parents. Louv claims that it's not television and video games that are keeping children away from nature—it's parents' fear of stranger danger. Today's moms and dads don't want their children playing outside, unsupervised, for hours.

America's schools have exacerbated the problem by drastically reducing or eliminating PE and recess, and by holding class outside only on rare occasions. The outside world, some teachers explain, is too distracting to be a setting for math or English. In our small town, when the new high school was built, some folks suggested that the classrooms have no windows. It was easier to manage the air circulation without them, so the argument went, and all that sunshine and greenery distracted from the serious work of learning. There was enough outcry from appalled parents that the window-snatchers were denied the fullest extent of their Orwellian vision. Now our high school has a mixture of windowless classrooms and rooms where the windows are so high and narrow that when the teachers and children sit at their desks, their view consists mostly of cinderblocks.

"Go outside," I told Julia on our third morning of home-schooling, "and take your notebook with you. Choose an object anywhere in the yard and write a page about it in as much detail as possible, without ever stating what the object is or exactly where it's located. Then bring the page to me, and I'll have to walk around our property and find whatever you were looking at, based on your description."

As I expected, she returned in fifteen minutes with half a page of sentences too broad to be of use. She had found something in the creek that was covered in moss and grass, but more than seventy yards of creek meander through our property, full of little islands that met her description.

"How can you be more precise?" I asked.

The best writers, I explained, have an eye for the telling detail. She must go back and determine what made her object unique. After ten more minutes Julia returned with much better sentences: "The object is two feet long and one foot wide, and ten inches tall above the water. The object is next to a moss-covered flat waterfall. It has a few dead weeds on it that have turned white. There is an arched rock near it."

With those directions I found the precise rock that she had in mind, and we sat together on the creek bank while I gave her a brief lesson in how to avoid using *it* and *is* so many times in her sentences.

By 12:30 that day, after indoor lessons in math and music, we prepared to go outside for an even longer spell. We had scheduled our first field trip for that afternoon. The coffee shop didn't count, nor did any trip within our town limits. The grocery store, the colleges, the local library—all constituted a daily part of community-based schooling. A "field trip" meant traveling at least twenty minutes out of town, something we would do on a regular basis over the coming months.

In many public schools, field trips are the latest victim headed for the chopping block, and not only because of budget concerns, which would be a lamentable but understandable excuse. Instead, the anti–field trip folk often cite the need for more test-prep time, while also questioning whether field trips hold much educational value.

This last complaint is the most mind-boggling. In my experience, one well-executed field trip can offer more intellectual content than an entire week of classroom exercises. I once took Kathryn out of school for a day to visit my sister, who works as a neonatologist at the University of Virginia's medical center. For half an hour Aunt Karen gave us a tour of the NICU (neonatal intensive care unit), where dozens of premature babies wrapped in blankets lay in thick plastic bassinets with tubes attached to their noses, their chests, and their feet. Kathryn stared at the computer monitors above each bassinet, watching heart and respiratory rates produce jagged lines that looked like the results of a lie-detector test, revealing the faulty lung, the inconsistent heart. Alarms beeped as oxygen rates exceeded or dipped below healthy limits. "The baby is rolling over," Karen explained, unruffled. "The baby is crying." Occasionally she turned a knob one notch forward or back.

I wondered if the visit disturbed Kathryn's eight-year-old mind. My adult consciousness told me that tragedies were unfolding in that room, along with miracles. Four nurses and one doctor hovered over the newest, tiniest arrival: a twenty-two-week-old boy, no bigger than a newborn kitten. His squiggling toes were the size of Dippin' Dots.

Later, Kathryn told me what had been on her mind: "I want to be a doctor like Aunt Karen. What should I do?"

We drove to the library and selected six children's books on human anatomy. At home, I searched in the back of a closet and retrieved a four-foot floor puzzle of the human body—the skeleton on one side, the organs on the other. Kathryn pieced it together, memorizing and reciting the names of every bone.

"Where can I buy mouse organs?" she asked the next day. Aunt Karen had her own laboratory where she and her assistants monitored living mice and performed experiments on refrigerated mouse lungs.

"Hmm." I hesitated. "We'll have to think about that one."

All of this enthusiasm stemmed from one field trip. In two hours Kathryn had seen babies tinier than she ever imagined and a hospital bigger than half of Lexington's downtown, and her aunt, whom she'd known only as a cooking, cleaning, nose-wiping mom, had been transformed into a person of life-or-death authority, dressed in a long white coat. Kathryn's vision of the world, and of her own future, had been significantly altered because we had taken her out of her usual classroom to another setting that was equally educational. Up until that point she hadn't witnessed many career options for women beyond various forms of teaching. She knew about elementary school teachers, dance teachers, and college teachers like me. But now she could envision herself as a doctor, and no homeschooling was necessary for that mental transformation—just a parent's readiness to supplement a child's schooling by visiting sites of learning around the community.

That's why field trips topped my list of priorities for Julia. The glory of our autumn lay in all the places she and I planned to explore.

Having said all that, I must now hang my head and confess that our first field trip was lame. We left home on our third school day to visit a new tourist attraction south of Lexington called *Escape from Dinosaur Kingdom*, which I hoped might appeal to Julia's paleontological bent. Mark Cline, a local artist and beloved town character, had built the place. Cline specializes in enormous fiberglass sculptures, glazed and elaborately painted, which he houses in an "Enchanted Castle" a few miles outside of town. Drivers can't miss the spot when heading south on Route 11: four sarcophagi, painted gold and blue and green, guard the white wooden privacy fence. Inside lie the remains of old elephants and hippos and Halloween monsters, a giant watermelon with windows, and imperial weaponry from *Star Wars*.

Dinosaurs are one of Cline's specialties; Julia had seen his "Cretaceous creations" years earlier on the street corners of a tiny neighboring town called Glasgow. Cline had convinced the town fathers that T. rexes and velociraptors hanging from the windows of abandoned buildings might encourage folks to visit their economically depressed crossroads. (Hey, it got our family to visit.) But now, Cline's dinosaurs had migrated farther south, and Julia and I were going to check out their new habitat.

On the way, we passed another Cline creation in a pasture to our right: a full-scale reproduction of Stonehenge, made from heavy Styrofoam and aptly titled Foamhenge. In the spring and fall, Foamhenge plays host to medieval festivals and college students' late-night drinking bouts.

"Ever heard of the Druids?" I asked Julia, and I inserted a brief history lesson into the drive.

After a few more minutes we reached the entrance to the Natural Bridge, the water-carved two-hundred-foot arch where Julia had disappeared on her first-grade field trip. The bridge is the sort of gorgeous natural wonder that should belong to our national park system. Instead, it has been transferred from one private owner to another, who in recent decades, have surrounded the site with sedimentary layers of kitsch. *Escape from Dinosaur Kingdom* was the latest addition, joining a wax museum, a toy museum, underground caverns, an equally cavernous gift shop, and the saddest miniature golf course imaginable.

For twelve dollars we bought two tickets to Dinosaur Kingdom and "Professor Cline's Haunted Monster Museum" (the two
couldn't be separated), then drove to an empty parking lot beside
a wooded hill.

Julia seemed a little creeped out by the surroundings.

"When you look at trees, do you ever see the faces of animals?" she asked.

I looked at the woods around us—shapes and lumps and colors and textures—but did not find them especially interesting.
"No, I don't see faces."

"I do," said Julia. "All the time. But never the faces of humans. Only animal faces. Birds and wolves and deer."

"Do you think that the spirits of animals live in trees?" I
asked.

"I think that animals live in trees," she replied, ever logical.

"You know," I said as I locked the car and dropped the keys
into my purse, "there was a poet named William Blake who lived
at the end of the seventeen hundreds, and once, when he looked
at a tree, he saw a host of angels singing in the branches."

For some reason, Julia didn't approve of this. "Mom," she said
sternly. "I don't *hear* things. And I don't see what's *not* there."

"Ah," I murmured. "Okay."

We passed through a gateway shaped like a monster's howling mouth, with gargoyle-topped columns on either side, before
walking up into the woods on a once-paved path, now a mixture
of broken asphalt and dirt. To our left, almost hidden in the trees,
a green-hoofed demon dangled a child from his claw; beyond
him, a small graveyard was filled with fiberglass tombstones. I
didn't tell Julia that I, too, was a little worried. Walking alone
through the Virginia woods toward an abandoned house/mon-
ster museum seemed like the rural equivalent of entering a dark
Manhattan alley. I feared that I might be leading my daughter

into a scene from *Deliverance*. At the trail's end, a giant skull with one revolving eyeball protruded from the side of a two-story turreted brick building. An enormous snake curled its way out one window, up to the chimney, where it swallowed a man's bloody leg. Recorded screams floated from the house's interior. The ticket taker on the porch stared at us as if we were the first people he had seen in months.

Luckily, Mark Cline's lovely, smiling wife appeared to our right.

"Have you come for the Haunted Monster Museum?"

"No, the dinosaurs," I said, and she directed us toward a wooden shack marked "Lost Caverns." When we stepped inside I realized that I hadn't done my homework on this attraction; the place had an unexpected narrative, posted on a painted sign:

It's 1863. While digging for dinosaur bones in the Lost Caverns, the Garrison family has discovered an entire valley on the other side filled with dinosaurs. Unfortunately, so has the Northern Army, who seek to use the dinos as weapons of mass destruction against the South. Can the Garrisons and their pet monkey Blinky stop them before it's too late?

God help us. This is why Mark Cline earns extra pages in the book *Weird Virginia*. With our nonrefundable tickets in hand, Julia and I passed through a "cavern tunnel" lined with imitation fossils of plesiosaurs and ichthyosaurs and other saurs of great variety, then entered a "valley" (read: pine forest) where velociraptors had cornered a cow while a screaming Yankee hung from the jaws of a T. rex.

All I could do was shake my head. Dinosaurs eating Yankees is the sort of bizarre sight that entertains tourists (a *Washington Post* reporter later dubbed the attraction "hilarious!" and "amazing!"), but when you live in our county, the endless references to the Civil War get very tiresome.

"Do you like this?" I asked Julia.

"Mom," she rolled her eyes. "There's a man's face poking through the stomach of a giant snake."

I looked, and she was right. A contorted face with eyes squeezed tight was pressing though a snake's belly, resembling Han Solo frozen in carbonite.

"There were no giant snakes in the dinosaurs' age," Julia protested. "And a pachycephalosaurus would not be standing alone like that." She pointed at a sculpture in the trees. "They lived in herds."

As we walked out, a motion-sensitive T. rex jerked its head forward and roared at Julia, so she backed up, walked forward, and made the head roar again, then did it one more time, until the dinosaur's head got stuck and locked in place, twitching and roaring.

On the drive home I thought to salvage the afternoon by stopping at a local farmer's produce market. "Country Hams! Homemade Honey! Apples and Tomatoes!" proclaimed the hand-painted signs. Here was a great lesson in the importance of supporting small farmers and eating fresh local produce. "Look at the sweet potatoes!" I said when we stepped out of the car. "Look at the string beans!" Bushels of fruits and vegetables filled the covered patio, some local (tomatoes and zucchini), some not (bananas and kiwi). The prices were a bargain, so I started filling plastic bags with yams and yellow squash, until Julia spoke up from her tentative stance beside our car.

"You sure you want to go in there, Mom?"

"Why not?"

She pointed up, and when I walked out of the shaded area, I saw that she was gesturing toward a row of T-shirts that hung

like an awning outside the patio. Some featured cartoon drawings of big-breasted women; others showed big-bottomed women
perched on Harleys, wearing thongs. The crowning touch hung
to our left: a T-shirt sporting the Confederate battle flag, with
the words "Never apologize . . ." emblazoned above the Stars and
Bars, and below: ". . . for being right."

"Great," I said, sighing. Instead of supporting corporate agri-
business, my dollars were going to fund the Grand Wizard of the
KKK.

The Confederate battle flag is a sore subject in our part of Virginia, with some people condemning it as an unequivocal symbol of racist hatred, and others saying, no, it's just an emblem of
Southern pride. VMI cadets used to include the Confederate battle flag in the background design of their enormous class rings,
until 1992, when a group of black cadets put their collective feet
down. "Why is it such a big deal?" John asked one of those cadets, who looked him in the eye and said, "My grandfather was
killed by a group of men who wrapped a Confederate flag around
his neck and hung him with it."

As for me, I hesitated outside that produce stand, torn between
my political principles and my desire for cheap sweet potatoes.

"If I go in, will you come?" I asked Julia.

"I guess so," she said.

I entered, half expecting to find a tattooed Hell's Angel behind the cash register. Instead, there was a smiling, warm elderly
man making friendly conversation with everyone in the place.
I wondered if he knew or cared that the T-shirts outside would
alienate a lot of potential customers. Maybe he did care. The last
time I drove by, the only things hanging outside were flags of the
Cherokee nation and an Irish brigade.

Driving home that afternoon, I asked Julia, "Why do you
think some people display the Confederate battle flag?"

She replied without pausing. "Because they hate black people."

"I'm sure that's true for some of them," I said, nodding. "But do you think there are others who just feel like Northerners act snooty toward them, and this is their symbol for showing that they are proud of being Southern?"

Julia didn't buy it. "People can be proud without saying that black people should be slaves."

When it came to moral questions, Julia usually divided the answers into right and wrong, with most human behavior falling on the wrong side. She had no tolerance for shades of gray, especially the grays of the Confederacy, and while her moral absolutism was often admirable, I wondered if it would serve her well in the future. During the course of her life, she was going to meet a lot of terribly flawed human beings, and it was always easier to dismiss people than to talk to them. For now, it was her prerogative to say that the emperor had no clothes.

✦

Fortunately, our next field trip remained free of any shadows of the Civil War. Julia and I had decided that as part of her art curriculum, she and I would take knitting lessons, which meant driving thirty minutes into some of the most beautiful farmland in Rockbridge County, to reach the Orchardside Yarn Shop.

We had made a preliminary pilgrimage to the shop back in August, with Rachel and Kathryn in tow. The journey involved a twenty-minute drive up the local interstate, exiting at a crossroads full of sprawling truck plazas, then turning away from the highway-view subdivisions, into rolling country hills where the farmers still struggled to maintain vast homesteads.

On the road that leads to the yarn shop, the houses are beautiful two-hundred-year-old affairs, some wooden, some brick, with wide porches and lily-dotted ponds, red barns, and silver silos. The Orchardside Farm waits four miles into this landscape, with its own two-story house, white wood with crimson shutters, and to the left, a small bright cottage where a grandmotherly, bespectacled woman serves as our region's knitting goddess.

A wide stream traverses her front yard, and driving over the water on her small concrete bridge is like crossing a river into paradise. Ducks and geese paddle the stream; peacocks roam the lawn. In the back of the yard a steep climb leads to a hilltop pick-your-own berry patch—two acres of raspberries and blackberries.

"Have you come to pick yarn or berries?" a young woman asked on that August afternoon, as my daughters and I stepped out of the car.

"Both," I said, and she pointed toward the white cottage.

Julia began picking feathers from the grass: long goose feathers and small, two-inch peacock feathers with fluffy bases and shining emerald tips. I called her to join her sisters, and the four of us walked into the air-conditioned space of the cottage.

Stepping into the Orchardside Yarn Shop is like entering a chapel full of stained glass; the walls are covered in shelves of bright, multicolor yarn—two dozen shades of blue, five variations on magenta. There, one finds yarns like beaded necklaces or tiny strips of tinsel. Yarns with names such as Glitterlash, Fizz Stardust, and Squiggle. Contemplative yarns: Zen, Yin Yang, and Space. Holiday yarns: Tropicana and Malibu. And everywhere: scarves, sweaters, purses, and baby hats knitted with kaleidoscopic effects.

To me, the place is as beautiful as an art gallery, as spiritual as a convent. Each stitch is another rosary bead, each scarf another proverb. In that chapel of yarn, women congregate on Saturday mornings, knitting and talking and laughing. Throughout the rest of the week they drop in and out like supplicants coming to leave a prayer. It would be educational, I thought, for Julia merely to sit in that room and absorb the ambience.

"We'd like to take knitting lessons," I said to the friendly white-haired lady behind the cash register. I pointed toward Julia, who was fingering yarn textures: cashmere and mohair and chunky wool.

"I'm here every Saturday morning," the woman said. "Lessons are ten dollars; children are free. I'll teach you a few things, and then you can stay for the morning, as long as you like, and keep asking questions."

"Saturdays are tough, because I have all three of my girls." Rachel and Kathryn were visible behind me, oohing over the "soooo adorable" mittens. "But Julia and I are homeschooling, so we could come any weekday, during regular school hours."

"We get lots of homeschoolers." The woman smiled. "I'm Sharon." She handed me a business card. "You'll need needles," she said, which I assumed would be an easy choice—I was wrong. The needles in that shop were as diverse as the women who used them: some tall, some short, some thin as shish kebob skewers, others fat as sausages. Most were made from traditional bamboo, a few were orange and purple translucent acrylic. "Knit Faster!" one brand urged, "with Turbo knitting needles!" I didn't want anything turbo in my car, let alone my knitting needles.

"These will do well for starting a scarf." Sharon handed me two pairs of bamboo needles. As for the yarn, Julia chose a shimmering ruby skein, soft as velvet. I flinched when I saw the price. If we bought three skeins, this would be a forty-dollar scarf. But if the beauty of the yarn inspired Julia, so be it. I bought one skein to get her going, and for me: a pale blue soft yarn perfect for a baby's hat.

"Three lessons should get you started," Sharon explained. "Give us a call when you're ready." With her card in my pocket,

I resolved to telephone in the next few weeks. Meanwhile, my girls and I walked outside and climbed the forty steps to the blackberry patch. A chalkboard at a little stand listed the prices: a pint for two dollars, a gallon for fifteen—one fourth of what we'd pay at our local grocery store. The picking proved easy if somewhat unadventurous—no arms scratched reaching through thick brambles for the best berries, no purple-stained clothes, no beestings. Here were neat parallel rows of bushes arranged as if at a vineyard, with huge black and crimson edible jewels thicker than my thumb. For half an hour, the only sound was the plunk of berries in plastic buckets, like slow rainfall on a tin roof.

Looking back, I realize that our afternoon at the berry patch had already provided Julia with the lesson in local agriculture that I had sought at the Confederate produce stand. The Orchardside Farm offered excellent fruit at a bargain price, giving us a chance to support the county's economy. I looked forward to returning once the school year began.

But life rarely grants such idyllic moments. When Julia and I scheduled our Tuesday morning knitting lessons in September, we learned that if you didn't come on Saturdays, your lessons weren't with Sharon. Instead, we were taught by another local woman who was perfectly nice, but she didn't teach children for free. And she didn't teach in the yarn shop; she preferred the nearby office, with its comfortable couch and coffee table. I didn't have the heart to tell her that we had come chiefly for the ambience of all that rainbow yarn.

Julia, meanwhile, could manage only a fifteen-minute attention span when it came to knitting. Her impatient fingers battled the needles and yarn, producing stitches that were often bulky or twisted; the teacher was always unraveling and telling her to try again. Invariably I released Julia to go outside, where she stalked the peacocks and free-range hens, while I received the knitting instruction to pass along in the evenings.

Although Julia didn't take naturally to textiles, our mornings in that corner of the county were time well spent. The introduction of knitting supplies into our home meant that for years to come, all my girls would take turns picking up the needles and yarn, sporadically trying and failing and trying again. Moreover, next door to the Orchardside Farm ("next door" meaning two hundred yards away) stood an equally wonderful spot, the Buffalo Springs Herb Farm.

Julia and I visited there after our first knitting lesson, parking beside a bank barn built in 1890, which was painted dark red with brown trim. Originally the bottom housed livestock and the top stored hay, but on that day the lower level held offices, and when Julia and I walked into the upper area, we were impressed by the cathedral-high roof that revealed open lofts where dozens of herbs and flowers in clustered bouquets had been hung upside down to dry. Around us, antique farm equipment lined the walls—a Christmas sleigh, a shaving horse (i.e., a wooden foot-operated vise). To our left stood a gift shop filled with woven baskets, potpourri, sachets, and soap (southernwood, pennyroyal, lavender, and peppermint) along with a wealth of spices (parsley, savory, and tarragon).

Most of the spices and dried flowers had come from a garden outside, where Julia and I headed after buying a few items. The garden resembled an Appalachian answer to the grounds at Versailles—tiny, but landscaped with meticulous care. Heirloom vegetables remained locked away behind a picket fence, but the rest of the gardens were open for the public to wander free of charge, and were bordered by a trellised walkway on the east, a small hill on the west, and the gardener's cabin at the southwest corner, with its log walls, stone floor, and two centuries of gardening tools on display.

Julia was in Nirvana, smelling and touching very gently, never picking or trampling. She wandered through the fragrance garden, the Mediterranean garden, the paradise garden. A small incline lay covered in twenty-three varieties of thyme—I hadn't known there was more than one—golden thyme, caraway thyme, longwood thyme, and all the varieties of creeping thyme (fairy and cosmosus, and orange spice). My favorite was "minus thyme," as if thyme could be subtracted back into some herbal past.

Julia lingered in the medieval garden, which was constructed like the ruins of a small stone chapel, with two-foot statues of saints tucked into stone nooks, a Celtic cross draped in vines, wind chimes dangling where the altar should have been, and small wooden benches that served as pews. When we sat down, Julia tilted her head: "Can you hear that?" Gregorian chants echoed so softly that a visitor would barely notice if she didn't take the time to stop and sit quietly. On our way out, I saw that someone had dropped pennies in the holy water.

Outside the gardens, across a broad green field, stood Wade's Mill, its water wheel turning. Julia and I headed there next, both of us dashing through the lawn sprinklers (September in Virginia can reach the upper nineties), so we entered the stone-and-brick mill still dripping. Inside that tall structure, giant gears pulled a four-story oval belt that operated huge grinding machines, producing white flour, wheat flour, and cornmeal, mixed with other ingredients and sold in little rope-tied bags: pesto flour, polenta, buckwheat pancake mix. Julia ascended the mill level by level, until she reached the outdoor platform beside the top of the wheel, where a long trough filled with water led to a moss-covered chute. She dipped her palm into the water and stirred. "It's cold and clear," she said, smiling, and I smiled back.

I looked upon that field trip as a great success, even though it served no big educational agenda. There were no facts for Julia to memorize about mills or gardens or bank barns; no quiz the next day. The excursion's purpose was largely aesthetic, allowing a child to absorb the beauty of the world and to admire what men and women could build when they set their minds to it. I sensed that Julia needed lessons in the marvels of human life as much as lessons in math and English. Much of the time she had spent in school seemed to have convinced her that human existence was a dreary affair filled with tests and worksheets and homework. And although hard work is an inescapable part of life, the world I wanted to show my daughter was also full of wonder—not only the wonders of wilderness (Julia was willing to acknowledge those), but of man working in harmony with nature.

We would return to that corner of the county twice in the coming weeks, journeying an hour round trip to reach the knitting cottage—a significant chunk of time in an average school day. Add all the field trips I had planned to Washington and Williamsburg, combined with frequent jaunts to the library, grocery store, and coffee shop, and Julia and I were destined to spend a lot of time on the road. Time is especially precious when you have only one year, so I wondered—what was the best way to use the car as a classroom?

Driving to the yarn shop, I sometimes turned on classical CDs and let Julia absorb Tchaikovsky while she stared out the window counting hawks that perched in trees alongside the highway. On longer trips, we brought along DVDs on history and modern art, followed by Julia's choices: *Dinotopia* and *Pokemon 2000*. But for most of our shorter drives, I turned off the technology and insisted on quizzing her in math and history and French. What is eight times six? I asked as we maneuvered between tractor trailers. Eight times seven, eight times eight? What's the difference between obtuse and acute angles? Take out a sheet of paper, I'd say, and draw a trapezoid. Indicate the length of its sides, then calculate the area.

Julia was thoroughly, invariably disgusted.

"We're in the *car*, Mom. Can't you give it a rest?"

When traveling on public school trips, she explained, the kids were allowed to play with Game Boys and listen to iPods.

"Public school field trips happen once every couple of months," I replied. "We are in the car every other day."

I tried to compromise by quizzing her for only the first half of every car ride—the longest I could ever hold her attention anyway. But even that intrusion was met with resentment. At root, Julia was a child who wanted to be left alone with her thoughts, and I valued that impulse. In our world of cell phones, text messages, and endless screens, most people spend far too little time engaging with their minds. Deep contemplation is an endangered art.

In Julia's case, however, the pendulum had swung in the opposite direction. She seemed likely to overdose on introspection. I remembered the words of Mrs. Hennis, Julia's first-grade teacher: "Julia is in her own world, and it's a wonderful world . . . but she needs to spend more time in our world." On car rides, I dragged her into my world by peppering her with questions. "*Quel âge as-tu, Julia?*" "What country first established colonies in New York?" "How do you find the circumference of a circle?"

Perhaps we would have been happier if I had engaged her in thoughtful conversations about the uses of mathematics or the complexities of historical events. But Julia was willing to have those conversations after three o'clock each day. The hours between 8:30 and 3:00 were the only time when she would agree to "play school," trying math computation, French conversation, or memorization of *anything*. I was determined to make the most of those hours.

Thus we established the roles that would become entrenched over the coming months: I was the drill sergeant and Julia was the dreamer. I wanted measurable progress, achieved through self-discipline and effective time management. Julia wanted a free-flowing and organic approach to life, where reading and math and music were pursued only to satisfy impulses of curiosity and pleasure, not to make "progress" toward societal goals. She wanted to live like Walt Whitman in *Song of Myself*: "I loafe and invite my soul / I lean and loafe at my ease observing a spear of summer grass." Loafing was Julia's joy.

I had done my own share of dreaming and loafing as a child, and I valued those hours as critical for building an imagination and nurturing a happy spirit. Still, I worried that Julia didn't show much motivation to succeed at her schoolwork, whether in our car or kitchen. When I told John, he just sighed and gave one of his "like father, like daughter" explanations: "When I was a kid I don't think I had motivation to do anything except play floor hockey, watch cartoons, and hang out with my friends. I didn't want to be anything or do anything until late in high school, when I first thought about going to college."

I told Julia that she needed to find a balance between dreamy reflection and structured tasks. Youth offered that rare opportunity when a girl could grow to become an accomplished athlete, a rock musician, a Rhodes scholar, or whatever she set her heart upon, if she could combine self-discipline with her imaginative visions. And so I gripped the steering wheel and pushed my reluctant child forward with her schoolwork.

One of my initial goals, as the cows and sheep and cornfields passed beside us, was to ensure that Julia learned her state capitals. I had been surprised, the previous summer, to hear that her fifth-grade peers would not be memorizing Bismarck, North Dakota, and Boise, Idaho. I viewed that task as an elementary rite of passage, and so had Julia's school, until a few years earlier, when they'd decided to drop it.

"You don't learn state capitals?" I asked a fifth-grade teacher.

"No," she explained. "And we don't require the children to spell the states' names correctly. We only want them to locate the states on a map, and learn their postal abbreviations."

Postal abbreviations? As in AK, AL, AR? That struck me as incredibly slack, another example of how the schools had lowered their standards to allow more time for test preparation.

The teacher saw no problem. "I don't think anyone learns state capitals anymore," she explained.

The next day I polled my freshman composition students at Washington and Lee: "How many of you learned the state capitals when you were in elementary school?" Of eighteen students from across the nation, fifteen raised their hands.

Still curious, I raised the subject with a couple of college friends whose daughter had just completed fifth grade in the Washington, D.C., public schools.

"Did Kerry learn state capitals?"

Yes, and their son would be learning them the following year.

"The kids in our district only have to learn the state postal abbreviations," I lamented, expecting these parents to commiserate.

The father merely shrugged. "Those can be useful." He was an economics professor at Georgetown, and he explained how a very smart colleague at another institution had been gathering oil statistics on Alaska, and was surprised that the numbers contradicted all of his expectations, until he realized that for months he'd been collecting data for the state abbreviated AL: Alabama.

Despite one professor's costly mistake, my daughter would learn her state capitals, thank you very much, at the rate of two or three per day, reviewing them each week on our trips to the yarn shop, coffee shop, and library.

Julia didn't seem to mind. She displayed a surprising talent for visualizing the U.S. map and naming all the states in geographical order. Beginning with Maine, she would run down the Atlantic coast, reciting each state and its capital sequentially, all the way to Florida. Then she'd move west: Montgomery, Alabama; Jackson, Mississippi; Baton Rouge, Louisiana; until she hit California, then north to Washington, and east across the Canadian border all the way back to Maine. The middle states were more of a jumble in her mind, but she learned their capitals dutifully, aided by a game that was our best homeschooling purchase, The Scrambled States of America.

I had bought several games during our summer homeschooling shopping spree: art games, science games, a Quantum Pad Smart Guide to the Fifth Grade. Some purchases turned out to be a dull waste of cash, but Scrambled States was so entertaining that Rachel and Kathryn frequently asked to play.

The game is a kind of slapjack, comprised of fifty cards that feature cartoon drawings of each state, along with its capital and nickname. Players arrange five cards face up, one of which should be slapped and tucked away into a victory pile in response to a prompt card. When the prompt read, "State capital has a person's name in it," Julia slapped Hawaii, because of the Lulu in its capital. I slapped Montana (remember Helena?). Sometimes the prompts were geographic: "Does the state border at least six other states?" Other times they were silly: "Is the state showing teeth?" All of the states had little smiling faces.

Between that game and our car-time practice, Julia learned her capitals in a few weeks, and I was once again congratulating myself on a job well done when a brief conversation burst my pedagogical bubble.

Our family was planning a trip to Chicago in the coming months, so I asked Julia, "What state is Chicago in?"

She shrugged. "Ida know."

"We've been there twice before," I reminded her.

Still no clue.

A dim realization swept over me. "Do you know what state Seattle is in?"

She cringed and muttered, "Oregon?"

"How about St. Louis?"

She cringed further. "Kansas?"

My heart sank. Here I thought that I was holding Julia to a higher standard by having her memorize state capitals, but in the end I was just being miserably traditional. She would have been much better served if I had asked her to learn the most important city in each state. After all, which city is more central to the history and economy of Illinois: Springfield or Chicago? What city should a child be able to identify in Washington: Olympia or Seattle? Most Americans know that St. Louis is located in Missouri, but few can remember that state's capital, Jefferson City. And why should they? (Sorry, Jefferson City folk.) In a big state like California, Julia might be wise to learn a few cities: Los Angeles, San Francisco, and maybe San Diego. Sacramento would not make the top of my list.

In the end, I had committed the same folly that so many teachers and parents deplore: requiring an elementary-grade child to spend a significant amount of time memorizing facts that she would not use on a regular basis, and would therefore forget within a matter of months. So be it, I consoled myself. Live and learn.

✳

In addition to our visits to the knitting cottage, Julia and I also tried field trips with other homeschooling families. Here was our opportunity for "socialization," that word so dear to critics of homeschooling. Here, too, was a chance to learn why other parents had chosen to bushwhack their own trails through the educational wilderness.

First came a trip to the Frontier Culture Museum—acres of reproductions of seventeenth-century farms—Irish, German, English, and American—located in a town forty minutes north. We drove there with Melanie and her daughter, Sara, whom we had met when their house was featured on an "alternative homes" tour. Each spring Lexington's Garden Club holds a "traditional" house tour, allowing folks to ogle some of the town's fanciest interiors. But that year Lexington's Healthy Foods Co-op arranged an alternative, which included a yurt and several solar homes with composting toilets. Sara and Melanie's remote rural house featured prominently on the tour, and was dubbed by my daughters as the "house of straw," because the walls were insulated with bales of carefully dried straw. A large tree stripped of leaves and twigs and polished smooth as marble rose through the interior of the house, so that Sara could sit in its branches inside her room. Outside, gnomish faces were carved into the plaster walls. The entire effect was luxuriously hippy, with large southern-facing windows that made the house passive solar, overlooking a manmade pond and a hundred or so acres.

While admiring her house, I learned that Melanie was an intermittent homeschooler. She had guided her older two sons through their elementary years before entrusting them to the local middle and high schools. Sara, her youngest child, had received one year of homebound kindergarten, before spending four years at our county's tiniest rural school—twenty-five children per grade. Melanie hadn't planned to homeschool again, but at the end of the fourth grade, Sara had begun to lobby hard. She was one of several children I would meet in the coming year who specifically asked to be homeschooled, wanting to spend more time learning at home with Mom. In the end, Melanie had given in, explaining, "You know, they grow up so fast."

So there we were on a September morning, two homeschooling moms, me a part-time professor and Melanie a part-time veterinarian, strolling with our fifth-grade daughters through replicas of seventeenth-century farms, complete with crops and barns and a smattering of livestock. On the German farm, Sara showed Julia how to pick up the chickens carefully and pet them like kittens. Luckily there were no ill-tempered fowl with sharp beaks.

By the end of the afternoon, Julia had learned much about the history of agriculture, from Colonial times to Sara's contemporary experiences. She had been able to touch and see and sometimes taste the differences in farmhouse life among various European countries, all the while getting fresh air, exercising her legs, and socializing with another child. The event met all of my requirements for a good field trip.

I followed this up by planning excursions with hardcore, long-term homeschoolers, families Julia and I had met at a fall potluck hosted by Claire, the mom who had been so helpful with all of my planning for the year. The mothers at her event (no dads in sight) ranged from devout Christians to confirmed atheists, and their kids ran the gamut from well-groomed preschoolers to well-pierced teens. Claire explained that each of these families homeschooled in their own, separate way, but they liked to gather for occasional group activities: theater productions and art workshops and communal algebra lessons.

One woman in the room couldn't be missed with her lovely copper-colored hair: Mary, mother to ten children ages three to eighteen. When I heard Mary mention "the Lord," I assumed she must have come to homeschooling (and all those children) through some religious compulsion. "Oh no," she said, laughing. Christianity was a recent development in her life. "I was a liberal feminist when I began homeschooling," she explained. Her oldest children had started out in the public schools, where she had worked as an occasional substitute teacher. But Mary hadn't liked what she saw. "I hated the Ritalin march," she explained, "all the children lined up at lunchtime to take their medication. I thought there couldn't be that many ADHD kids."

Ritalin was not a school mandate; it was the choice of parents and doctors. But in Mary's eyes, the urge to succeed in the public schools' controlled environment had contributed to a medicated generation. Mary loathed the schools' emphasis on behavior modification, every classroom with its chart on the wall, listing children's names on paper tennis shoes or race cars or baseball bats, each name falling down the chart from green to yellow to red, depending on a child's behavior. Nor did Mary like the incentives for good behavior—"If you stayed green all week you could visit the treasure box!" For her, traditional schools were too managerial, preparing children for the corporate world or factory life. A stubborn iconoclast with an MFA in poetry, she valued creativity and freedom above all: "Kids need time to be creative as children. In the adult world they'll have plenty of time to meet other people's expectations."

In addition to being a poet and screenwriter in the scattered moments not devoted to her kids, Mary had a special flair for science. That fall she was planning a three-day fossil study, and she invited Julia and me to come along.

A few weeks later we joined Mary and a handful of other homeschoolers in the basement of a church, where an amateur paleontologist had spread part of his fossil collection across a table. He spent an hour explaining about the digs he had been on, and how fossil lovers could buy and sell specimens on the Internet. Every time he mentioned dinosaurs, Julia waved her hand and talked with such eager abandon that my pride in her knowledge was balanced by my sensitivity to the group. I kept putting my hand on her knee and murmuring, "Let the other kids speak, Julia."

A week later we gathered in that same basement to hear Mary expound on trilobites—when they lived, where they lived, the details of their primitive anatomy displayed on handouts. Finally, in the third week, five moms and nine children crowded into Mary's fifteen-seat van and she piloted us an hour south, through the rolling pasture between the Blue Ridge and Alleghenies, with one little carsick boy threatening to vomit half the way.

That drive gave me a chance to ask a few other moms why they had opted for lifelong homeschooling. The most succinct reply came from a woman with striking curly black hair and dark eyes, whose daughter looked like a beautiful Greek princess. "Why are you homeschooling?" I asked, and she looked me right in the eye: "Have you heard what sort of language the children use in the public schools?"

I knew what she meant. There were a lot of sassy kids at Waddell Elementary, steeped in the language of Happy Bunny—imagine the Easter bunny with an attitude: "I'm happy, don't wreck it by talking." Rachel, our verbally precocious middle daughter, had an ear especially attuned to edgy vocabulary. In the second grade she had tried a bout of experimentation with profanity that had left her babysitter puzzled: "Where did Rachel get the potty mouth?"

I had responded with feigned innocence: "Oh, you know how it is. Once they go off to school, they hear everything." In fact, Rachel had heard plenty of bad words at our house. Between

John's military mouth and my occasionally roiling temper, our eight-year-old was starting to sound like Richard Nixon.

As I looked out the window of Mary's van, watching the Blue Ridge Mountains parallel the highway, I knew that I was one of the parents whose slack habits had contributed to the schools' verbal cesspool. Fortunately, after a few conversations on the difference between good words and bad, Rachel had cleaned up her act, but I discovered over time that I didn't mind the occasional *shit*, *damn*, or *crap* so much as the shallow drivel that many elementary-age children were absorbing from American pop culture: daily discussions of who was and was not cool, whose clothes were pathetic, what boy was *hot*. Compared to all the gossip about social winners and losers, Rachel's second-grade profanity sounded downright eloquent.

Now Mary had pulled off the highway, and after a few miles of winding country lanes, she had reached the site of our excavation: an unprepossessing dirt hill right beside the road—no marker, no parking area, just Mary's childhood recollection that this was a good place to dig. With one mother standing in the road to slow passing cars, we sat on that incline of clay and shale and attacked the dirt with small picks and hand shovels.

Within fifteen minutes everyone had found a fossil except me and Julia. I was starting to think that short-term homeschoolers were deficient in the art of digging, when Julia hit a trilobite vein. The effect was like a miner's first discovery of gold. Julia was thrilled, doubling her pace. For half an hour she carved out pieces of shale, peeling layers apart gently, uncovering trilobite fossils the size of my thumbnail. The earth was full of buried treasure more precious to Julia than any pirate's hoard.

"It's cool that you can find fossils right beside the road," she said. "I mean, you usually think of fossils being out in the desert.

But here they are, right in the dirt. And these are older than the dinosaurs."

We went home with shale fragments wrapped in tissue paper and packed in individual jewelry boxes. To this day Julia has two pieces tucked away in her bedroom drawer—homeschooling relics, as tangible as the bones of saints.

.✻.

One final trip capped our fall: a three-day mother-daughter excursion to Washington, D.C. Although I had worked in Washington for two years, and had visited annually for the past eighteen, I had never set foot in the National Archives, the Supreme Court, or the Library of Congress. Homeschooling offered the chance to fill the gaps in my own education, let alone Julia's. We packed our itinerary with sights new to both of us, along with our old favorites: the museums of Natural History and Air and Space.

What a glorious sense of escape, to leave town after a Thursday college class, with only one child in tow. John could manage Rachel and Kathryn for three days; he could make their lunches and drive them to school, chauffeur them to playdates and dance class and birthday parties, feed them, read with them, tell them to brush their teeth and take their baths and go to bed. I was free—free in a way I hadn't experienced in years.

On the drive, Julia and I listened to books on tape (after some obligatory math and history quizzing, which she lamented noisily), but when we crossed the Potomac, my job as tour guide began. "Look at the Kennedy Center," I said. The Lincoln Memorial, the Washington Monument.

"What's that building on our left?" I asked.

"The White House," Julia answered.

"What branch of government is run from the White House?"
"The executive."

Inside the National Archives' Rotunda, we stood before the Constitution, preserved in helium under glass.

"Isn't it impressive?" I asked, but Julia shrugged.

She found the space dark and dull, the Declaration of Independence yellow and faded, a mere ghost of its former self. Julia was more interested in lunch than in the Bill of Rights. And yet, two years later, when I asked if she remembered the Archives, she said yes, it was "very cool" to see history preserved. That struck me as a statement about the nature of homeschooling; it was an experience liable to be valued mostly in retrospect, once memory had filtered out the discomfort of sore feet and the growling of a child's stomach.

Although it would take years for Julia to appreciate the Archives, she did seem to show an immediate interest in the Supreme Court interior. There, she sat quietly while a guide explained what we would be seeing if the Justices were in session. I was impressed with Julia's silent concentration; she seemed absorbed in the tour guide's words. But when we walked outside and I asked her to write a paragraph about the experience, I learned what had monopolized her attention:

Hi, I'm Julia and I just went to the Supreme Court. Inside I saw the Supreme Court's courtroom. It had one eagle on each flagpole. We saw that golden animals were carved into gates that rimmed the right and left hand sides. If you go one floor up there is a basketball court called the highest court in the land.

The courtroom's human history and function held little interest for my daughter; her eyes were searching for any animal presence in the room. "I kept imagining the animals coming to life and climbing off those golden bars," she told me later. "Even the fish, swimming in the air . . . I never do that with humans. I never imagine statues getting up and walking around."

There were plenty of animals to interest Julia inside the old Library of Congress, which we visited next. Zodiac symbols decorated the central hall's marble floor, and Julia stood on Capricorn's bronze goat while peering up at the names of Milton, Shakespeare, and Dante inscribed in a heaven of stars and angels. The Library had just reopened after years of renovation, and the colors were almost fluorescent, all peach and aqua and white. It looked like an elaborate Italian palace, full of intricate Corinthian columns, sculpted staircases, shimmery mosaics, and sparkling stained glass. The main reading room glowed with rose and tan marble arches leading up to the rotunda, where statues of Newton and Herodotus and Moses peered down from the ether.

"I think this is the most beautiful room in Washington," I murmured to Julia.

She wasn't impressed. Sure, it was pretty, but as she noted on our way out, "What's the point of a library where you can't even check the books out?"

Julia chose instead to linger in the glassed-in botanical gardens beside the Capitol, where she could commune with orchids and bromeliads. She also felt at home inside the National Museum of the American Indian, donning buffalo skins and beating on drums. She loved the television screen that showed cartoon stories of Native Americans transformed into stars in the night sky. "I could have watched that all day long," she mused.

Washington is a homeschooler's paradise, not only because of the museums and monuments at every corner, but because so much of it is free. At 6:00 p.m. we attended the daily complimentary concert at the Kennedy Center's Millennium Stage. An Irish harpist performed with a percussionist and a tap dancer, and when she told the crowd that we were welcome to dance, Julia stood and waltzed in the aisles.

Our chief expense came from restaurants, but even those were educational for a ten-year-old. Lexington has no Thai café, no Indian or African food. In Washington we could enjoy them all, especially my favorite: Ethiopian. Julia, child of my heart, was happy to eat with her fingers, tearing bits of spongy injera bread to pick up minced lamb, shredded cabbage, and pureed lentils.

As for our lodging, we stayed with the college friends whose children had faithfully learned their state capitals in the D.C. public schools. Their mother was a Justice Department attorney who, years earlier, had argued and won a case before the Supreme Court. Spotting the opportunity for one final lesson, I prodded Julia: "Remember what you heard at the Supreme Court today? How each lawyer has thirty minutes to present a case to the Justices? And how the Justices grill the lawyers with questions? Wendy is one of those lawyers—she stood in that courtroom and answered the questions, and she won her case. Do you want to ask her anything?"

Yes, at the end of the day my fifth-grader had a pressing question for the accomplished attorney. The most important question of all.

"So, where are your toys?"

CHAPTER SIX

➤➤The Winter
of Our Discontent◄◄

All's fair in school and war.

JULIA

IF HOMESCHOOLING HAD BEEN AN ENDLESS STRING OF FIELD
trips, wandering through museums and parks and concert
halls, Julia and I would have been happy all year. Away from
home, reveling in freedom and space, we enjoyed the pleasures of
hands-on learning. But field trips are the exception, not the rule.
In between our sporadic travels, the kitchen table waited with its
hours of math and grammar and science—and as most parents
can attest, extended spells of homebound mother-daughter contact are a recipe for trouble.

Most homeschooling books don't mention these troubles; they
don't dwell on shouting matches and slammed doors. Perhaps
other homeschooling households are more placid than mine, or
perhaps the first foray into homeschooling is always rocky, and
years of practice are required to smooth the path. But I suspect
that even the best homeschooling families have their ugly moments, from minor annoyances to major fights, and at the risk of
inviting the social worker to my door, I will tell you about ours.
Here, in order of increasing aggravation, are all the things that

began to go wrong for me and Julia, as the hopefulness of fall gave way to the gloom of winter.

To begin with—something small.

Before launching into the regular fifth-grade math curriculum, I had thought to give Julia some sense of where numbers come from, and why they are necessary. Our public library has an excellent children's book called *The History of Counting*, written by an archaeologist named Denise Schmandt-Besserat. The book begins with the numberless systems of simple societies, and with a mixture of brightly illustrated pages and clearly written text, it demonstrates how the rise of cities in ancient cultures made precise methods of counting necessary.

"Look at this page," I said to Julia one morning in early September. "Did you know that there are people living in the world today who don't use numbers at all?"

Julia settled beside me on the living room couch while I read aloud:

For example, the Paiela, who cultivate orchards in the highlands of Papua New Guinea, count by pointing to parts of their body. The number 1 is called "little left finger," 11 is "left neck," 16 is "right ear," etc. This way of counting is called body counting. When the Paiela go to the marketplace, they trade and bargain by pointing to their fingers, wrists, elbows, shoulders, neck and nose. This way of counting is sufficient in communities that have no use for large numbers, because the people themselves produce most of the food and things they need. (The largest number of the Paiela is 28, shown by the two hands clenched together.)

Here was a drawing of a handsome brown-skinned man with a bone through his nose, his torso facing the reader with arms down, palms forward, head turned to his right, naked except for a skirt of long white feathery fronds. Numbers outlined his upper body, extending from the tips of his fingers, up his arms, around his head, and down to his opposite hand.

"How would you say nineteen in the Paielas' language?" I asked Julia.

"Right shoulder."

"What about five?"

"Left thumb."

We turned the pages and saw cultures that counted with pebbles, and the ancient Egyptians using oval stone markers to represent each sheep.

"Isn't this interesting?" I said.

Julia turned away, staring out the window toward the mountains.

"What's wrong?" I asked.

"C'mon, Mom," she sighed. "It's *boring*."

Boring? People in the twenty-first century who survive without numbers beyond twenty-eight was boring? I looked at my beautiful daughter leaning away from me on a pillow, strands of dark brown hair falling in swirls beside her cheeks, and I immediately recalled T. S. Eliot's *The Love Song of J. Alfred Prufrock*:

And would it have been worth it, after all
. . .

Would it have been worth while,
To have bitten off the matter with a smile,
To have squeezed the universe into a ball
To roll it toward some overwhelming question,
To say: "I am Lazarus, come from the dead,
Come back to tell you all, I shall tell you all"—
If one, settling a pillow by her head,

Should say: "That is not what I meant at all.
That is not it, at all."

There I was, armed with my pile of books and games and puzzles and field trip itineraries, trying to reveal the wonders of the world to this yawning creature. And there she was, running the tip of her finger across the pattern in the upholstery, intimating that I had no comprehension whatsoever of her mind: "That is not what I meant at all. / That is not it, at all."

I don't know what I expected from my ten-year-old. Boundless joy at a book about numbers? Mesmerized interest in the tribes of New Guinea? Naturally a little girl wouldn't share all of her mother's interests, but I did assume, in those early days, that Julia would meet me halfway. I thought that once we embarked on homeschooling, she would stop equating teacher with torturer, and muster enough enthusiasm, enough sense of intellectual adventure, to give each new subject, and each new book, a cheerful try. Julia, however, could be remarkably dismissive of topics that didn't immediately spark her interest.

"Shall we watch this award-winning film on George Washington?" I would ask, and Julia would merely sigh. Dullsville.

A concert featuring the Cleveland String Quartet? Ho hum.

A speech at W&L by Jimmy Carter? "Oh, Mom, do we *have* to go?"

Yes, often we *had* to go. Much as I understand the need to follow a child's interests, how does a ten-year-old know where her passions lie unless she is first introduced to the myriad possibilities in the world? A child might skip one concert, but should she skip math because she dislikes it? Or science? Or history? Some unschoolers would say, "Yes, she'll come back to math in her own time." But short-term homeschooling doesn't allow time for the child's interests to catch up with the curriculum, and I believe in the daily discipline of math and writing and music for any school-age child.

I usually required Julia to complete the tasks I had planned for the week, whether they appealed to her or not. Remember that boring essay on Fahrenheit and Celsius? I insisted that she write the whole thing, for the sake of having finished what we started. This meant that I had to squeeze the paragraphs out of her over the course of five days, which was kind of like running a soggy shirt through a dry wringer. She probably would have written a better essay on a more appealing subject, and in the coming months I tried to offer many choices: If you don't like this math book, what book would you prefer? If the metric system is boring, what science topic do you want to write about? And yet, the wringer approach was sometimes necessary, because even when we chose topics that Julia enjoyed, she could still, like any ten-year-old, display an immense capacity for foot-dragging.

Take, for instance, our fall-term focus on natural history. We had decided to study Peter Ackroyd's *The Beginning*, a book that follows the evolution of life from the Big Bang through cavemen. The pictures were vivid, the text was well written, and the subject was right up Julia's alley, with its angry T. rex on the cover. We planned to complement each chapter with art projects and videos and writing assignments, focused on different time periods: Precambrian, Paleolithic, multiple ice ages.

In theory, it sounded great. In practice, the first time I asked Julia to read a chapter, she managed about three pages before closing the book. I soon discovered that this child, who could remain absorbed in fiction for hours at a time, had a very limited attention span when it came to nonfiction. Julia was happy to learn nonfiction from films and TV: the History and Discovery channels were fine with her, and Eyewitness videos, with their catchy opening music, white backdrops, and thirty-minute length, were ideal. But when it came to reading a single chapter from a children's biography, she balked like a recalcitrant mule. Dinosaurs might hold her interest for half a dozen pages; she could rarely stomach human beings for more than a few paragraphs.

This surprised me, because in the first through fourth grades, Julia had often checked out nonfiction books from the library, usually on nature and sometimes outer space. But now I realized that she had never read those books from cover to cover. She had sampled them, scanning the pictures and dipping into paragraphs here and there. And why not? She was a child, not a college student (something I, with my professorial habits, had to constantly remind myself). I tried to suggest novels for Julia with historical subjects, for the sake of sneaking a little nonfiction into her brain. Mary Pope Osborne's *Magic Tree House* series had been wonderful for Julia in the second grade, incorporating history and science into a magical adventure. But now, in the fifth grade, Julia had such a strong preference for fantasy that it was hard to interject versions of the real world into her reading. I supposed that I should be glad she was eager to read anything at all; perhaps an interest in nonfiction would emerge later in life.

Nevertheless, since *The Beginning* was the centerpiece of our science and history, I wasn't willing to give it up. Instead, we spent several mornings reading the book together. I would read a paragraph, then Julia would read one. Or sometimes I would read a chapter on my own, then deliver the information in the form of a mini-lecture, with questions and answers. Either way, the process was much more labor-intensive for me than I had anticipated, and we wound up skimming much of the text.

When faced with Julia's bored indifference, I would sometimes set aside a book, a film, or the entire plan for an afternoon. With no standardized tests looming, no required facts to memorize, we had the flexibility to stop, regroup, and adjust the plan.

As I saw it, our curriculum was valuable as a starting point. We had a set of clear goals; how we achieved them could be a matter of trial and error.

So as for that beautiful counting book? I put it away. And what else did we abandon over the course of the year? How many books and games and plans were relinquished as lost causes? I'll mention just a few.

There was, for instance, my plan to conduct verbal lessons with Julia while going on outdoor walks. I had imagined she and I might talk about history, poetry, and geography while getting some exercise and fresh air. (Elementary school teachers can chuckle at my idealistic expectations.) Although little John Stuart Mill was capable, by age five, of sustaining long talks while strolling with his father, my lovely child of nature displayed a two-minute tolerance for conversation before she would run ahead of me to pick Queen Anne's Lace growing at the side of the road.

"Thank you," I would say when she handed me a bouquet. "And what do you think brought about the end of Mayan civilization?"

"Oh no!" she would respond. "A dead rabbit!" And off she'd go to stare at whatever mangled corpse graced our path that day. (On our road, the daily fare can range from possum to ground hog to skunk. I soon got tired of making lessons out of squished squirrels.)

Surrounded by the glories and horrors of nature, Julia had no interest in abstractions; world history or American government couldn't compare with a scuttling chipmunk. On most walks, she bounded like an unleashed golden retriever, chasing after cardinals or blue jays, returning to my side only briefly before running again. Given space, Julia always preferred running over walking, darting down sidewalks and grocery store aisles, rarely attentive to teachers and parents saying, "Slow down Julia! No running in the halls!"

The few occasions when we managed to blend outdoor walks with a clear academic agenda came when Julia maintained a leaf journal. With a field guide in hand she was content to slow her pace, walking from tree to tree on Washington and Lee's campus, taking photographs, doing leaf rubbings, distinguishing the eastern white pine from the short-needled loblolly. She recorded ash, elm, and oak according to their kingdoms and phyla, and wrote a descriptive paragraph on each one.

"Remember those times when we took pictures of trees and wrote about them?" she said to me a year later. "I liked that. Let's do that again."

And yet, once the gold and crimson and saffron shades had vanished from our landscape, much of the initial luster of homeschooling vanished as well. When the air grew cold and the trees fell bare and we retreated more and more indoors, Julia and I started to seriously grate on each other's nerves.

In a large classroom, or a larger homeschooling family, there would have been other children to dilute our one-on-one contact. My attention would have been diverted, and Julia would have had time to daydream, and to chart her own imaginative course over the hills and valleys of learning. It was hard for her to have my maternal eye focused so frequently upon her—imagine Sauron's eye in *The Lord of the Rings*—and any mother who observes one child intently is bound for unpleasant discoveries.

I soon found that my eldest daughter had an enormous flair for whining, a veritable gift for discontent. Her repertoire of grievances spanned all the injustices of a child's world, from teeth brushing to room cleaning to the daily grind of math and grammar. "I *hate* fractions . . . I don't *want* to proofread . . . Why do I *have* to practice my violin?" Homeschooling can be especially exhausting when every bout of productive work is preceded by ten minutes of lamentation, and I found myself repeating the classic parental refrain: "You could have finished the job by now, in the time you've spent complaining about it."

How foolish I had been, to have believed that Julia's complaints over the past two years had been caused by her distaste for the public schools. I had assumed that all her griping stemmed from an institutional cause; surely she would be a cheerful learner once I granted her this break from the old routine.

If only it had been that simple. My daughter, I soon realized, protested about all structured schoolwork, whether it took place in a classroom or a kitchen. She might have been pleased with pure unschooling if freed to choose her daily direction, but that, from my perspective, was not an option. Math and spelling and science all had to be studied, regardless of a ten-year-old's habitual petulance.

"Glass half full," I kept saying to Julia. "Glass half *full*."

"Halfway isn't good enough," she replied.

I began to wonder if my child had a genetic predisposition toward grumbling. This must be a matter of nature, not nurture, I told myself, because Rachel and Kathryn, born into the same household, the same model of parenting, and attending the same schools, did not share Julia's propensity to balk noisily at all schoolwork. In fact, my chief concern about Rachel was the excessive time she devoted to her homework. Far from complaining about it, she threw herself into her assignments with such high standards that in future years my efforts would be torn between trying to get her to lighten up and encouraging Julia to work harder. As for Kathryn, encountering the rituals of public school for the first time, including weekly homework, she didn't blink. When I mentioned that I never had homework in kindergarten, she found my comment a curiosity, but not a rallying cry. Only

Julia, keenly attuned to social injustice, saw the adult world as infringing way too much upon her childhood. Whether in the form of homeschooling or a traditional classroom, education and lamentation went hand in hand.

Her complaints reminded me of Julia's toddler years, when my pockets were full of pacifiers to soothe her screaming outrage. Now I was offering games and puzzles and outdoor science experiments as intellectual pacifiers with only moderate success, and on her most petulant days I could feel myself getting resentful.

Instead of protests, I think I would have liked a small measure of gratitude. That might sound selfish, but it would have been nice to have a teacher appreciation week in homeschooling— some recognition from Julia that Mom was spending a lot of time trying to make her education livelier and more fun, so maybe she should give the complaints a rest.

My only consolation came from other frazzled moms, similarly exasperated with their querulous children. "It's terrible," one British mother explained, describing her son's behavior with a term that I liked: whinging. "I asked him just yesterday, when did you become such an incredible whinger?"

Fifth grade, a few mothers explained, was an especially trying time for girls—the beginning of their transition from childhood to adolescence. A few of Julia's classmates had started their periods; some looked like fourteen-year-olds, their bodies had developed so fully, so suddenly. Along with this physical development came a host of emotional struggles: eating disorders, debilitating self-criticism, obsession with popularity and fashion and dating. Sadly, the behaviors once associated with girls' teenage years now seem to be ensconced by the end of elementary school.

Julia displayed none of this preteen angst; she couldn't care less about clothes or boys or social ladders. I told myself that her loathing for structured schoolwork was mild compared with the self-loathing that some of her peers were expressing. Still, that didn't take the edge out of her complaints, or mine.

Faced with growing frustrations, my first response was predictable—I got mad at my husband. This homeschooling, I told myself, might be less exhausting if John was more supportive.

John had been skeptical about the whole homeschooling concept, predicting that I was going to drive myself crazy. And rather than admit he might have been right (too much to ask of any wife), I started to focus on all the subtle ways he was contributing to my insanity.

At the beginning of the year he had willingly jumped aboard our homeschooling train once it started to leave the station. On Tuesdays and Thursdays from noon until three, John was ready to welcome Julia at his VMI office, for lunch and lessons in the flute and conversational French. In preparation, Julia and I had visited the French teacher at our local middle school and had purchased the same textbook she was using, noting how far the first-year French class usually advanced. We didn't expect Julia to maintain a middle-school pace; our town's sixth-graders study their language five days a week. But we hoped that John's fluency (from years of study and travel in France) would give Julia a solid start.

I was especially adamant about leaving Julia in her father's care, not only for the sake of my mental health, but also to thwart the idea that homeschooling is the sole territory of stay-at-home moms. Homeschooling is sometimes labeled as antifeminist—an enterprise that keeps women occupied at home, focused on their children and incapable of pursuing a career. This label has always bothered me, first, because homeschoolers are a diverse bunch of women and men, and second, because, in my mind, "feminism" is defined not by the voltage of one's career, but by the ability to make choices—to choose to be a full-time doctor or a full-time mom, or something in between. In my case, I wanted to combine homeschooling with a part-time job, something plenty of homeschoolers, female and male, manage across our country. But flexible options are possible only when homeschooling moms and dads receive support from spouses and partners, grandparents and friends. If I wanted to blend homeschooling with professional work, that meant getting help from John.

He seemed willing enough when September rolled around. "Today was great!" Julia wrote in her journal after her first day with Dad. "I went to the library, and I even had Dad start to tutor me in French and flute. Which is great because I don't get to see him that often anymore." John's typical schedule involved evening rehearsals three days a week, football or basketball games on weekends, and out-of-town trips every month. A three-hour block of time with her father was a special treat.

Unfortunately, after the first week, those three-hour blocks quickly dissolved into fifteen-minute chunks. It seemed that John's office was a bad setting for homeschooling (no surprise there, many working parents will affirm). With 150 band students, John often had cadets streaming in and out of the room. A thirty-minute flute lesson might suffer two or three interruptions, and with his telephone and computer beckoning, John spent as much time on email as on Julia's French.

Meanwhile, once the novelty wore off, Julia began to lose interest.

"When we started," John explained, "it was all new and interesting, so she paid attention to me. In the first two weeks we'd spend an hour on French and an hour on the flute each day, and everything went well. But after that, she figured out that she could just blow me off."

Like me, John assumed that if he got Julia started on an assignment, she should be able to work independently for half an hour. Occasionally that worked; more often, when I came to pick her up at three o'clock, John would be off at a meeting while she was absorbed in computer games.

"What did you do with your dad today?" I'd ask.

"A little bit of French," she'd reply, not looking up from the screen. "A little bit of music. Mostly we hung out at the weight room."

The VMI weight room. Imagine a vast monument to sweaty testosterone, full of football players and warriors-in-training, working their abs and biceps and pecs while blasting songs from The Killers and Drowning Pool. That family-friendly space was destined to become Julia's alternate classroom, as John's need for daily exercise competed with her need for academic instruction. While Dad tried to break his latest bench press record, Julia went next door to the cardio room, full of treadmills and stationary bicycles and, most important, a TV hanging down from the ceiling. Julia had no qualms about monopolizing the remote control; John was often amused to walk in and find a room full of macho cadets watching the Powerpuff Girls—Bubbles, Blossom, and Buttercup—saving the world with their tiny, muscle-free physiques.

As the weeks passed and the weight room prevailed, I thought, "Okay. No problem." Since John thrived on daily exercise, he could be Julia's PE teacher. In the coming months, they ran the steps at VMI's football stadium, jogged around the parade ground, and practiced sit-ups and push-ups. They tried a little racquetball, and John timed Julia running around the outdoor track. When it came to physical education, he had one clear objective: "All I have to do is get Julia sweating."

This all sounded great to me, so long as John and Julia kept up with their other subjects. Sadly, that didn't happen.

One evening in October, John came home from a late jazz band rehearsal, dropped his keys and trumpet case on the hall table, and collapsed on the couch.

"Julia's stopping flute," he announced.

"But you've only tried it for one month," I protested.

"She isn't making progress."

Julia, he explained, had learned the first few notes with ease, but when it came to "going over the break" (when all the lifted fingers must be placed back on the air holes at once, while pressing down an octave key), she'd hit a brick wall. It was hard. She got frustrated. She fell into tearful tantrums, which provoked dry-eyed tantrums from John. The two of them spent as much time arguing as playing.

"Anyway, she's not practicing," he said.

"You've never practiced with her at home," I responded.

"She should practice on her own."

By then I was gritting my teeth, a habit I had developed after the birth of my children. My maternal frustrations are recorded on the whittled-down edge of my left incisor. "I've spent four days a week for the past four years," I said, "getting Julia to practice her violin. You could spend one night a week working on the flute with her."

John shook his head. "That's your thing, not mine."

There we were, caught in an old family argument—the same argument that echoes in households across America, wherever parents debate whether a child should be required to practice a musical instrument.

John and I have very different perspectives on the matter. I come from a family where, at age seven, every child was signed up for one year of piano lessons, followed by several years of any instrument the child preferred. My mother viewed music as an essential part of a child's education, as relevant as science, history, or math. Although my brother gave up his French horn after a few years, my sister is now an excellent cellist as well as a doctor. As for me, I earned money with my violin all through high school, playing at weddings and parties and pops concerts, and working as a strolling, gypsy-clad violinist in an Italian restaurant that my mother described as "whorehouse red." These days I still perform with a small local symphony—the legacy of a mother who sat her children down and required them to practice.

But John perceives different legacies in the world around him. He sees children whose natural love of music has been squelched by parents who pushed them to practice. His parents never pushed. Their family piano was used primarily as a mantel for holding framed photographs. John's first taste of music lessons came in the seventh grade, when band instruments were introduced at his Catholic school. He persuaded his parents to purchase a Bundy student trumpet, and from there he proceeded to be the worst trumpeter in his grade. He didn't practice; he didn't learn to read music; band class was a weekly humiliation, so he quit. Music didn't come up again until the ninth grade, when his brand-new high school started a band program. When the director learned that John owned a trumpet, that was enough qualification to sign him up. Inspired by excellent teachers, John surprised everyone by practicing steadily, majoring in music, and ultimately becoming a college band director. Still, he views instrumental music as a choice, not a requirement—a pleasure for those few people who have the desire and the discipline.

"You should play the violin because you enjoy it," he often says to Julia, whenever she complains about practicing—which is my cue to glare at him from my seat at the piano bench.

"It takes a few years of practice," I insist, "to get comfortable enough with an instrument so that you can really enjoy it." And then I look over at Julia. "Do you want to quit the violin?"

"I want to play," she invariably responds. "I just don't want to practice."

And so we slog on.

✦

Flute lessons, however, were a battle I was not willing to fight. Julia was getting plenty of music education with her violin, and she objected to double duty on instrumental music. The flute had been my concession to our local school system, which has no string program. The small middle school Julia would be attending the following year offered band as its only in-school music, and in preparation, Julia's peers were picking up trumpets and clarinets and saxophones. If she wanted to join them in the fall, she needed to start practicing.

Julia's flute, however, soon returned to its shelf in VMI's instrument room, and I wouldn't have minded its disappearance, except that her French lessons didn't seem to be faring much better. John readily admitted that he had no curricular plan for French—no schedule for what they should achieve each week, or each month. His approach to language instruction was entirely free-form; they would start at lesson one and go from there.

"Bonjour!" he said to Julia on the first day. *"Je m'appelle John! Et toi?"*

On day two he repeated the same few words, as he did on days three and four. Sometimes he offered written assignments; sometimes he skipped French altogether. The results were unsurprisingly slow, since real progress in a foreign language requires daily practice. Two sessions each week couldn't impress a new vocabulary upon Julia's brain.

"You know," John said, sighing, "I'll go over how you say hello and 'how old are you,' and 'where's the bathroom,' and in three days she's forgotten everything. She has no concept of keeping it in her head and using it as a language that other people actually speak."

I suggested that he speak a little French to Julia each day at home, but John was even more averse to homework than our daughter. French would have no place in his afterschool hours.

Much as I would have liked for John to throw himself into this homeschooling venture, I couldn't ask much more of him. A parent must be fully committed to homeschooling in order to make it work, and while in some households that determination is shared by both parents, who feel equally responsible for the child's progress, in many families the mother serves as the chief homeschooler. A working dad might be more active in the social, athletic, or religious aspects of homeschooling, but mothers often handle the academics. Especially in our case, since John had never been sold on the idea of homeschooling, this was my project, and my burden. If Julia was going to learn French, I would have to learn it, too.

Initially I asked Julia to teach me what she had covered each week with her dad, since teaching is the best way to reinforce one's own learning. But Julia's knowledge was too vague for her to pass it along. I tried instead to study the French textbook with her, slowly, page by page, asking her little questions, such as the ages of her family members: *"Quel âge a ton père? Quel âge a ta soeur Rachel?"* Driving in the car, I would inquire about the time: *"Quelle heure est-il?"* And where were we going? And what time should we arrive? When grocery shopping, or buying gas, or sitting at the coffee shop, I inserted little French terms and questions into our routine, encouraging her to ask me questions as well, to try to get a tiny conversation going.

In the end, it was the blind leading the blind. I never learned enough French to progress beyond the simplest sentences, and my pronunciation was guesswork. Even when we practiced daily,

Julia had little memory for the language. Her vocabulary grew at a snail's pace.

Pitiful as our efforts proved, we remained far ahead of any foreign language instruction Julia would have received at her elementary school. There, her exposure would have been limited to one hour after school, once a week, for one semester, with a college student who might manage to introduce the children to a smattering of foreign vocabulary, culture, and cuisine. These days, even that one-hour slot has been dropped from the "after-school enrichment program."

Waddell's teachers explain that due to state mandates, there is no time in the day for foreign language instruction. But in my dream elementary school, all of the teachers would use a little bit of Spanish in their daily routine. When asking children to take out their books, why not say it in Spanish? Why not call children in from recess with a Spanish phrase, or teach the numbers one through twenty in Spanish as well as English? With new phrases added each year, the students and teachers might jointly develop a beginning grasp of the sounds and concepts behind an important foreign language. Meanwhile, at our house, I've bought the Rosetta Stone package for French, in case any other child wants to give it a try.

✳

Back in 2005, when faced with Julia's slow progress in French (and math and spelling), I began to resort to an age-old parenting technique: bribery.

"What use are Roman numerals in our world today?" I asked Julia one afternoon.

"Probably not much," she answered.

"No, not much" I agreed. "But I'll give you a quarter every time you find a Roman numeral being used in our town, or in our lives."

Julia's eyes lit up.

"Up to a maximum of two dollars," I added.

Her smile drooped. Still, she reached over to me, took my wrist, and tapped the glass on my watch. "Give me a quarter," she said. The short hand on my Timex was pointing between XII and I.

When my children were small I thought I would never pay them a penny beyond a weekly allowance in exchange for chores, but my high ideals faltered one afternoon in the public library, when I was speaking to a child whom I admired. She was a highly intelligent and mature girl who excelled at so many activities—music, dancing, writing—that I had occasion to stop and praise her. I don't recall the exact impetus. A recent recital or a recent poem? Whatever the compliment, she smiled at me, leaned forward, and said very quietly, "My parents pay me to do it."

I was shocked. Her parents were my vision of the ideal mom and dad—a bright, friendly, and accomplished couple raising bright, friendly, and accomplished children. And they were using money. Or at least that was the child's perception. Had the parents been present, they probably would have offered a rush of hasty explanations and qualifications.

After my initial, self-righteous *tsk-tsk*, I paused to consider the matter. All around me parents and teachers were coaxing children with "rewards" of endless variety: toys after a dental appointment, candy at the end of a violin lesson, "Smarties" sweets at school for children who aced a test. Julia's tennis coach, whom she met for occasional private lessons as part of her homeschooling, wielded quarters like prizes at a carnival game. Knock down the orange cone on the service line, and you'll get another coin.

I cringe at the thought of paying children for good report cards, dishing out a certain number of dollars for every A. Although some parents swear by it, to me, that sort of financial transaction taints learning with the stench of hard cash. Our family's alternatives, however, are far from virtuous. Sometimes when our girls all bring home excellent report cards, we "reward" them with a family dinner at a nice restaurant. Or occasionally I'll buy them small stuffed animals. These are celebratory acts, I assure myself, not bribes. It would probably be less expensive just to pay for each A.

On the one occasion when I resorted to a big cash transaction with a child, there were clear benefits and even clearer drawbacks. It happened because Kathryn had been slower to swim than her sisters, staunchly refusing to put her head underwater. Summer after summer, we paid for swimming lessons, bought fancy goggles, coaxed and pleaded, but Kathryn remained adamant. She watched her friends wiggle like tadpoles through the pool, and envied their joy at jumping off diving boards. Still, she strolled through the water, stirring the pool with her fingertips and sometimes dogpaddling in shallow depths with her neck straining above the surface.

Then, suddenly, one summer day, after offering my usual pointless words of encouragement, all of my parental standards flew out the window. I looked my youngest daughter in the eye and said, "I'll give you twenty dollars if you'll put your head underwater right now and swim."

Her mouth fell open. To Kathryn's six-year-old mind, twenty dollars was a pirate's fortune. Andrew Jackson was a rare visitor in my wallet, let alone my children's piggy banks. Shocked into action, Kathryn eyed the expanse of liquid around her and, with grim determination, she pulled her goggles over her eyes, took a deep breath, and plunged. Lo and behold, she didn't emerge sputtering and resentful, taking the cash and never wanting to try again. On the contrary, she liked it. She loved it. For the next half hour she dove and splashed and jumped into the deep end from the side of the pool, delighted to be submerged. It was like the conclusion to *Green Eggs and Ham*—the surprising pleasure in the thing most dreaded. "And I will eat them in a boat, and I will eat them with a goat . . ."

Amazing, I thought. Maybe a little bribery was not such a bad thing. I had just saved myself a bundle in the swimming lessons I would now cancel for that summer.

But there was a larger price to pay; there is always a larger price. Julia and Rachel, who had overheard the episode, insisted that they, too, be paid twenty dollars for some aquatic feat. Julia would start swimming laps and Rachel would learn to do a head-first dive.

This wasn't what I had in mind; their achievements would have come eventually without payment, and sixty dollars was going to break my mommy bribery budget. But my girls insist on equal treatment with the unflinching standards of a stern judiciary. They had me, and they knew it.

Any parent who has stooped to pay a child for some miscellaneous achievement knows what comes next: the dreaded day when a nine-year-old stands before you and says, "What will you pay me if I do _____?"

"I will pay you with a hug and a kiss and my sincerest admiration," I replied when that day occurred in our household.

At which point the child snorts, "Yeah, right."

Model parents will nod and say, "That's the problem with our society: young people who don't act for the sake of pride, only for profit." And yet, the world of child rearing is never black and white. My girls, like most children, pursue their passions without coaxing. The question is how to encourage children to complete all those other tasks that they might find onerous, but that parents know to be essential. Stern discipline can be effective when it comes to household chores, but it's probably not the best tactic for getting a child to read. So why not offer a small reward every time a reluctant reader finishes a certain number of books? Our local library includes prizes in its summer reading program. Is that a vice?

"Set a goal," I said to Julia a few times during our home-schooling, "and we can agree on an appropriate reward."

Julia proposed serious goals: to advance through all the exercises in her violin book, or to score 100 percent on a Saxon math test. (Although she learned math concepts quickly, Julia tended to be very careless when taking tests. A perfect test was a rare achievement.) In exchange, she suggested lunch at her favorite restaurant, or a small dragon statuette.

One might imagine that our homeschooling would become an expensive proposition, with all the restaurant bills and little prizes. In fact, although Julia liked the idea of setting goals, she rarely had the daily discipline to see them through. If I pushed and prodded, she could make regular progress toward a chosen reward. More often, the prizes disappeared into the fog of school.

After a while I began to wonder if we were on track to achieve any of our goals. Julia's knowledge of natural history seemed about as solid as Swiss cheese; her memory for math facts came and went with the tides. Her French vocabulary was minimal, and her spelling remained shaky; words that she mastered one week appeared in mutilated form on the next week's essay.

By the end of December, I was lying awake at night riddled with self-doubt. Were we making enough progress to legitimize the sacrifices? Or, in Prufrock's words, *Would it have been worth it, after all? Would it have been worth while?* Because, make no mistake, homeschooling requires major sacrifices.

I worried, for instance, about the social life that Julia was missing. Back on Halloween day, when all the children at Waddell Elementary had dressed up in costumes and paraded through the school's neighborhood (with a handful of John's drummers leading the way), Julia had stood beside me on the curb watching her sisters march by in butterfly wings and princess regalia. When the principal spotted Julia among the crowd, she came over and gave her a hug, and I felt sorry for my daughter, exiled from the happiest rituals of the school year.

"Are you sorry to miss this parade?" I asked.

"No, not really," Julia replied.

"What *do* you miss?"

She sighed. "The parties."

Waddell Elementary was a party heaven, with Thanksgiving mini-feasts and Christmas cookie decorating, Valentine baskets and birthday cupcakes—all the pleasures that craftsy, cake-baking moms can insert into a school day.

Sometimes I would try to offer substitutes. One winter afternoon I took Julia to our local tea room, which offered extravagant hats and scarves and sequined gloves for girls to wear while sipping teas with names like Moroccan Madness. Although I aimed for a festive mood, Julia smiled weakly from beneath her feathered hat. She appreciated the sugar cookies and raspberry sorbet, but a mother in a boa does not constitute a party. Rachel and Kathryn, however, imagined the scene with envy, and the compensatory outing I scheduled for them never fully assuaged their sense that Julia was receiving an inordinate amount of Mom's attention.

Sibling jealousy soon became a problem in our household. Kathryn suffered the greatest pangs. For years she had been accustomed to monopolizing my attention, beginning each morning by searching me out in the house, climbing onto my knees, and pushing away my computer keyboard or the book I was reading. In restaurants and concert halls, movie theaters and puppet shows, she tended to migrate to my lap, apparently determined to remain as close to my womb as possible.

"We forgot to cut the umbilical cord on that one," John would often say as she crawled into our bed.

When Kathryn saw my maternal efforts focused on her eldest sister, she responded decisively. In the evening, if Julia and I were lying side by side reading a book, Kathryn would come and pry her way in between us. If Julia refused to budge, Kathryn would lie flat on top of my body until I had to stand and shed her, limb by limb.

"I want to be homeschooled," she began moaning by November, once the novelty of kindergarten had worn off. "Why can't I stay home like Julia? I want *you* to teach me."

"Maybe when you're in the fifth grade," I answered. Her clinginess seemed like a good reason *not* to homeschool her.

While Kathryn physically battled for my attention, Rachel often appeared at the side of my bed sporting puppy dog eyes and saying, with sniffling melodrama, "No one loves the middle child." Then she would laugh and turn away, but only halfheartedly. That winter Rachel developed the habit of standing up in the middle of family dinners and walking over to John or me to speak directly into our faces, insisting on eye contact while she told a long story. If our attention wavered for a second, she would say, "Mom! Dad! Listen!" and start her long tale again from the beginning, so that we might hear the opening sentences three times before she finished.

"I'm jealous of Julia," she confessed one morning, "because she gets to go to the coffee shop so often." I've paid a fortune on peppermint mochas since that day, trying to even the score in Rachel's mind.

Back in 2005, John and I attempted to soothe our unloved middle child with plenty of one-on-one Rachel time. When John traveled to France that winter with his jazz band, he didn't take Julia along to practice her *parlez-vous*. Instead he invited Rachel, treating her to six days in Paris and two in Normandy. She came home sporting a smile and a pink beret.

And yet, for all our efforts at equally doled out love, by midwinter the entire family was suffering the strains of homeschooling: Julia was whiny; Kathryn was resentful; Rachel and John were brooding. As for me, I was ready to strangle someone.

Part of my problem was the annual despair of February. In Virginia, February is the cruelest month. Winter stands entrenched in a brittle gray landscape, draining the human spirit of all color. In our drafty old house, even when I wear my coat indoors, I can never quite get the chill out of my bones. Julia and I sometimes spent February mornings soaked in a scalding Jacuzzi beneath inches of bubbles, trying to stay warm while we watched snow flurries outside the bay window and talked about the early colonists in New England.

February is a miserable month for teaching—the interval when students have lost their fall enthusiasm and spring remains too distant for hope. Valentine's Day provides only a weak counterbalance to all the darkness and depression that can freeze the human heart in February.

My heart felt especially cold that winter, hardened by months of mother-daughter power struggles, and suffering the cabin fever that comes with winter homeschooling. To escape our homebound malaise, Julia and I tried a mid-winter field trip to Washington. One of my college roommates was a curator at the National Gallery, and she had assembled an impressive exhibit on Dada, gathering works by artists from all over Europe. College friends from London and Cincinnati were coming to celebrate the exhibit's D.C. premiere, and Julia and I joined them for three days of ice skating, concert-going, and, of course, art.

Dada, however, is not the sort of art to cheer a wintry soul. The exhibit opened with films clips from World War I: horses wearing gas masks, soldiers dying by the thousands in muddy trenches, others coming home *sans* legs, arms, and faces. The parallel with the Iraq war was all too clear.

Dada is heavy for most adults, let alone a ten-year-old. Julia didn't care for paintings of discombobulated human forms, scraps of newsprint scattered helter-skelter on canvases, and piped-in recordings of Dada "poetry"—clipped fragments of verbal nonsense. "These guys must have had serious nightmares," she murmured. "I wouldn't want to meet them in a dark alley."

She was equally unmoved by Marcel Duchamp's *Fountain* (an upside down urinal); nor did she appreciate the moustache and goatee he had scribbled on a copy of the Mona Lisa: "You know, I can say the five blades on my ceiling fan represent a star. Does that make it art?" Still, she enjoyed Sophie Taeuber's marionettes, which looked like whimsical predecessors to Tim Burton's *The Nightmare Before Christmas*, and she discovered a dark beauty in the collages of Kurt Schwitters—bits of multicolor paper, metal, fabric, cork, and leather arranged in a controlled chaos.

That three-day weekend provided a brief respite from our February blues. Back home in Lexington, Julia took out her gift shop Dada kit and randomly dropped strips of paper, gold wire, and clipped newsprint on a piece of yellow paper. Behold! Art. But soon enough our usual tensions resumed: the whining, the teeth gritting, the boredom and blowups. More and more my frustrations emerged in brief fits of anger, which produced especially ugly results. Just as there is no place like home, there is no anger like homeschooling anger.

My friends invariably act surprised when I raise the touchy subject of maternal rage. "But you're so calm," they say, "so patient," and I used to agree. Decades ago, in a college interview, when an Amherst admissions officer asked me for one adjective to describe myself, I shrugged and replied, "Mellow."

Parenthood changed that. After ten years of child rearing, I discovered that deep down inside, I am as much of a control freak as anyone else. For what is homeschooling but an act of control? An attempt to make the amorphous world of education conform to an individual's or family's concrete vision. Ultimately, children cannot be controlled, real learning cannot be forced, and the effort to do so yields minor explosions.

Hence the nickname that Julia assigned me halfway into our dreary winter.

She dubbed me "the Volcano," because of my tendency to swing from a state of calm green dormancy to a heap of spitting lava. In my defense, I reminded her that volcanoes give plenty of warning signs before they erupt. I would usually ask Julia to do something three times before my tone changed into what John calls my "monster voice": a low-pitched, sharp-edged bark he swears he never heard during our first nine child-free years of marriage.

"It's so out of character for who you really are," he told me one day. "I'd never even seen you raise your voice before we had kids. I guess the girls know how to pull your chain."

I prefer to think of my "monster voice" as the dulcet tones of a drill sergeant instructing some poor private to "Do it *NOW*!" Unfortunately, drill sergeants don't fit the sentimentalized American vision of motherhood. Once, when I mentioned my occasionally volcanic state in a homeschooling article for *Brain, Child* magazine, a man responded by saying that I should get some anger management therapy. (To which the only appropriate response is, "Give me a ——ing break.") There's plenty of anger in American society, and some of it might require therapy, but if all moms had to consult a psychologist every time they blew their tops, most U.S. households would be bankrupt.

Years ago I never would have confessed to getting storming

mad at my kids. I thought it was shameful—an unacceptable loss of control. Mothers were supposed to be endlessly loving and encouraging. We were supposed to resemble Carol Brady or Shirley Partridge or June Cleaver, unfailingly good humored in the face of enormous exasperation. Now, in the new millennium, I find those saccharine maternal stereotypes to be as unhealthy as Barbie's grotesquely arched and tiptoed body.

Nevertheless, I tend to feel very guilty whenever I lose my temper. Once, when I asked John if he thought my monster voice was a problem, he laughed: "Are you kidding me? I come from an Irish-Catholic family with screaming and throwing shit and hitting and physical violence. Your angry voice is nothing. You are the UN, and my family was like Kosovo and Serbia."

But angry words can be as hurtful as blows, and in the throes of homeschooling, I did utter some harsh, embarrassing words. The worst emerged in February—the dark night of the homeschooling soul—during a math lesson.

All year Julia had been following a two-track math schedule, with her time divided between concepts and computation. Week by week she learned new material—from Roman numerals, to place value, to dividing decimals and fractions—and although these gave her little trouble, basic computation was another story. Multiplication tables slipped from her memory with the same speed as the rules of spelling. I wondered if the two were handled by the same portion of the brain.

One morning, while reviewing another of Julia's especially careless tests, I asked her,

"Julia, what is six times four?"

She shrugged. "Eighteen."

"Six times *four*," I repeated.

She gazed up at the ceiling, more interested in swirls of plaster than arithmetic. "Twenty-six?"

"Julia!" I snapped. "Don't be a dumbass!"

That got her attention. Her eyes widened. Her jaw dropped. "You called me a dumbass!"

At which point I launched into rhetorical maneuvers worthy of Bill Clinton.

"I didn't say you *were* a dumbass. I told you *not to be* one. There's a difference."

Julia shook her head. "You called me a dumbass."

"You're obviously not a dumbass," I continued. "You're a very smart girl. But if you don't use your brain and pay attention to what you're doing, you're going to *appear* to be a dumbass." I sighed. "Let's just finish correcting this test," I added. "How would you fix the next problem?"

"How should I know?" Julia said. "Since I'm such a *dumbass*."

Clearly she was a very sharp girl and Mom was the dumbass, because for the rest of the day, and occasionally in days to come, she wielded my insult like a get-out-of-jail-free card that exempted her from any need for thought.

"What was the Magna Carta, Julia?"

"Gee, I guess I'm too much of a dumbass to remember."

"When was Jamestown founded?"

She shrugged and pointed to her head. "*Dumbass*, remember?"

✦

Bad as things were at that point, they got worse. We hit bottom one morning in late February, when Julia was practicing her violin.

There's something about the sound of a novice violinist that churns up all of my internal lava. Maybe it's the high-pitched rasping or the notes that remain forever flat or sharp. Math errors, misspelled words, mangled subject-verb agreement, are nothing compared with the torture of an out-of-tune violin. While grammatical mistakes lie silent on a page—turn your eyes away and you can pretend they don't exist—the screech of a flat fiddle is inescapable.

"How can you tell when a violin is out of tune?" Julia joked just the other day.

"I don't know," I said. "How?"

She smiled. "If the bow is moving."

I wish I'd had a sense of humor about it during our home-schooling. Instead, I began each practice session inwardly telling myself to remain calm, not to get annoyed, which was difficult, since Julia usually began with five minutes of complaint about having to practice at all. Each time, I explained how her new teacher had high expectations. Esther Vine, Julia's Mormon violin teacher, had moved back to Utah, taking with her our days of Rainbow violin books, with their multicolor pages and cartoon drawings. Now Julia had advanced to serious music—the first movement of a Seitz concerto—and her teacher took new students only if the child agreed to practice at least five times a week. "We'll make sure that happens," I had promised Ms. Porter back in August, so now I felt a contractual obligation to hold up our end of the bargain.

Julia didn't mind playing through a piece; she just hated the idea of going back and correcting her mistakes. No matter how bad a cadence sounded, she plowed ahead. Practicing her concerto was like running the mile at school; it didn't matter if she wound up limping across the finish line; so long as she completed it, she figured she had done her job.

"Stop," I would say after an especially mangled measure, and Julia would keep playing. "Stop," I'd repeat, while the music continued. "*Stop!*" I'd catch her bow in my hand and lift it from the strings.

"When I say 'stop,' that means *stop*. . . . If you mess up a phrase, you need to go back and work on it. Practice it ten times, or thirty times; whatever it takes."

If Julia learned a note wrong, she tended to stick with it, as if she had established a tradition that should not be broken—which might give the impression that she was a poor violinist. On the contrary, Julia was very good, for a ten-year-old. It was her talent, I explained, that made me insist.

"If you were lousy, I would let you quit. In fact, I'd want you to quit, to spend your time on something where you had more potential. But people are born with certain gifts, and one of yours is music. You should take the time to develop your gift."

I nurtured no secret dreams of Julia performing professionally; I just wanted her to reach the stage where she could enjoy music as a social event. Two more years of practice and she could play in our community orchestra, sight-read string quartets with friends, or join a bluegrass group. But all my visions came crashing down during our homeschooling.

One afternoon, Julia was playing a passage in her concerto, which she had memorized with a wrong note, an F natural instead of an F sharp. The melody didn't sound bad with an F natural; it just wasn't right. Performers, I told her, can't change the composer's notes. They can't pick and choose which sharps to play.

She played the passage again, with an F natural.

"Wait," I said, and she kept on playing. "Stop!"

She continued on.

I walked over and lifted her bow from the strings. "See this note here," I pointed at the top of the page on her stand. "It's an F *sharp*. Try it again."

Once again she played an F natural, racing forward like a runaway train.

This time I lifted the violin from her hands without asking (a very rude action; good violin teachers always ask permission first). "Here's what the passage is supposed to sound like." I played it with the proper notes.

Julia took back her violin and played an F natural.

By now I had gritted another millimeter off my left incisor. Reaching forward, I pulled her third finger a half inch up the fingerboard, to the F-sharp position. "That's the note you need to play. What's the problem?"

She played the passage again with the same, ingrained F natural.

"Sharp, sharp, *sharp!*" I said.

Natural, natural, natural, she played.

Was she doing this deliberately, to torment me? Or did this child of nature instinctively cling to all things natural? Or— most likely of all—was she never listening to what I said, tuning me out as she had tuned out so many teachers before, playing the notes that had settled into her brain, right or wrong, oblivious to all instruction?

By now my voice had crescendoed from mezzo piano to forte. "It's an F *sharp!* Why won't you play the *#&%$ *F sharp?*"

One more time she tried it. She started at the beginning of the passage, winding her way through a series of correct notes, correct rhythms, correct dynamics, and then, at the moment of truth: F natural. At which point I leaned over and swatted her across the top of her head. It wasn't a hard swat, not the sort of thing that would hurt, knock a girl backward, or leave even the faintest tinge of pink. An inch of tousled hair, poking out from behind her ear, was the extent of the physical damage. The emotional damage, however, will probably ripple back to me for years to come.

On television, a swat across the head is the stuff of comedy—

a hallmark of *The Three Stooges* (but who wants to be a stooge, especially mean-spirited Moe?) and the Skipper on *Gilligan's Island* (but he always used his hat against his little buddy, never his hand). In reality, there is nothing funny about a mother swatting her daughter on the head, particularly in our household, where corporal punishment is supposed to be off limits. (In fact, when Julia was six years old and especially disobedient, I once spanked her on the side of her thigh. After eyeing me with surprise, and noting my flustered, guilty face, she laughed and taunted me, "Mommy's a spanker! Mommy's a spanker!")

Now I wished that she would mock me, laugh at me, make light of the situation. Call me a swatter or a smacker or a walking Mount St. Helens. Instead, two things happened. She played the F sharp, but she did it with tears in her eyes.

"I'm sorry," I mumbled. "That was way out of line."

I tried to assuage my guilt with lame excuses. "It's just that you were driving me crazy, the way you wouldn't play such a simple note."

Julia wouldn't even look me in the eye.

"You can put your violin away," I said. "We're done for the day."

Done for the day, done for the week, done with all of it. Julia took refuge in a book while I retreated to my bed, where I stared at the ceiling and wallowed in a sea of self-recrimination. I was a lousy homeschooler and, what's more, a lousy mom. I should probably not have had children in the first place. I had never been one of those women whose body aches with maternal instincts, someone who feels her life will be incomplete without a child, eager to hold other women's babies, to read board books and buy onesies and push a stroller through a park. I should have settled for Wordsworth and Bishop and Eliot, and never trusted myself with these precious little lives.

Because what had come of it? I had struck my daughter for something so trivial as an F natural. Homeschooling had brought out the worst in me. It had turned me into a sputtering, head-swatting monster. And the more I brooded over my failures, the more I was certain: this homeschooling had been a mistake. It was time to quit.

CHAPTER SEVEN

➤➤Turning Point◀◀

*The importance of writing is the one
thing Mom and I agree on.*

JULIA

THE NEXT MORNING IT WAS HARD TO GET OUT OF BED—
hard to face my daughters and look at myself in the mir-
ror. I didn't want to contemplate the ugly features I'd
developed as a homeschooler: my own little *Picture of Dorian
Gray*. Better to stay under the covers and sleep it off for a few
hundred hours.

Not that I had the option. Most days I can barely grant myself a few hundred seconds. As I huddled under our blankets that
morning, trying to stay warm in the winter's pre-dawn hours,
those extra ten minutes meant that our family's schedule would
be rushed. Rachel and Kathryn might be a minute late to school,
and at Waddell Elementary, if a child is one second late, the parent is supposed to park her car, get out, and walk inside, then
stand as a silent, contrite witness while the school secretary fills
out a tardy slip for the child to deliver to her teacher.

I rarely bother with that. If my girls are substantially late, I'm
willing to sign them in, but if the bell rings as we pull up, or if
we are within the two-minute limit, I drop them off and skulk
away. I figure children can retrieve their own tardy slips without

the school's attempts at disciplining already rushed and harassed parents. Even the word *tardy* annoys me. Nevertheless, the thought of those little white slips and their pink carbon copies, and the stern letters of admonition sent home after three late arrivals, was enough to launch me out of bed. I got up, grabbed my robe, roused Rachel and Kathryn, made their lunches, fixed their breakfast, poured John a cup of tea (one teaspoon of sugar, one dribble of cream), looked in the girls' shared room ("Why aren't you dressed yet? Hurry!"), searched for shoes and socks ("It's okay if they don't match! You're wearing long pants!"), signed homework sheets and field trip forms, brushed and braided Kathryn's hair, cursed inwardly as Kathryn pulled out her imperfect left braid, braided that side again with added care, lamented the half-eaten bowls of cereal on the kitchen table, and handed my girls buttered bagels through the window of the car while John yelled, "We don't have time for that!" Then I stepped back and sighed while the three of them pulled out of the driveway with forty seconds to spare.

Mornings like that are reason enough for some families to homeschool. I know a local woman whose kids sleep until 9:30 while she enjoys her coffee and paper, a morning walk, and a leisurely shower. In her house, school begins at ten, and by two, the children have finished all of their lessons. I envision their home as an island of peace in the morning, while throughout their neighborhood, families scurry around grouchy and stressed. More arguments take place in our house between 7:30 and 8:00 a.m. than at any other time of day.

Yes, one might say, but those late-sleeping children will never be prepared for the early morning grind of the working world! And maybe that's true. But there are many working worlds in our country, with various working hours, and why must children be indoctrinated so early into the hassles of adult life?

I pondered that question as I closed my door against the February chill. Walking into the kitchen, I sat down and warmed my hands on a mug of tea, blowing ripples across its surface. That day Julia could sleep late. Left undisturbed, she would doze until ten, which suited me fine. I needed time to think.

Glancing at the counter to my left, I saw Julia's journal, which beckoned with its oh-so-pretty Thomas Kinkade cover. I picked it up and examined that cover carefully for the first time: a painting of a stone cottage trimmed by multiple shades of blue. In the middle, an azure door was matched by azure shutters and eaves, topped with silvery blue shingles and a background of trees and sky that faded into a gray and pink twilit haze. In the foreground, a willow tree leaned over the cottage's left corner, while dozens of plants bloomed simultaneously, perpetually. Snapdragons, red, pink, and purple, lined a hand-hewn wooden fence, and tall puffy shrubs buffered the entire scene, covered in miscellaneous blossoms that ranged from bluebonnets and scotch broom to daisies and lilac.

This, I told myself, was the American idealized vision of home. Home was a place where every window glowed with orange and golden light, while tiny threads of smoke rose from the tops of brick chimneys. Home was a warm and sheltering nook, so inviting that even animals seemed drawn to it. Five blackbirds congregated on this painted roof, while a cat watched from a fencepost. To the left, free-range hens pecked in a pebbled walkway leading through a gate that remained always open.

It struck me that Julia, for her daily journal, had chosen this paradisal image of home. Here, home was a haven of safety, beauty, and warmth, not a setting for anger and stress. Not a place where a frustrated mother called you a dumbass or popped you on the head for playing an F natural. What a betrayal of hopes my recent behavior had been. Obviously I was not living up to Thomas Kinkade's vision of the world.

I thought of the March family in *Little Women*. Even amid financial hardships and the troubles of war, their house was warmed by love, doled out under the guiding light of Marmee. And theirs, too, was a homeschooling house, where Jo was tasked with teaching little sister Amy, in protest against the tyranny of Amy's knuckle-rapping schoolteacher. Of course, Jo deplored the idea of homeschooling her sister; she probably popped Amy on the head many a time. And Marmee, whose sticky-sweet name sounded too much like marmalade, confessed to having a fiery temper and a bitter tongue: "I am angry nearly every day of my life, Jo." Even in the most idyllic households, anger and frustration could simmer just beneath the surface.

Still, I hated to compare myself to Marmee. I never did like *Little Women*, and in fact, neither did Louisa May Alcott, when she was first writing the book. She found the task dreary and dull and would have stuck to writing potboilers, if it weren't for her somewhat despotic father, who pushed his daughter to complete the highly marketable project.

The question for me, on that cold winter morning, was how hard a parent should push a child toward success. Should a parent "push" at all, or merely nudge and coax and pray? In the lives of many successful women there has lurked some form of parental despot, prodding, insisting, and sometimes punishing. I wondered: Was a touch of tyranny essential in parenting? So many parents of my generation seemed to allow their children to tyrannize them.

I took another swallow of tea and opened Julia's journal. Julia always let me read the pages with impunity, since she rarely used them for personal feelings. In fact, her first entries were little more than silly scribblings:

A dragon is gold,
A goblin is mold,
And the fairies have to be sold.

The wise one was told,
Even though he was old,
He still could not fold,
The evil cold.

In the first few weeks of homeschooling, Julia had viewed her journal as a boring chore. Compelled to write one page after school every Monday through Thursday, she had conformed to the letter, if not the spirit, of the assignment. She had filled her initial pages with short, terrible poems in large print, with double spacing between lines and quadruple spacing between stanzas. Her goal was haste, not quality; she sometimes completed her page in five minutes.

I had been tempted, in our first month of schooling, to insist that she fill each page with thoughtful, single-spaced writing. This silly verse, I had wanted to say, was beneath her intelligence. Luckily, I never intervened. For once, I displayed amazing self-restraint, remaining patient even through the lowest forms of doggerel: "Twinkle twinkle little mutt, / Do not think I am a nut."

Now, as I flipped through the more recent pages of Julia's writing, I was reminded that a mother's silence is often more effective than her words. After weeks of jotting down hasty drivel, Julia had decided to put her journal to better use. She had begun to compile a dragon encyclopedia, filling her pages with descriptions of imaginary Fire Dragons, Cat Dragons, Were Dragons, and Water Wyverns. "Warrior Dragons," she wrote, "are one of the most interesting dragons that have been":

*They were the first dragons to paint their eggs. They also
have a stinger on their tails that detaches at a speed of five
milliseconds! Sometimes when detached it reaches over 1000
miles per hour. Warrior dragons' wings have three sets of wing
membranes [spelled "mendbrains"] so that if one part of the
wing is damaged, the dragons can still fly. They breathe fire
and have a way with their tails so that the stinger grows back
in two seconds flat!*

At last, Julia was actually writing. These pages were not composed to silence an insistent mother; they were meant to satisfy
a ten-year-old's imaginative thirst. As a result, the sentences
weren't scribbled quickly, with oversize type. Here was single-
spaced cursive, with subsequent entries that built upon earlier
ideas:

Dragon Eggs

*Warrior dragons paint their eggs with special symbols that
give the baby dragons their small unique ability to run a bit
faster or fly a bit better. But the reason why fairy dragons
paint their eggs is for helping the eggs to not get eaten. So
they usually paint a reptilian eye pupil on the egg . . .*

As I studied the progression in that little blue book, from
hasty riffs on a single rhyme to intricate, creative sentences, I told
myself that here, in my hands, lay tangible proof that something
had been accomplished in our homeschooling. Julia had begun
to write from her heart, and as a result, her ideas, her sentence
structure, even her grammar, were improving.

That brief moment at my kitchen table served as a minor
revelation. How wrong I had been, for the past several weeks,
to have fretted over all the things that were going badly in our

schooling. What a fruitless waste of time, to have worried about incomplete tasks, abandoned goals, misspelled words, and miscalculated equations. Instead, why not celebrate everything that was going right?

I should have known that the real test of our academic success would lie in Julia's writing. After all, I am an English teacher—not a French linguist, not a scientist, certainly not a mathematician. For twelve years I had taught college students how to write papers and analyze literature, and my chief academic goal in homeschooling had been to encourage Julia to write across the curriculum, drafting essays on everything from fantasy novels to colonial life.

Closing Julia's journal, I walked into our dining room, where our family computer stands in a corner cabinet. There, from the shelf above the monitor, I took out Julia's portfolio, which held most of her formal writing from the year. Inside were pages and pages of essays, three times as much writing as her peers were doing—more writing, in fact, than Julia would ever complete in any of her middle-school years to come.

Thumbing through the early pages, I stopped at Julia's first book report, on a novel called *Crispin*, by the children's author known as Avi.

"What should you include in a book report?" I had asked Julia back in September.

"The title of the book," she answered.

"That's a good start."

"And the author?" she added.

"That's important, too. But what else?"

She shrugged. "Stuff that happened in the story?"

"Yes, that's called the plot. But what other information should you include?"

Julia was stumped, because what else did a book contain besides the stuff that happened?

Laura Brodie

"How about your own analysis of the book?" I suggested.

"What do you mean?"

"Well, did you like *Crispin*?"

"Yeah," she nodded.

"Why?"

"Because it was good."

"What made it good?"

"The writing."

"What made the writing good?"

"I dunno."

"Every good book is successful for different reasons," I explained. "Some books are funny, some have beautiful descriptions, some have exciting adventures, some have great characters. If you know what makes a particular book good, then you'll know what makes each author unique. Is Avi talented at writing action scenes, or dialogue, or describing a place?"

Julia wound up writing two brief paragraphs:

Crispin Critique

Crispin is good because of all the different settings and adventure. I like the settings a lot because they are so different but also so alike. I liked the adventure because it's so exiting [i.e. exciting] yet so dramatic.

But I don't like how his on-the-run life stopped so quickly. Because as soon as he saw Bear his on-the-run life stopped short, and a minute later, was gone for good.

It was rough, but it was a start. My college students still write about how things are "so different but also so alike." That, I explained to Julia, doesn't say much.

My students also suffer from repetitive vocabulary. "See how you've used *like* in three sentences in a row?" I said to Julia.

"How can you change that? What's one synonym for *different*? And how else can you say 'on-the-run life'?" That day marked Julia's first acquaintance with a thesaurus.

We also talked about larger questions of content. What made the story exciting and dramatic? Could she describe some of the settings? Why was Crispin's life "on the run," and who was Bear? These sorts of questions occupied every week of our autumn homeschooling, and now when I turned to Julia's most recent book report, the benefits were clear:

Martin the Warrior

In a mysterious place called Redwall, there is a stoat called Badrang who has a fort next to the sea. He has long dreamt of a fort to call his own, and now he has one using the slaves he has captured in fighting. One of those slaves is a young mouse named Martin.

Martin has a warrior's spirit and a hate for the stoat. When he stands up to one of the captains, Badrang ties him to a log post and leaves him there until morning, but during the stormy night he meets a mouse named Rose who is on the outside of the fort looking for her brother Brome. Martin agrees to help her if she keeps the deadly seagulls off of him in the morning . . .

When compared with Julia's *Crispin* sentences, these paragraphs were a model of eloquence. They contained more color and detail than her previous work, with none of the awkward stiffness. Here, after briefly getting mired in the word *call*, she had experimented with her verbs, and had used more dependent clauses to make the sentences flow. Admittedly, the content was mere plot summary; analysis would have to follow. But Julia's writing had made a clear step forward.

Flipping through more pages, I saw that her research had also improved. Over the past few months I had required Julia to complete several author studies, just as her fourth-grade teacher, Mrs. Gonzalez, had recommended. As a book lover, Julia had welcomed the reading. In the fall she had devoured all six volumes of *The Chronicles of Narnia*, in anticipation of Disney's November release of *The Lion, the Witch, and the Wardrobe*. Together we had watched the movie *Shadowlands*, starring Anthony Hopkins and Debra Winger, to learn about C. S. Lewis's life. Julia found that film tedious, but she did enjoy reading Susan Cooper's *The Dark Is Rising* trilogy, as well as two books by Natalie Babbitt, three by Avi, several *Redwall* installments, and Christopher Paolini's five-hundred-page sequel to *Eragon*, titled *Eldest*. With Lewis, Cooper, Avi, and Paolini, Julia had researched each author on the Internet ("Find three sources," I said, "and don't just rely on Wikipedia!"), and she had composed essays on each writer, with a biographical paragraph or two, a few sentences on each book she read, and occasional attempts at introductory and concluding paragraphs, which sometimes amounted to introductory and concluding sentences.

When it came to doing research, her early efforts were shaky. With Lewis, she had displayed a child's fixation on death:

> *I think that C. S. Lewis was a very experienced writer, and had great tragedies in his life. His mother died when he was a kid, and his wife died of cancer. But he did get three wonderful years with her when her cancer subsided, only to return again! C. S. Lewis died on the same day President Kennedy was assassinated. But his books live on today.*

Three months later, when she researched Christopher Paolini, Julia was handling an author who was eighteen and brilliantly alive, so she found more to say:

Christopher Paolini is the author of Eragon *and* Eldest.
He was born on November 7, 1983 in Southern California,
and lived for some years in Anchorage, Alaska before
moving to Montana. He was homeschooled all his life and
was surrounded by the Bear Tooth Mountains. Christopher
Paolini has a sister named Angelina, which is where he got
the herbalist's name in Eragon *and* Eldest. *He also got some*
of the scenery from home, like the mountains in the Spine,
and the valley which holds Carvahall . . .

The fact that Paolini was homeschooled seemed to inspire Julia. She marveled that a home-educated sixteen-year-old could make a million dollars writing about dragons. Paolini was leading her dream life, and Julia set about writing in her journal with added vigor.

Reading Julia's portfolio was like perusing the before and after shots that fill so many women's magazines and television shows. Look at the amazing transformation! Before and after a trendy diet, before and after a professional makeover, before and after a stint on *What Not to Wear*. Julia's writing was now sleeker, more stylish, more beautiful. Admittedly, one reason for the improvement was purely cosmetic; her later essays were typed, while the earlier work was handwritten. Our computer was now checking her spelling and grammar, and computer screens tend to inspire more verbosity than mere pencil and paper. Still, the bare fact that Julia had learned to type represented yet another significant achievement.

The previous year, Waddell's gifted program coordinator had recommended typing for Julia's homeschooling curriculum. Typing, she explained, was a valuable talent in middle school. These days many ten-year-olds have already honed their typing skills through years of computer access, but I had steered Julia away from keyboards for much of elementary school, believing that children should be immersed in books before they are immersed in technology. At the start of our homeschooling year, Julia was still pecking at the keys with one finger.

Now, as I thought back over the weeks in which Julia learned to type, the process seemed analogous to our entire experience of homeschooling. It had been a matter of me planning and insisting, Julia complaining and resisting, all leading up to the crucial question: When was it time to quit?

Back in August, I had tried to buy a fun typing game for Julia, not realizing that plenty of free games are available on the Internet. The Webkinz site—sacred oracle to so many grade-school girls, including my Kathryn—includes a typing game. But as a novice homeschooler, I didn't know about these options, so I thought to purchase something online. A basketball game—where children could shoot virtual hoops while positioning their fingers at ASDF JKL;—had garnered the most enthusiastic reviews. Alas, my primitive PC didn't have the Windows operating system necessary to run that program. Instead, I settled for SpongeBob SquarePants, with his Bikini Bottom typing tournament, filled with maritime games. (Imagine a motorboat accelerating down an underwater raceway, speeded by a child's typing, with slops of seaweed splattered on the windshield at every error.)

Julia hated it. After a few tries in early September she grew weary of SpongeBob's high-pitched nasal words of encouragement: "One key at a time, baby, one key at a time. . . . Don't get sand in your britches! . . . Just think how hard this would be if you were a clam!" The only game she appreciated was Do Ray Mi, where the computer played one musical note for each typed letter, plunking through some sailorish tune, à la "The Irish Washerwoman's Song." Anyone who has heard "The Irish

Washerwoman's Song" knows that there is only one rule for performance: the faster the better. Julia had a musical incentive to
increase her typing tempo.

Nevertheless, she complained. "Do I have to use this stupid
program?"

"You have to learn how to type," I replied, "and this program
is all we've got."

Over the next few weeks, Julia's lamentations combined with
SpongeBob's nasal cheerleading to produce an intolerable duet.

"Okay," I relented. "You don't have to practice typing as part
of your regular curriculum, but each time you misspell one of
the words in your spelling journal, you'll owe me five minutes of
SpongeBob."

That was a mistake. Learning a new skill can be a joy or a
duty, but it should never be presented to a child as a form of punishment. Julia complained as much as ever, until, after a few more
weeks, she wore me down.

"I'll make a deal with you," I said. (My homeschooling often
resembled a domestic version of *Let's Make a Deal*.) "If you can
complete the level-ten quiz at twenty words per minute, you can
quit SpongeBob."

Level ten was not very high; I could have insisted that she
go much further. But it was high enough to give Julia a solid
foundation in typing, while not being so distant that she would
despair. That light at the end of the tunnel inspired her to type
with added determination, and within a few weeks she had met
her goal.

Letting Julia quit taught me one rather obvious lesson about
the value of quitting. Freed from the obligation to type, Julia
sometimes revisited the program voluntarily. In moments of
boredom, or when fooling around on other computer programs,
she would occasionally stray back to Bikini Bottom, and tinny,

computerized strains of "The Irish Washerwoman's Song" would float past my ears as I wiped the kitchen counters.

All of which brings us back to mid-February, as I assessed the typed and handwritten contents of Julia's portfolio. Flipping through the pages, I remembered my feelings from the previous afternoon: the impulse to quit, to say, "Enough. Move on."

But if Julia was making good progress, why not push forward? Wasn't her portfolio proof that my method was working?

Far from it. Although Julia's writing had clearly improved, the cost of that improvement had been too great. Over the next few days, whenever a friend would ask about our homeschooling, my answer would be blunt: "It's been an academic success, but a maternal failure." Sure, Julia could produce excellent work if I behaved like a harpy and held her feet to the fire. But how long should a mother dangle her child's toes above the flames?

I thought of my friend Todd, the history professor who had homeschooled his son for six weeks. He, too, had seen clear academic benefits from homeschooling, but the tensions had almost destroyed their relationship, and it seemed that my methods were on the verge of being equally destructive.

The essays that rested in my hands had not been written with the same joy apparent in Julia's journal. All of this eloquence and creativity had been produced begrudgingly, every paragraph accompanied by another protest. Admittedly, "joy" might be an unreasonable expectation; few children embrace essay-writing with unfettered glee. Still, part of my goal in homeschooling had been to reduce Julia's misery, and it seemed that over the past few months I had only managed to give her misery a new name. I had granted her a break from traditional schooling, but not a respite from oppressive expectations. Maybe it was time to give her a break from me.

But what would it mean to "quit" in mid-February, when

three and a half months of the school year remained? We certainly couldn't quit math—math required daily practice, and our carefully mapped out curriculum filled nine months. Ratios, probability, and variables all lay before us. Besides, I had an English major's intimidated reverence for math; math was serious business and must progress full speed ahead.

In other areas we had more leeway. Take the violin, our primary source of conflict. Julia was scheduled to play in a mid-May recital—nothing fancy, just twenty parents gathering in a college music classroom to hear fewer than a dozen children perform one piece each. In preparation, she had started to learn the first movement of a concerto, and reneging on her obligation would set a bad precedent.

The post-recital months were a different story. The summer offered a lesson-free hiatus, and come September, Julia would be so busy with her new middle-school routine, with its homework and tennis team practice and afterschool clubs that I couldn't guarantee she would practice five times a week. The prodding required on my part might once again transform me into a maternal version of the Incredible Hulk, a roaring, button-popping, discolored vessel of rage.

Maybe, come summer, it would be time to try the John Brodie approach to music education. Require nothing of the child, and let her take the initiative. I could offer to play duets with Julia, and encourage her to join the local orchestra, but the weekly pressure to prepare for a lesson could be lifted.

And what should happen with our other homeschooling subjects? What pressures could I eliminate on that score? I remained at the table for another half hour, imagining all the ways Julia and I could stop what we were doing, or at least change course.

Our winter had been tainted with too much stress and guilt. We needed a new direction, one that would allow me to express more love and appreciation for Julia, and maybe even feel a little better about myself. We needed time to heal our mother-daughter wounds.

✳

When Julia eventually came downstairs, shuffling and groggy, she folded her arms on the kitchen table and rested her face on them sideways.

"What time is it?" she murmured.

"Nine forty-five."

"Why didn't you wake me?"

"I wanted to let you sleep."

"No math this morning?"

I nodded. "No math today."

Math was our early-morning subject, tackled first each day to make sure that it didn't fall by the wayside as the afternoon advanced. Even that scheduling decision was probably one of my homeschooling mistakes, for although I am a morning lark, my mind sharpest before noon, Julia is a night owl, drowsy and ill-tempered in early daylight. Maybe that explained why her math facts remained blurry in her mind.

"No violin today, either," I said. No out-of-tune scraping. No ugly head-swatting scenes.

"I want to apologize again for yesterday. I shouldn't have yelled at you and hit you on the head. There's no excuse."

Julia shrugged. Apologies were useless without some form of action, and in the coming year, she would explain that she didn't even care about the head-swatting. She only cared about being called a dumbass.

"I want to make a deal with you," I continued, sliding into my Monty Hall routine. (Let's show Julia what's behind Door Number One!) "In the future, if I ever lose my temper or even raise my voice, we can stop homeschooling for that day. You won't have to do any more schoolwork. Which doesn't mean that you can watch TV or play computer games, but you can read whatever you like for the rest of the day. How does that sound?"

Julia sighed. "Good, I guess."

(But wait! There's more! Show Julia what's behind Door Number Two!)

"There's something else," I began. "I've decided that you don't have to write any more essays for the rest of the year. You're done with writing nonfiction. All the writing you'll do will be your own stories and poems, and your own chapters of novels. Whatever you like."

"No more author studies?" she asked.

"Nope."

"And no social studies or science essays?"

"That's right."

"What will we do, if we aren't writing?"

Good question. I had never given Julia a science or social studies test. Although I had verbally quizzed her on names and dates and scientific facts, in our schooling, written tests were reserved for spelling and math. When it came to science and social studies, her only assignments had been to make posters and write essays focused on atoms and molecules, astronomy and prehistoric life. Now we'd be putting an end to all that.

"Well, with science, you can keep doing experiments." (We had fiddled haphazardly with balloons and dirt and potatoes and magnets and electrical circuits.) "But you won't have to write about what you learn. And from here on out you can choose whatever science subjects you want to study for the rest of the year. What interests you?"

Julia paused for a moment. "Birds," she said, "and flight."

"Okay, so we'll go to the library and check out books on that."

"And what about social studies?" she asked.

I sighed. Our adventures in social studies had been a curious, and somewhat depressing, odyssey. History, I had discovered, is a tricky subject to teach when your pupil has an intrinsic bias against human beings.

When reading *The Beginning*, Julia had been happy to learn about the evolution of animal life. Walking fish and giant sloths and saber-toothed tigers all sounded great. But when *Homo sapiens* entered the picture, she had tuned out completely. Mankind was utterly unappealing, especially drawings of hairy Neanderthal men. Perhaps she would have preferred pictures of smooth-skinned Adam and Eve.

I doubt it. At heart, Julia seemed to nurture a slightly misanthropic streak. She was comfortable with human beings when they appeared in ones or twos, but when people congregated, they produced war, urban blight, bigotry, and the destruction of the rain forests.

Julia's art testified to her preference for animals. She frequently drew elaborate pictures of creatures, both mythical and real, devoting hours to the scales on a single snake. As for human beings, she sketched them quickly, thoughtlessly, with a first-grader's techniques—circular heads, rectangular legs, ears like a heart divided in half. It seemed as if she did not want to observe human beings in detail; stick figures sufficed for the planet's most destructive occupants.

For such a creature-centered child, social studies presented a unique challenge. There were few human civilizations that Julia admired. The Incas gained her respect, with their mysterious ability to move five-ton rocks across rivers, valleys, and mountains to build Machu Picchu. "The state made them drink beer," Julia wrote, "so that even when they were exhausted they would be relaxed." She composed a seven-paragraph essay on these ancient Peruvians, but three of the seven paragraphs described bloodshed and havoc: the Incan civil war, the slaughter and destruction wreaked by Pizarro (whom Julia always called Bizarro), the pillaging of Machu Picchu by thieves. As for the Spanish invaders:

> *None of the soldiers were given a chance to enjoy the riches; they were all killed over a span of time. Francisco Bizarro was killed by his men (before they were). You may feel sorry for the Spanish, but remember that they wiped out three great civilizations; the Maya the Inca and the Aztecs. But don't be sorry for the Incas either, remember that the Inca captured neighboring tribes and made them work.*

When it came to human history, everybody was guilty.

After the Maya, Aztecs, and Incas, Julia had transitioned into Native American cultures, where she felt an instinctive sympathy for the Sioux. (I can imagine Julia as a Sioux child in a previous life, a girl with a name like Running Wolf—riding horses, honoring nature, keeping her hair in braids that wouldn't get tangled.) But the history of the Sioux is a tragic tale. "This is a true story," Julia wrote at the end of another depressing essay:

> *. . . it is a story of bloodshed and abuse. Crazy Horse was shot while being restrained by soldiers. Sitting Bull was shot when he refused to go into custody. In fact the only Sioux chief that wasn't murdered was Red Cloud who signed the treaty that closed the Bozeman Trail. Every Indian that was in America was forced onto a reservation or was killed unless they married a white man or accepted the white man's ways.*

And she didn't even mention Wounded Knee.

Julia's perspective got even darker when we moved on to Caucasians; after studying the Sioux, the lives of the early Pilgrims seemed pretty drab. I suggested that she write an essay on a strong woman in early America, hoping that a woman's life might provide a counterbalance to all the killing Julia seemed to find in the lives of men. Settling on a female role model, however, was easier said than done. Whom should she choose? Betsy Ross? No way. What 1950s version of gender roles promoted the sewing of a flag as the female contribution to the American Revolution? Pocahontas and Sacagawea seemed a little more exciting, but Julia recognized that their chief role in history was to serve as helpers of men, and they were ultimately co-opted into white expansionist ambitions.

Abigail Adams and Dolley Madison possessed admirable qualities, but I feared that Julia was unlikely to appreciate the subtleties of these women's epistolary skills, nor was a ten-year-old liable to grasp how a wife's sharp intellect could advance the career of a more blunt-witted husband. One book on Molly Pitcher briefly held Julia's attention; Molly seemed like a model of rough-edged girl power, once she set aside her job as the guys' water girl. Her glory at the cannons, however, was a momentary flash in the pan.

I wanted Julia to study a strong woman who consistently challenged the status quo, so I suggested Anne Hutchinson, that famous thorn in the side of the clerical leaders of early Massachusetts. Hutchinson, I explained to Julia, was banished from the Massachusetts Bay Colony after holding discussions in her home where she questioned the teachings of the male clergy. She and her family were forced south in the footsteps of Roger Williams, the nonconformist minister who founded Providence Plantation. Not far from Providence, Hutchinson and a small band of followers formed a tiny community called Rhode Island.

I had hoped that the life of a strong woman might inspire Julia. Instead, she found the reading boring and the writing tortuous. Our library had no children's book on Hutchinson, although they had ten on Betsy Ross. (They've since acquired two Hutchinson books, at my suggestion.) Julia's research was limited to a few Internet sources and one page in a history text devoted to dozens of Puritan men. Although she had produced eight paragraphs on the Sioux with little coaxing, when it came to Hutchinson, she managed only three, and that trio came as easily as blood from a stone. Even to most adults, the nuances of Puritan religious doctrine are about as comprehensible as Mandarin. I didn't expect a fifth-grader to grasp the subtleties of Hutchinson's trial, but I hoped she might be impressed with this woman's tough-mindedness. Instead, Julia absorbed another lesson in the evils of mankind:

> *Hutchinson was known for having meetings with women where she expressed her beliefs that Indians should be free, all you have to do is have faith to get into heaven, and women should not be men's slaves. In other words they should have freedom of thought and religion. But then in a trial she was banished from the colony because of it.*

For Julia, history always morphed into antisocial studies.

She wasn't alone in her skepticism. Today, plenty of children express doubts about the inherent greatness of America and the supremacy of mankind above all other creatures. Some parents blame the public schools' emphasis on "political correctness" for producing a cynical generation, and wonder how our children will ever learn to be patriots if we dwell on the horrors of slavery, the slaughter of Native Americans, and the centuries of discrimination against women. Better to emphasize classic tales of blue-eyed heroism.

But what some folks call "political correctness," I call honesty. Julia, I had determined from the start of our homeschooling, would be educated with forthright discussions about racism, sexism, and all the other nasty "isms" of human existence. If that made her less than idealistic about the world around her, so be it. Love of country, I once told Julia, should be open-eyed, just like love of family. You should see all the flaws and yet still know that you are a part of the group and should struggle to preserve it.

So—should Julia keep writing about social studies?

"No," I told her. "But you do have to keep reading American history, since by the end of the fifth grade you're supposed to be familiar with all the highlights, up through the Civil War." Midway through the year I had purchased the Smithsonian's *Children's Encyclopedia of American History*, which offered three hundred glossy pages of colored photos and drawings, documents and timelines, mixed with lively text. That snazzy book summed up the major events in every era; if Julia carefully reviewed the first 110 pages, she'd have a good survey of all the American history a fifth-grader needed to know.

"Reading? That's all I have to do?" Julia asked.

"Reading and conversing and thinking," I responded. "Can you handle that?"

Julia stood, walked to my side of the table, and gave me a big hug. "Thanks, Mom."

CHAPTER EIGHT

⤜The Rites of Spring⤛

Spring is so freeing, when the weather is
warm but there are cool winds that smell like
water and the color green.

JULIA

THUS BEGAN A NEW CHAPTER IN OUR HOMESCHOOLING. With history and science relegated to afternoon reading and conversation, Julia embarked upon seven weeks of creative writing, devoting all of her computer time to short stories, poems, and scraps of soon-to-be-abandoned novels. She wrote twenty-five typed pages of fiction, and as always, her mind dwelled upon a fantasy world in which creatures were the heroes, oppressed by human villains.

"Once there was a beautiful palace in the sky where unicorns grazed on clouds," her longest story began,

> *. . . in fact they had a whole sky kingdom! The sky palace seemed to be made out of fog and glass. The king and queen, however, were not so enjoyable.*
>
> *The queen came from a place called Rome, and had flown up on a kite. She was rarely seen without having puffy dresses on, and had raven black hair now, but when she came she had an old robe, tattered old shoes, and some kind of smell about*

her like horses, dust, and sweat. She, in fact, was a woman
gladiator who had been in an arena busy fighting men when
she stole a giant kite from the grasp of the emperor's children
and flew off.

Watching Julia absorbed in her stories for hours, I understood the impetus behind unschooling. John Holt, who spurred the unschooling movement in the 1970s with his revolutionary book *Teach Your Own*, believed that children were natural learners who would absorb the most knowledge and skills if freed to pursue their individual interests, and if encouraged to gain insight from the daily activities of life. It's a pedagogical approach too loose and liberal for most parents, but in Julia's case, there was clear value in letting her throw herself into her passions, without a parent or teacher forever interrupting, dividing the day into fifty-minute segments and saying, "Stop what you're doing . . . Change gears . . . Time for math. . . . Time for social studies."

If Julia had been entirely unschooled for the year, she might have focused on science experiments for four or five days straight, followed by three weeks of short-story writing and a two-month immersion in Greek mythology. In the end, an unschooled approach might have been closer to the "real world," where a carpenter can work on one house for months, or a painter struggle with one canvas for weeks. The division of children's attention into arbitrary time slots is an artifice established for the convenience of schools, and is not designed to match the development of the human brain.

One thing is certain: if Julia and I had been unschoolers, our house would have been cleaner. Most unschooling websites stress the importance of children learning while doing chores; "household responsibilities" are a regular mantra. The idea falls somewhere between pioneer-style homesteading and Emersonian philosophy, promoting the notion that humans learn best by doing, not by sitting in a classroom. By contrast, today's public school parents often complain that their kids have little time to help around the house. Children are so burdened with homework and afterschool activities, staying up late to finish assignments, that parents hate to ask much more of them. I've often watched my house devolve into a grubby mess while I remained reluctant to enlist my girls' aid—their noses were too deeply buried in their schoolbooks. The appeal of unschooling grows in proportion to the grime in my kitchen.

During those mornings when Julia was busy writing, she and I led a charmed existence. Gone was the anger, the conflict, the profanity. Gone was my need to oversee, harangue, and correct. I didn't have to ask Julia twice and thrice to settle down and get to work. While she wrote, I made great headway on grading and reading and laundry, and during her ten-minute breaks, she helped to empty the dishwasher and fold sheets. In those hours I began to lighten up about her education; I tried to enter the Zen of homeschooling, and let her learning emerge more "organically," a favorite unschooling term. Those placid mornings went a long way toward healing the wounds of our stormy winter.

And yet, despite all of its appeal, Julia and I barely dipped our toes into the unschooling pond. With reentry into the public schools looming, I was willing to loosen the reins for only a few hours each day. At other times, I insisted that we maintain a traditional approach to French and music and, above all, math.

Math is the unschoolers' Achilles' heel. The website Un schooling.com claims that "Geometry can be found in quilt making, algebra in painting a room," but I can imagine middle-school algebra teachers rolling their eyes. Yes, math is present everywhere in the world around us, and hands-on application is key to all education, but house painting is no substitute for daily practice with equations. Every day throughout the spring I still required Julia to practice math and spelling and violin exercises. Unsurprisingly, during those hours, she continued to fall into long periods of whining and foot-dragging that left me praying for the patience of Job.

Hanging over my head was my promise to cancel school for the day if I raised my voice. Given my track record, one might assume that Julia enjoyed plenty of abruptly truncated school days throughout the rest of the year. In fact, only once in the coming months did we have to drop everything and read for a day—which doesn't mean that I got grouchy on only one occasion. Far from it. But Julia's calm hours of creative writing helped to lower my stress level, and when trouble inevitably emerged, I found that if I couldn't always control my temper, I could at least control my volume, which I reduced to a hissing simmer.

"I always know when you're angry," Rachel said to me one morning in March. "Because you get all stiff and shivery."

That might sound unhealthy. Better to let one's feelings out, some moms might say. Better to erupt in minor spurts than to compress all of one's frustrations deep inside the heart's core, where they'll ultimately explode with Vesuvian force. In my experience, however, it's often preferable for a mother to stiffen and twitch, apoplectic with annoyance, than to speak angry words. "Behold how much wood is kindled by how small a fire, and the tongue is a fire." That's how one of the characters in Marilynne Robinson's *Gilead* puts it.

My verbal pyrotechnics didn't always require an audience. When possible, I tried to utter my angriest thoughts alone, outside, to the nonjudgmental trees. I felt like Midas's wife, whispering her secrets to the river reeds. Usually my self-control was rewarded, because children morph from devil to angel hour by hour, transforming a mother's thoughts from bile to honey. If

I could weather my tempests, Julia would inevitably stop complaining and produce some wonderful piece of art or writing that ushered out all of my internal sunshine.

"Look at this," she would say, and show me a pencil drawing of a phoenix rising from its ashes, thirty-two feathers drawn with individual attention. At ten, Julia's drawing skills vastly exceeded my own.

"It's beautiful," I smiled. "*C'est magnifique.*"

Meanwhile, as spring advanced, the weather provided the external warmth that had been absent from our lives over the past few months. Purple crocuses dotted the lawn, followed by jonquils and daffodils, growing in clusters in the woods beside our creek, and with each burst of color, Julia and I shed our chilly moods. She brought me daffodil bouquets, their yellow heads drooping, and I cut sprigs of forsythia that shot like fireworks from the vase on our hall table. These were our peace offerings, symbols that familial love can be renewed along with flowers and trees and grass.

Despite all my previous tantrums, Julia never seemed to hold a grudge. Perhaps it was the gaps in her memory; my outbursts slipped from her mind as quickly as the state capitals. Or perhaps she never took me as seriously as I took myself. Even in the midst of my bleakest winter fits, she often maintained a sense of humorous patience: "Breathe deeply," she told me as I gritted my teeth. "Count to ten."

"You know that I love you, even when I'm angry," I said to her on those occasions.

"Yeah," she replied, sidling up to me on the couch. "I know."

❖

By April we were celebrating the return of regular field trips, including our most memorable history lesson: three days in

Virginia's "historic triangle" of Jamestown, Williamsburg, and Yorktown. Jamestown, site of the first permanent English settlement in America, was planning to celebrate its four hundredth anniversary the following year, and in preparation, the state of Virginia had joined with private donors to build a huge living history complex, called Jamestown Settlement, next to the original historic site.

"I've been wanting to visit this place," I said to Julia one afternoon, pointing to the settlement's website on my computer screen. "I've never been to Jamestown, and we can spend a day in Williamsburg, too."

"Can we visit Busch Gardens?" Julia piped up.

"No," I shook my head.

"Can we go to Water Country USA?" she asked.

"That's not even open for the season . . . But we can stay at a hotel, and eat at restaurants," I said, trying to coax her.

She was unimpressed.

"And you won't have to play the violin," I added. "Or do any math."

"Not even in the car?" she asked.

"Okay," I bargained. "We'll listen to books on tape instead." We had a deal.

Driving though the Virginia Piedmont on an early April morning, past the scrubby pines and into the marshy Tidewater region, I explained to Julia why our state wanted to shine a spotlight on Jamestown. Virginia hoped to remind the rest of the country about the Old Dominion's important role in early American history. This was, in part, another North-South thing. Virginia had long been annoyed that the Massachusetts pilgrims often got top billing for founding America. *Schoolhouse Rock* features cartoon Puritans crashing into Plymouth Rock, but it doesn't ever mention John Smith and the Jamestown crew.

When we reached historic Jamestown's national park and began to walk around, Julia and I overheard a park ranger jokingly curse the "damn Yankees" for stealing Virginia's thunder in the colonization race. The ranger went on to inform his tour group that pilgrims searching for religious freedom made a better founding legend for our country than the truth behind Jamestown: rich members of a joint stock company scouring the New World for profit.

Historic Jamestown featured a small museum and archeological excavations, a church and a statue of Pocahontas, and best of all, a working glass house, where Julia stared for twenty minutes at artisans crafting vases and pitchers from balls of molten sand. The glass house stood beside a small beach, where wavelets from the James River broke onto the white shore. Julia threw bits of pine bark into the water and watched a small ferry crossing the half-mile stretch, where the James widens as it approaches the Chesapeake Bay.

"Who would have thought that there would be beaches at Jamestown?" she said.

"What were you expecting?" I asked.

"A port," she explained. "A small city with more boats."

*

Some boats were waiting at the national park's fancy new neighbor, Jamestown Settlement. That's where most of the cars had been headed when Julia and I turned off to see the original Jamestown. Many of those tourists would never visit the authentic site, now that a living history complex had been built next door.

"*We're* the real McCoy," one miffed ranger complained. "Jamestown Settlement is just a replica." Julia and I nodded in sympathy before skulking over to contribute our dollars to the newcomer.

When we pulled into the Jamestown Settlement parking lot, we faced a brick building so large it looked more like a hospital than a museum/café/educational center. Inside, the structure boasted not one but three gift shops among acres of museum displays. Julia and I walked straight through the building and outside, to the living history sites. There, on the banks of the muddy James, floated replicas of the three ships that had brought the early colonists: the *Godspeed*, the *Discovery*, and the *Susan Constant*.

These were Virginia's answer to the *Niña*, the *Pinta*, and the *Santa Maria*. Julia and I strolled aboard the surprisingly small decks, then climbed below to see the cannons and supply barrels, and tiny officers' beds built into the wooden hull. The beds were so small that even Julia, who promptly climbed into one, could not stretch out her four-foot-ten-inch frame. She and I sat down on a rough-hewn bench and played crazy eights with a hand-drawn deck of parchment cards.

"It's nice," Julia said as we exited the *Susan Constant*, "but it's too pretty." The ship's hull was painted yellow, blue, and brown, with decorative flowers and stripes. "It doesn't look hundreds of years old," she explained.

"It's supposed to look like it would have in 1607," I replied, "when the colonists first arrived."

Julia eyed the ship critically. "After four months at sea, do you think it would look like that?"

She had a point. In fact, the entire settlement had a slightly Disneyfied appearance, with colorful ships neatly docked and a well-maintained wooden fort containing structures built of clay and wood: small storehouses hung with dried tobacco and smoked ham, an armory, a blacksmith's shop, a church. Julia ran from building to building like Goldilocks, trying out all of the straw mattresses and preferring the four-poster bed in the governor's two-room cottage.

Living history was much more fun than social studies on a printed page. Julia loved posing in a soldier's metal helmet and breastplate, and carrying empty water buckets on a wooden beam across her shoulders. While my own inclination was to walk quietly from place to place, Julia had no qualms about noisily questioning the blacksmith and tobacco farmer. "What's this called?" "What does that do?" Could she touch it, throw it, shoot it?

She liked it all, even though she realized that the "settlement" didn't capture the ambience of the real colony. Back in the early 1600s, Jamestown was a desperate, marshy place where the vast majority of colonists died of malaria and starvation. These well-fed reenactors, neatly shaven and freshly bathed, wearing straw hats and knee breeches and drawstring cotton shirts, couldn't re-create the anguish of their antecedents, some of whom had dug up dead bodies in order to eat them.

The written materials throughout the settlement acknowledged the grim truth: starvation and slavery and the gradual destruction of the Powhatan culture. Julia was too busy touching tobacco leaves and flintlocks to read the printed placards, but I found them enlightening—another lesson in all that a parent can learn while homeschooling. My childhood memories of Jamestown were limited to visions of Pocahontas saving John Smith's life, but nowhere, in film or painting or book, did the settlement teach that old story; too much doubt had been heaped upon John Smith's journals. I made a mental note to stop repeating the old legend to Rachel and Kathryn.

"Did you know that Pocahontas's real name was Matoaka?" I asked Julia. "Pocahontas was her nickname." I didn't add that *Pocahontas* meant "little wanton"—a nickname some historians define as "frolicsome," while others view it as an insulting term for a girl who liked to play games with strange boys from foreign lands.

"It says here that during her teenage years Pocahontas was taken captive by the English and held hostage." I pointed at a placard. "They wanted to trade her for English prisoners and weapons and tools."

"I can't believe you read all the little tablets," Julia replied. "I just walk around and scan everything, but you stop to read the signs."

"When I was a kid I didn't read them, either," I explained. "But when you get older you slow down and get curious about the history. Besides," I added, "these cards show me how much I don't know."

I had embarked upon nine months of homeschooling with the innocent assumption that Julia and I would be reviewing a lot of the same history and science that I had encountered as a fifth-grader. That assumption was particularly naïve when it came to science. Our knowledge of the universe changes on a daily basis, and much of what Julia had learned in the fall about natural history—the Big Bang, tectonic plates, feathered dinosaurs—was undiscovered country when I was a child. Now, at Jamestown Settlement, I was reminded that history, too, constantly evolves. Narratives are transformed according to each teller's perspective, and are influenced by the ongoing discovery of new records and artifacts.

I realized on that day that if I were to homeschool beyond the elementary grades, I would feel enormous responsibility to learn more than I already know about science and history. At the fifth-grade level I already felt inadequate as a science teacher, knowing so little about chemistry and physics and the scientific method. At Jamestown, I saw that if I were to teach history to a middle-schooler, I would want a few weeks of advance reading on every subject we studied—just to uncover the latest facts, to find the best books to share, and to communicate the importance of historians' methods, from proper documentation to the value of primary sources. One of the joys of homeschooling comes from how much parents and children discover together, but I can understand why some homeschoolers rely on the Calvert curriculum or the Charlotte Mason method, or any of several models available on the Internet that guide a parent year by year through all the ins and outs of math and history and science. For one year, Julia and I could wander free from prescriptive models, but as a long-term homeschooler, I would probably seek more guidance, just to avoid the worry that my knowledge was out-of-date.

Someday Julia might be similarly humbled by the obsolescence of her knowledge. On that April afternoon, she was concerned only with scraping out charred bits of a tree trunk that a Powhatan reenactor was carefully burning and carving into a canoe.

"Do you like this place?" I asked Julia as we prepared to leave.

"I like dressing up," she replied, "and I like scraping deer hide with an oyster shell."

As for me, I liked letting my child learn from other people who knew much more than me.

*

The next day Julia and I drove twenty miles to Colonial Williamsburg. Our family had visited the site twice in the past, walking the gravel lanes and watching horse-drawn carriages led by coachmen in knee breeches and triangular hats. On previous visits, however, we had always been the unticketed second-class citizens, barred from almost every interior, grasping at scraps of history as we glanced into the windows of the millinery and cobbler's shop. Now, in the name of homeschooling, I swallowed hard and paid sixty dollars for two tickets, which granted access to the entire town.

We began our day with a visit inside the Governor's Palace, where the tour guide earned her money by parrying Julia's constant questions. As usual, I resorted to whispering in my daughter's ear, "Let the other people speak. Be patient. Don't wave your hand so furiously." Fortunately the tour guide was a matronly good sport who quickly took the situation in hand. She dubbed Julia her junior tour guide, which meant that the ten-year-old "guide" must wait for all the "guests" to ask their questions before she peppered her older "colleague" with inquiries. The tour guide kept Julia at her side, where she could prevent my curious child from touching the swords and armor on the walls. Steel blades seemed to have a magnetic attraction for Julia's fingertips.

At the end of the tour one woman approached me and said, smiling, "Don't worry about your daughter asking too many questions. I'm a schoolteacher, and it's wonderful to see a child who is interested enough to ask any questions at all."

Of course she was right. My own tendency to be quiet and unobtrusive when clustered in a group of strangers didn't need to be imposed on Julia. Still, that teacher could not see the worrisome trend that my maternal eyes spotted in my child. During that tour, I once again noticed how Julia did not acknowledge herself as one among many. When the group moved from room to room, she initially tried to jostle her way to the front, as if this were a race she must win. She had no instinct for letting others go first, and no inclination to listen to strangers' questions. Call it childish self-absorption or something more clinical, Julia might as well have been enjoying her own private tour, she was so oblivious to the crowd.

I breathed easier when we stepped outside, where Julia could wander the boxwood maze in the Palace Gardens, or skip down Duke of Gloucester Road singing aloud. I bought her a pennywhistle in an outdoor market, and she walked the streets composing tunes on the spot, utterly unconcerned that no one else around us was playing a musical instrument.

Her chief delight was *The Revolutionary City*—an outdoor theatrical production consisting of more than thirty professional actors and amateur reenactors, who spread throughout a few cordoned-off blocks on Main Street. That afternoon's performance featured scenes a colonial citizen might have witnessed between 1774 and 1776, when America was on the brink of war. The production began as Julia and I sat in the grass outside the large brick Capitol; an actor playing Lord Dunmore, governor of Virginia, appeared on the balcony to announce that, in response to acts of rebellion in Boston, King George had dissolved the Virginia assembly. From there, Julia followed a procession of actors and tourists down the street, moving from scene to scene. Here was a loyalist daughter dressed in pink calico defending her father's political views and lamenting how all this revolutionary fervor was infringing on her social life. And here, gathered surreptitiously behind one house, a group of African slaves debated whether they should join the Continental Army and gain their freedom at the end of the war. Julia ran from building to building, listening to everyone, asking questions and joining in debates—precisely what the actors encouraged, although most of the onlookers were blasé adults like me, happy enough to watch, but not eager to play the game.

Looking back, I view that day as a great homeschooling pleasure, even though plenty of American families have enjoyed the same Williamsburg experience without ever having to dabble in home education. One might insist that Julia could have absorbed her colonial lessons on any well-planned family weekend; homeschooling wasn't necessary. In our family's case, however, that's not quite true. Had Julia's sisters been present, the event would likely have degenerated into arguing, poking, and kicking. In less than two hours I would have been hurrying for the exit.

With Julia as my only charge, I managed to find a bench in the shade and settle down with a novel, frequently glancing up the street at my child, safe in the hands of other educators. Julia was happy, and we stayed all afternoon. That night we slept in a motel on the York River, with the tiny historic district of Yorktown at our backs, within a mile of the spot where the French Comte de Rochambeau helped to block the Chesapeake Bay so that a stranded Cornwallis, denied reinforcements, was compelled to surrender.

These days, if you ask Julia who Cornwallis was, she usually doesn't remember. She does recall, however, the jellyfish in the shallow York River, small and white translucent creatures pulsing up to the water's surface then sinking back down to the sandy bottom, trailing little fish in their tentacles. To Julia, the lessons of the landscape were more memorable than history lessons, and that was okay with me. When she revisited Cornwallis in high school, in the two years when all of her American history would be repeated, I hoped she would recall wading in the York River, peering into the cave where Cornwallis hid, and walking around the battlefield. Our field trip had given her a tangible reference for bringing to life the words in a textbook.

✦

Arriving home from our mid-April travels, Julia and I had reached the final stretch of the school year, and once again we had to adjust our daily schedule. I was committed to teach a six-week intensive class at Washington and Lee called Reading Lolita in Lexington, based on Azar Nafisi's memoir, *Reading Lolita in Tehran*. Now I would be spending six hours each week discussing Nabokov, Fitzgerald, and Austen with twenty-five students, while guiding them through the history of Iran and Islam, from Cyrus the Great to Mahmoud Ahmadinejad. Every second week would bring another stack of student papers.

"You're going to have to spend more time with Dad," I explained to Julia. "I'll be home on Tuesdays and Thursdays, but on Monday, Wednesday, and Friday afternoons you'll need to stay at VMI."

Not a good plan, one might think, given John's busy schedule and the lure of the VMI weight room. But John's work always settled down by late April, with the cadets busy preparing for exams and mid-May graduation, and in recent months John had begun to show some promise as a homeschooler.

The previous fall, in the wake of Julia's aborted flute lessons, John had picked up some of the home-ed slack by assuming a new role: art teacher. He was much better suited to the task than I. After Julia's knitting lessons, I had assigned her various art projects; "Sculpt a velociraptor. Draw some Mayan hieroglyphs. Sketch a medieval knight according to the instructions in this how-to drawing book." I had tried to think of projects that matched Julia's units in science and history, but in my artless ignorance, I could offer her no practical advice. "Looks good to me" was my constant refrain as I admired her sketches and clay creations.

My own artistic efforts had withered in the sixth grade, when a teacher presented my drawing to the class as an example of what *not* to do. She had told the class to draw her face, of which she was obviously proud, and although I had tried my best, at the end of the period she had held my paper up beside her aquiline nose and lamented: "This doesn't look anything like me!" Couldn't I see that her hair had a dark sheen far superior to the generic straw that I had sketched? After that I carefully avoided art for the rest of my school years, such is the power of one bad teacher.

John's encounters with art were consistently happy. He came from a family blessed with artistic genes, from his sister painting murals in her daughter's bedroom, to his great-grandfather painting murals inside Rockefeller Center. John preferred sculpting; he specialized in small, cartoonish clay figures—four-inch cadets in full regalia with sabers at their sides, or three-inch hockey goalies doing half-splits to block a puck. Two years ago, after teaching Julia to play chess, he had sculpted a set for her: dinosaurs confronting dragons. Gathered on one side stood pterodactyl knights, triceratops bishops, and his-and-her T. rexes serving as king and queen. Facing them were purple dragons perched on turreted castles, Chinese dragon knights holding emerald balls, and pawn hatchlings breaking through oval eggs. When I saw him paint the figures, I remember thinking: Does this child know how much she is loved?

Since November, John had been overseeing Julia's art projects, and in the process he had learned to appreciate all the art teachers from his past. "Now I know why those teachers always started with an apple or a glass," he remarked one afternoon. "Julia and I started out trying to draw the front of Scott Shipp Hall" (one of VMI's castle-like buildings). "I was planning to do the whole thing, so I could show her how to draw shadows. But you know what? We spent an hour just drawing part of the roof."

Art lessons gave John and Julia a wonderful chance for father-daughter time. "We'd do drawings together," John recalled months later. "I'd do one and she'd do one. We drew faces, we drew each other, we tried to draw trees. Art was so much easier than music."

This was a strange comment from a band director, but apart from reading and creative writing, art was the only activity Julia would happily pursue for hours, without constant oversight. While John met with cadets, Julia painted still life watercolors of fruit that he had arranged on his desk. While he conferred with administrators, she built an Aztec temple out of sugar cubes, painting it gold with red drops spattered on the stairs. "Blood," she explained. "They threw the bodies of their sacrificial victims down the temple steps."

In art, John had found his homeschooling niche. Years later, I would feel proud to arrive home and see him in the yard with our girls, kitchen chairs arranged in the grass behind short easels, a small table cluttered with brushes and paints and mugs of water, while they all concentrated on acrylic paintings of the Blue Ridge Mountains.

Now that spring had come, and I would be leaving Julia with her dad three afternoons each week, I gave John an extra charge. "You can teach Julia about the Civil War," I announced one morning in his office. Placing our *Children's Encyclopedia of American History* on his desk, I opened it to the 1860s and said, "Knock yourself out."

John didn't flinch. He's a Civil War enthusiast, the sort who makes a biannual pilgrimage to Gettysburg, and who lies awake at night reading volume after volume on generals and battles and the trials of foot soldiers. In our earliest, child-free years of marriage I followed him to Antietam, Appomattox, and Shiloh, but while John felt something spiritual at most battlefields, I was thoroughly bored, kicking my toes into the side of yet another earthwork.

"What better place to study the Civil War," I told Julia, "than at VMI, on ground shelled by Union troops?" After VMI's cadets marched up the valley in May of 1864 to help the Confederacy win a brief victory at the Battle of New Market, the Union's General Hunter marched down the same ground, burning crops as he went. When he reached the outskirts of Lexington, he set up cannons across the Maury River from VMI, and proceeded to bombard the place. John showed Julia the Union cannonballs still embedded in the back walls of VMI's barracks.

He also took her to the VMI museum, to see the bullet hole in the sleeve of Stonewall Jackson's leather coat, from the day in 1863 when he was accidentally shot by a Confederate soldier. (Jackson died of the ensuing gangrene.) But Julia was too troubled by Jackson's stuffed horse to care about the general's coat. Little Sorrell, VMI's monument to taxidermy, had recently been refurbished by a Smithsonian conservator, inspiring the cadets to feature in their student newspaper a picture of the horse wearing platform shoes and a tilted ball cap, with a caption that read, "Little Sorrell: Pimp My Ride."

Julia wasn't impressed. "Little Sorrell looks creepy," she said. "After all his service to his country he gets cut open and made into a big, dead doll with glass eyes."

In fact, she was skeptical about VMI's entire culture. Another girl might have become enamored with military regalia, spending so much time on the campus of a military college, surrounded by men in uniforms, gray and green, and young cadets wearing crisp white trousers and gray jackets. College boys who usually slouch around in jeans and T-shirts can resemble Prince Charming when decked out in gold buttons and white gloves. But they didn't interest Julia. VMI's culture was too masculine, too regimented, and too anti-individualistic to appeal to her idiosyncratic mind. In fact, our most memorable homeschooling event that spring turned out to be an antiwar protest, prompted when VMI announced its choice for graduation speaker: Donald Rumsfeld.

VMI's senior class had made the pick, raising groans from the college's moderate professors and quiet grumblings from career Army officers who hadn't liked Rumsfeld even before he became secretary of defense. Now that the Iraq War had descended into a muddled mess, with Rumsfeld hovering on the brink of resignation, he seemed like a bad choice for graduation day. Nevertheless, each year VMI's seniors are allowed considerable leeway in choosing their speaker, and Rumsfeld was slightly more legitimate than the cadets' selection a few years earlier: G. Gordon Liddy.

An impending visit from Rumsfeld was a rallying cry to all Lexingtonians who had opposed the Iraq War from the get-go, and I was solidly among those ranks. I had spent seven months prior to the U.S. invasion working with area Quakers to plan local rallies, organize carpools to D.C. marches, and distribute hundreds of self-designed red buttons that looked like little stop signs reading, "No War Against Iraq." During those months, Julia, Rachel, and Kathryn had become accustomed to waving signs at local protests, and although my activism was a touchy subject at a school like VMI, the best antiwar speech I ever heard took place at that college, when the International Studies Department held a forum on the possibility of war in Iraq. In a surreal moment, General Anthony Zinni explained to a packed crowd of eight hundred cadets and civilians why invading Iraq was a bad idea. As he put it: "I've spent the last ten years watching this guy, Saddam Hussein. And I'm here to tell you, he ain't Adolf Hitler, and he ain't Osama Bin Laden. He's Tony Soprano. He's a gangster . . . and he's not worth the life of a single lance corporal." It was like a scene from a Vonnegut novel, to watch hundreds of uniformed cadets howling with cheers as a general told them about the lunacy of a war in which they would soon be fighting.

Once the war started, I had converted my activism into support-the-troops mode, but Rumsfeld's visit was an irritation too great to be ignored. One faculty wife suggested that a group of VMI spouses should disrupt the speech, standing up halfway through and pulling out banners previously hidden in our purses. Lexington, however, is a very polite community, and the local peace activists opted instead to gather at the northern entrance to town, where a bridge crosses the Maury into Lexington. With the turreted walls of VMI visible in the background, protesters would occupy the sidewalk along the bridge and advertise their anti-Rumsfeld sentiments to all the passing drivers.

"Julia and I are going to join the protest against Rumsfeld," I told John a few days before the event. "I think it would make a good civics lesson."

John looked up from his computer with eyebrows raised. He usually responds to my activism with a "That's nice, honey" wave, and a repetition of his old refrain: "Just don't get me fired." This time he was more specific.

"Make sure that it's not your face on the evening news, okay?"

The night before the protest, Julia placed a big white poster on our kitchen table and got out our Magic Markers. I wrote the words: "Support Our Troops: Fire Rumsfeld." Julia handled the pictures: a line of toy soldiers along the bottom and, above them, a cannon with flames emerging from the word *Fire*.

"Do you understand who Rumsfeld is?" I asked Julia.

"Not really," she admitted.

I explained to her about a president's secretaries, but I think she envisioned female typists. So I told her that Rumsfeld was a man in charge of the military who had pushed hard for war, when peace was still an option. These days, I explained, most Americans feel that our involvement in Iraq was a bad idea, costing a lot of lives and money. Julia could fathom all of that.

The next morning, we gathered at the bridge with forty people—a tiny number by urban standards, but a large crowd for little Lexington, where most peace vigils draw fewer than a dozen usual suspects. One person had dressed as the grim reaper, pacing with his scythe; another wore a grotesque George Bush mask. Everyone brought posters and picket signs and banners, and drivers who supported the anti-Rumsfeld message honked and waved. Others passed by stone-faced.

Keeping our promise to her dad, Julia held our big poster in front of our faces when two television cameras scanned the scene, and that night, the protest accomplished its objective: major news channels covering VMI's graduation included clips from the bridge. Whether the event accomplished any teaching objectives, I can't say. After fifteen minutes of yelling, "Down with Rumsfeld!" and "Stop the War!" Julia soon lost interest. She disappeared behind the line of sign-waving adults, and when I searched her out after another half hour, I found her sitting with her back to the bridge's concrete railing, hidden behind the crowd, reading a fantasy novel while all the ugly thoughts of war and politics slipped from her mind and into the river below. I supposed I couldn't expect a fifth-grader to be filled with political passions, especially a child like Julia, who had a very limited interest in the troubles of human beings. Had we been trying to save whales, or free monkeys from a science lab, her imagination might have been sparked. I could see Julia as a stubborn tree sitter. But as for some old, stuffy guy named Rumsfeld? Julia didn't really care.

"Can we go eat some lunch?" she asked.

"Sure," I said. As we walked off the bridge, she rolled our poster into a more useful object: first a megaphone, then a percussion mallet, which she beat on the hood of our station wagon.

"What did you think of the protest?" I asked across the car roof as I looked for my keys.

She held the rolled poster to her eye, telescope-style. "It was okay, I guess."

"What would have made it better?"

"An after-party," she replied. "With lots of creamy dips and crackers. You could have talked politics with the adults, and I could have watched TV."

Years later, when I showed Julia her comment, she remarked: "Did I really say that? I think what I meant was that if I cared about a political cause, I would rather go to a party than to a protest. Or maybe to a restaurant, where half the profits were going to support the cause. But I'm not the kind of person who wants to stand around holding a sign for hours, and I think most people feel the same. I mean, even at the protests in Washington, they have to have a rock band there just to get people to come."

※

Back in 2005, as the cadets packed up their barracks' rooms and drove off with their parents, our year of homeschooling was rapidly drawing to a close. One week after the protest, Julia's violin recital took place, suffering only one glitch. When we arrived at Washington and Lee's music building, the accompanist shuffled through her piles of piano music and exclaimed, "Oh no!" She had left one book at home; Julia would have to perform her movement of the Seitz concerto a cappella.

"Do you mind?" I asked Julia.

"Why should I mind?" she responded.

One of the advantages of tuning out social norms was that Julia never appeared nervous when performing before an audience. As a child, I had suffered through annual violin recitals with my bow arm trembling and my stomach clenched, so I admired my coolly confident daughter, who seemed unconcerned with any eyes upon her. No piano accompaniment? No problem. Julia took the floor unfazed, and in the first long stretch of rests, where a piano should have been playing the orchestral part, she lowered her violin and sang the melody with unself-conscious abandon. Inspired by her gutsy solo, I joined her (though more quietly), and her violin teacher occasionally piped in as well. In the end, Julia had her accompaniment, and she concluded with a dramatic, deep bow.

Watching her fiddle away, I doubted my decision to stop her violin lessons. She was the most advanced little string player in the room, and now all of her progress would slow to a snail's pace. But I feared that if we continued her lessons, hatred of practicing would turn into hatred of me. We had to choose between progress on the violin and peace in our household, which is why, after the recital, Julia packed her violin away in its case and stuffed it underneath her bed, where it would accumulate dust in the coming months.

Now that we had reached the countdown until the end of the school year, I suffered a major attack of last-minute anxiety. Had Julia learned enough? Would she be prepared for the sixth grade?

I've since learned that end-of-the-year panic is very common among short-term homeschoolers. One acquaintance in Northern Virginia told me that she and her middle-schooler, who had stayed home for a year, spent all of June cramming math, because she feared she had neglected it throughout the spring. In my case, math wasn't the problem. For the past month Julia had been taking Saxon math tests at the rate of three per week, reviewing all of her knowledge, practicing test-taking skills, and reassuring me that no concept had been left behind. As far as I could tell, her math skills were fine; my anxiety came from an unexpected corner.

In early May, Julia and I had visited our local independent bookstore, a comfortable, cat-inhabited space with a big children's section, where we often lingered, reading silently in the cozy chairs. Usually the bookstore offered a calming experience. On that May afternoon, however, I made the mistake of glancing at the children's education shelf, and there was E. D.

Hirsch, perched atop his hill of cultural literacy, espousing *What Your Fifth-Grader Needs to Know*. I picked up the book, flipped through a few pages, and soon found my mind filled with dread. Julia knew nothing of feudal Japan or early Russian civilization. She had never been introduced to scientists such as Elijah McCoy or Ada Lovelace. Even some of Hirsch's third-grade essentials, on Constantine and the Byzantine empire, would have left her dumbfounded. Oh God, I shuddered. Should Julia try to cram in some of these facts before the end of the year?

Hirsch's curriculum is a noble vision, especially in the area of history. While Virginia hammers home American history and government in elementary-, middle-, and high-school classes, giving far less attention to the larger world, Hirsch focuses on international history and geography—a much more colorful approach, suited to our increasingly global lives.

But despite its strengths, for the average parent whose children have never followed Hirsch's sequential plan, his books are an exercise in paranoia. Even with my Ph.D., I didn't know all this stuff, and that recognition alone should have given me a clue. I should have rested assured that it was possible for a person to lead a thoughtful existence, get into a good college, and pursue an intellectual life without having her brain crammed with a specific list of cultural facts. Julia might not know about the dynasties of China, but I bet Hirsch's disciples couldn't tell the difference between a Parasaurolophus and a Pachycephalosaurus. The important thing was to nurture a child's desire to learn, to encourage her intrinsic curiosity about the world, and to show her how to find the answers to cultural questions as they arose. I set Hirsch aside with only a mild sense of guilt.

The next shelf of titles, however, was harder to dismiss. Here stood the *Summer Bridge Activity Books*, full of worksheets designed to keep a child academically hopping during the summer months. I had bought one of these books years ago, when Julia was approaching the third grade, but I had quickly put it away. Inside lay the same joy-sapping grammar and math worksheets that kids confront daily in the public schools. I'm all for summer learning when it takes the form of reading and writing, art and music, athletics and outdoor play, but true-false science quizzes make me cringe. The last thing a child needs during the summer is more multiple choice and matching.

Nevertheless, on that May morning as Julia migrated toward the bookstore's toy section, I opened the fifth-grade book. Julia would be far ahead of this game, I assured myself; these paperbacks followed the lowest common denominator in the public school curriculum. Thumbing through the pages, I found that Julia was well advanced when it came to math and grammar. So far, so good. Unfortunately, the book contained subjects I had never considered. One page featured the bones in the human skeleton—apparently standard knowledge for ten-year-olds. Another included hundreds of spelling words that children were supposed to know before entering the sixth grade.

"Hey, Julia," I called into the adjoining room, where she was busily arranging a landscape of African safari animals. "How do you spell *exception*?"

"*E-x-e-p-t-i-o-n*," she said.

"How about *descent*?"

"*D-e-s-e-n-t*?"

My heart sank, so I tried one more word. "Julia, how do you spell *Wednesday*?"

"*W-e-d-n-e-s-d-a-y*."

Okay, so my spelling-journal approach had at least cemented a few pragmatic words into the phonetic bog within Julia's brain. But now I was stricken with petty fears—exactly the reaction these books try to elicit, since parents' anxieties and competitive impulses are a powerful trigger for consumer spending. Worried that Julia wouldn't be prepared for the sixth grade, I paid the fourteen dollars, and for three weeks in May I required my daughter to cram spelling words and memorize bones.

The human skeleton was easy enough to master, with the help of our tangible bodies and a four-foot floor puzzle. Julia and I sang in the car: "The humerus is connected to the . . . femur." The spelling of abstract words, however, was a hopeless chore. In those last frantic weeks of our homeschooling, Julia memorized dozens of words for one test, then forgot them by the next week. By May 20 I'd given up, chiding myself for having ended the year with this desperate spelling marathon. It had been ridiculous to add last-minute goals to our curriculum—the paranoid mistake of a novice teacher. Homeschooling requires an enormous amount of faith in oneself and one's child. I needed to trust that Julia had absorbed plenty of knowledge throughout our year, and that she would keep learning day by day as her life continued. Chagrined by my frivolous purchase, I dropped the *Summer Bridge* book into our recycling bin.

With May now drawing to a close, only one task remained for our school year. Julia needed to take some form of standardized test and mail the results to our local school superintendent. So long as she scored above the lowest twenty-fifth percentile, she could advance to the sixth grade.

The mere mention of standardized testing conjures anxious memories from my childhood—the misery of three-hour exams that grew harder every year, prompting repeated nightmares of arriving at a test unprepared. After my last comprehensive graduate school exam, I remember thinking: "I will never again take a serious test. Never, never, never."

But when it came to Julia's testing, there was no reason to worry. Following the advice of several homeschooling friends,

I bought the fifth-grade California Achievement Test from an online service, and when the test arrived in the mail, I was surprised at what an innocuous little exercise it was. The test was comprised entirely of English and math—no science or social studies units that Julia might not have covered. In addition, the test was administered completely on the honor system, with no proctor required to monitor the process. In other words, this was a cheater's paradise. Any parent, sibling, or stranger could have filled in the answers, and although the test gave clear instructions on how much time to allot for each section, I knew homeschooling families who allowed their children unlimited time. Those parents objected, philosophically, to putting time constraints on children, and justified their practice by pointing to Virginia's SOL tests, where students are granted plenty of extra time.

Julia had the freedom to take the five-part test at her leisure—scattered across one week, or crammed into one afternoon. She chose to tackle one section each day of the week, faithfully sticking to the prescribed time limits. That faithfulness was sorely tried on her first math test; when I looked over her shoulder after the first ten minutes, I saw that she had completed only five problems.

"Why are you going so slowly?" I interrupted.

"You told me to check my answers," she replied. "So I'm doing each problem twice."

"No," I smiled. "Complete the entire test first, then go back and check your answers in whatever time you have left."

Julia barely finished that exam on time, but the other tests posed no problem. In fact, many of the questions were shockingly simple.

"Which of these numbers is even?" one test asked. "39, 81, 42, or 73?"

"I think this question is testing your English, not your math,"

I explained to Julia afterward. "Some children might not know what *even* means when it's applied to numbers." I could imagine no other reason for asking fifth-graders to distinguish between odd and even numbers.

At the end of the week we mailed Julia's testing booklet and answer sheets off to the designated P.O. box. A few weeks would pass before we received the paperwork showing Julia's scores, which alternated between the ninety-seventh and ninety-ninth percentile on all tests. In the meantime, a standardized exam seemed like a pretty dull way to end a child's school year. The test was a requirement, not an accomplishment; Julia felt no sense of pride. What should we do, I wondered, to acknowledge the successful completion of a year of homeschooling?

At Waddell Elementary, the fifth-graders were preparing for a graduation ceremony, where every student would walk the stage and receive certificates of achievement in reading and math and music. A few top students would get special prizes, and I wondered if Julia should be given some sort of award: A framed diploma? A blue ribbon? In the past, she had never cared about certificates; they disappeared among all the other miscellaneous school papers. But she did like ribbons, especially big blue ones with frills. However, I couldn't imagine assigning a first, second, and third place to homeschooling; this wasn't an art contest or a horse show.

Instead, I arranged for Julia to bask in the glow of some warm, human praise. The previous year, her fourth-grade teacher had offered to read Julia's writing at the end of the year. It was important, she had explained, for children to share their work and receive recognition for a job well done. And so, at the beginning of June, I scheduled an afterschool meeting with Mrs. Gonzalez.

"Oh, how lovely." The veteran teacher smiled when Julia placed her portfolio on a table in front of Mrs. G. Julia had decorated the cover with green and red and blue mountains; inside, a dragon sketch was tucked into the jacket pocket. The portfolio writings were divided into author studies, creative writing, science and social studies essays, and miscellaneous work.

"You wrote about Susan Cooper!" Mrs. Gonzalez beamed. "I love Cooper. And you studied the ice age, and the Aztecs and Incas!"

While Mrs. Gonzalez read a few of the essays, Julia strolled around her old classroom, touching books and bulletin boards and lifting a piece of chalk to sketch a dragon's head on the blackboard.

"Do you know what I like best?" Mrs. Gonzalez called out, and Julia came to her side to look down at the pages.

Mrs. G. pointed to a poem called "Old Barns": "In a cow pasture / Stands our neighbors' barn / Here a hundred years / Housing cows and larks . . ." "Your writing is wonderful," Mrs. Gonzalez said, smiling, and she gave Julia a big hug. That small act of commendation was exactly the prize that I had been seeking. A hug from a favorite teacher beat any certificate or ribbon. It was a loving, physical stamp of approval—recognition beyond the usual praise from Mom or Dad. The fact that the approval came from a public school teacher seemed to represent a human bridge between the worlds of government education and homeschooling.

All that remained now was for me and Julia to clean our house. Homeschooling is a messy affair, with posters and puzzles and glue sticks scattered on mantels and tables and counters. Over the next two days, while her sisters packed up their school supplies, Julia would recycle piles of math sheets and store away half-used spiral notebooks. I began to reclaim our dining room, which had served as a cross between a science laboratory and an art studio. Finally, after searching under beds and couches and coffee tables, I carried two stacks of books to the public library, checkbook in hand to pay the overdue fines.

"You're done?" A homeschooling acquaintance seemed surprised when I ran into her at the circulation desk.

"Sure," I replied, somewhat taken aback. "Tomorrow is the last day of school."

The woman smiled. "Our family keeps going straight through July, then we usually take a break in August."

"Wow," I murmured. "Good for you."

Once again, my rookie status as a homeschooler was on display. It had never occurred to me that Julia and I might continue with math and grammar and spelling through June and July, but of course there was no reason for homeschoolers to follow the public schedule. A three-month summer break makes little sense outside agricultural communities, and plenty of today's teachers deplore the long summer vacation, because of all the catching-up that has to be done in September.

Julia, however, would not have tolerated a single hour of schoolwork beyond the public limit. She was accustomed to the idea of a finish line, a June date toward which she could sprint like a marathon runner in her final Olympic lap. With two sisters in the public system anticipating the joy of their last day, it would have been cruel to ask anything more of Julia, or of myself. I, too, was steeped in an academic worldview that craves June as a light at the end of a long, dark tunnel.

When we picked up Rachel and Kathryn on the last day of school, Julia gave her annual cheer of delight from the backseat of the car. Usually that howl of pleasure makes me smile, but that year I felt a little sorry to see my daughter so gleeful. Despite all the freedoms of our homeschooling year, all my efforts to make it stimulating and fun, Julia still experienced the last moments with a sense of visceral release. In the end, our version of homeschooling had not escaped the worst aspects of school: the pressures of daily work, the crush of high expectations.

That's the problem with short-term homeschooling, some long-termers might say. Real home education doesn't involve a mere break from traditional schools; it requires a whole new approach to life and learning. Parents and children must be willing to opt out of the competitive, overscheduled culture that currently dominates American education, if they really want to get the benefits of homeschooling. And it takes more than one year to accomplish that.

Nine months was not enough time for me and Julia to break our institutionalized habits and decide for ourselves what we truly valued in education. I almost wished that she and I had another year to try again, without the steep learning curve that we had climbed so painfully throughout the winter. But if Julia and I had taken more time to fully master homeschooling—if we had tried one more time to craft a year of glorious, conflict-free success—how could Julia ever return to the public system? Many families who try short-term homeschooling never go back to traditional schools; they are so pleased with their new-found freedom. For us, however, continued homeschooling wasn't an option. Julia needed more time away from Mom, in a place where she could observe hundreds of other human beings, and learn what behaviors she admired and deplored. As for me, I wanted more time alone. The writer's life is a solitary venture, and in the hours before noon, when I am most productive, I yearned for the silence of an empty house to allow characters and worlds to take shape in my mind. One year of homeschooling had provided a wonderful break from my usual routine, but I needed an end date, too.

Nevertheless, as I drove my girls to our local ice-cream shop for celebratory sundaes, it occurred to me that this really wasn't the last day of school. If I had thought of it at the library, I would have told my homeschooling acquaintance that, yes, Julia and I would be continuing straight through July as well. Not only because every well-planned family outing can constitute a day of homeschooling, but because one big educational adventure remained ahead, an event that I viewed as the culmination of Julia's entire experience.

For years John and I had been hoping to fly out west for a three-week vacation, to show our children canyons and mountains and desert landscapes far different from anything they had seen in the eastern United States. This summer seemed like the ideal occasion, because now the trip could provide the perfect capstone for Julia's year. Over the past few months, while Julia had been busy crafting stories and taking math tests, I had scoured the Internet, booking campsites and hotel rooms and searching for cheap airfares. In the process, I had mapped out an itinerary that resembled a fireworks finale, with multiple bursts of natural beauty coming in quick succession. From late June through mid-July we would be camping in the Rockies, strolling through Yellowstone's geothermic wonders, motorboating on Signal Lake at the foot of the Grand Tetons, mule riding through hoodoos in Bryce Canyon, walking along the Virgin River at Zion, lodging among Luxor's faux-Egyptian splendor in Las Vegas, admiring the Bellagio fountains by day and Cirque du Soleil by night, hiking into the southern rim of the Grand Canyon, driving through Monument Valley after a visit to the Navajo National Monument, and marveling at ruins in Mesa Verde National Park.

I didn't call this "homeschooling" because I didn't want to taint our plans with that dirty word *school*, but I viewed these weeks as the ultimate field trip, designed to reinforce much of Julia's curriculum. What better way to appreciate the shifting of tectonic plates than to stand among the Rockies' Aspen range?

How better to witness the power of supervolcanoes than to watch Old Faithful erupt? Julia's study of dinosaurs would culminate among the fossils at Dinosaur National Monument, in Utah, and her unit on Native Americans would include dancing in a pow-wow in Cody, Wyoming, and touring the Anasazi's Cliff Palace, in Arizona. Since half of our evenings would be spent pitching a tent and cooking over an open fire, that, too, would be educational, and I planned to ask all three of my girls to keep a daily journal.

And after those three weeks, what other trips might our family plan? What cities and countries might we show our children? What mountains and lakes and rivers? What planetariums and Broadway shows and art museums could we visit? What conversations could we have at the kitchen table, about news and politics and books and the subjects our girls were studying at school?

So long as children lived under our roof, ours would be a homeschooling family, turning off the TV to spend more time talking and reading and going for walks. That June afternoon, as I watched my girls scoop sprinkles and hot fudge and cherries from the tops of their sundaes, I promised myself that at least until my daughters were teenagers, I could be the guiding force in their education.

Julia smiled at me from behind her Oreo moustache, and I smiled back. This is not the end, I thought. This is one more beginning, among all the new beginnings to come.

Epilogue: Back to School

I will remember the coffee shop, and the trip to Jamestown. . . . And if I ever have kids, maybe I'll homeschool them for a while.

JULIA

WHEN I LOOK BACK AT OUR YEAR OF HOMESCHOOLING, one memory stands out.

Julia is riding a bicycle on our country road. The bike is typical Wal-Mart fare: purple and pink with bright white tires and silvery ribbons that stream from the handlebars. It's too small for Julia, whose knees rise at right angles as she pedals very slowly, not fast enough for the wind to lift her hair.

"Pedal faster, Julia."

I am jogging at her side in blue jeans and sandals, sweating through a Mr. Whippy T-shirt as I hold on to the right handlebar.

"You've got your balance now. I'm going to let go for three seconds."

"Don't let go, Mom!"

"Just for three seconds."

I let go and count three milliseconds aloud, grabbing the handlebar before Julia topples to the left. A pickup truck approaches behind us, and we steer her bike over to the tall grass mingled with Queen Anne's Lace at the side of the road. The stranger in the truck waves as he passes, and I wave back.

Then Julia is in the middle of the road again, and I am running beside her, letting go for three seconds, four seconds, and five. Now she's pedaling faster, and I'm huffing and puffing, saying, "That's it! You've got it! Keep going."

I let go, and Julia speeds ahead, down the straightaway beside our neighbor's sloping meadow, where the cows have paused to lift their heads and watch me as I cheer.

That was one of our PE classes in September, scheduled as conscientiously as kickball or crab soccer would have been scheduled at Waddell Elementary. It might seem strange: you'd think that a ten-year-old would know how to ride a bike already. Most children master the feat somewhere between ages four and eight. But traffic on our road comes too fast to make the street a child's playground, and our neighborhood has no cohort of bike riding kids to inspire my girls. Our house is situated too far from town for a child to ride a bike to school or the library, and most of our family excursions take place on mountain trails, not roads suitable for bikes. As a result, none of my girls had learned how to ride a bike, an omission that nagged at my conscience.

On that September morning, when I saw Julia turn at the end of the street and pedal back toward me, I told myself: Even if we accomplish nothing else over the next few months, our home-schooling will have been a success. Homeschooling had given us the time and motivation to achieve something important, to master a skill that was long overdue and that might have been neglected for years to come, with all the busy-ness of school and homework, dance class and music lessons.

✦

Three years have passed since that September morning, and now I can tally a host of small achievements that homeschooling made possible. Our year of learning prompted us to step inside buildings I had always walked past, such as the U.S. Supreme Court, the National Archives, and the Governor's Palace at Williamsburg. It inspired us to purchase a wealth of educational materials—card games for math and art and history, puzzles for geography and anatomy, and CDs of French songs. None of these purchases was essential; homeschooling can be accomplished on a shoestring budget, using materials available in nature and at the public library. Nevertheless, all these new items, combined with the inspiration of Julia's example, have left a lasting impression on our family. These days, Kathryn knits, rides a bike, and plays the violin, while Rachel lies beside me in bed with Julia's French book in her lap, saying *"Dors bien, Maman." "Toi aussi, Rachel. Dors bien."*

Above all, homeschooling enabled Julia and me to understand one another more deeply—to witness each other's flaws and strengths and practice the art of patience. I wish I could claim that my angry outbursts have disappeared, and that I am now a model of meditative calm. But who would believe it, especially in a house with four opinionated females? Truth is, the emotional weather in our family alternates between sunshine and storm, with the occasional hurricane looming (never more than a category two). Homeschooling taught Julia and me to comprehend each other's tempests, and to appreciate all chances to bask in warm, cloudless love.

And yet, for all the successes I could recount, my memories remain tinged with the sadness of lost opportunities. What would I do differently, if I had the year to do again? How could I have made Julia's education a little more joyful?

Looking back, I fear that with my professorial habits and constant admiration for John Stuart Mill, I tended to treat my ten-year-old like a miniature college student. Accustomed to teaching young people twice her age, I approached my little pupil as a short, scruffy-haired adult—my coffee shop companion and knitting buddy, not my little girl. Plenty of children yearn to be treated as adults, but Julia's instincts have always pulled in the opposite direction. For her, the grownup world holds no allure, other than the freedom to abandon school. Throughout our year, Julia would probably have liked more chances just to be a kid, running free and clowning around.

Recently I discovered a wonderful book called *Educating Esme*, the diary of a young woman's first year of teaching in Chicago's public schools. Esme Codell taught the fifth grade, and in reading about the quirks, fears, and dreams of her students, I can see how young ten-year-olds really are, and how desperately they want to play. Grandparents are probably able to look at children with such eyes, to appreciate their incredibly fragile youth, and know the value of skipping and shouting and eating candy while you can.

Esme Codell knew how to have fun with kids. In her first year, she planned a Fairy Tale Festival that included a fashion show: "Is fur still 'in' for the Three Bears? What is Cinderella wearing to the ball this season?" She also built a time machine for her class—a huge cardboard box covered in aluminum foil, with a flashing red ambulance-style light on top. The side of the box included dials to imaginatively set the century and place where a child wanted to travel. Inside were beautiful books, and a cozy space for reading alone with a flashlight. No child ever complained that the time machine was a fraud; they emerged from the box with stories of extravagant worlds they had visited.

"Wow," I thought as I envisioned that silver box with its flashing light, "I wish I had read this book before teaching Julia."

Here was a wealth of creative ideas for sparking a child's imagination. Of course, Ms. Esme's pupils were inner-city kids who did not arrive at the fifth grade with Julia's academic skills. They had to be inspired and entertained just to be coaxed into reading, whereas Julia took to books like a bird in flight. Perhaps reading outside on a hammock was just as fun for a child as reading inside a decorated box? I doubt it. A hammock is not a time machine, not a gateway into a spaceship, a safari, or a haunted house. In our average homeschooling day, Julia had many opportunities to absorb the beauties of nature, but not many chances for wild, imaginative adventure.

To Julia's ten-year-old mind, my idea of "fun" was probably as dull as my definition of "cool." I remember a math game we sometimes played in the name of "fun." Julia and I shuffled a deck of cards with all the jacks, kings, and queens removed, then dealt five cards each. Using addition, subtraction, multiplication, and division, we had to separately contemplate the numbers before us, and produce an equation that equaled 1, then 2, then 3. For instance, if Julia's cards read 5, 10, 3, 8, and 4, she might write "$((5 \times 3) - 8) + 4 - 10 = 1$." Then she would deal five new cards and construct an equation that equaled two. Then three, four, and so on, with new cards dealt for each step on the ladder. Together she and I advanced until one of us was stumped. The highest number Julia reached, one wintry day, was twenty-three.

Card games struck me as a creative approach to math, but Julia found them only mildly entertaining. One morning, she peered at me over the cards and said:

"Why don't we ever do holiday worksheets?"

"What do you mean?"

"At school we do decoding worksheets, like at Halloween, where the answers have ghosts and vampires in them."

She meant the kind of puzzle where every correct equation yields a letter to be inserted into a blank space at the bottom of the page. The spaces provide the punch line to some tepid joke: *What happened to the guy who didn't pay his exorcist? He was repossessed.*

Laura Brodie

"You like those worksheets?" I asked, somewhat amazed.

"Everybody likes those." Julia sighed, exasperated with my blunt, middle-age brain.

I had always dismissed those exercises as more useless pulp in the weekly stacks of paper that Julia brought home. It had never occurred to me that she enjoyed these activities, and wanted me to copy them. Julia wanted Thanksgiving hangman games with words like *cornucopia*. She wanted Christmas word search puzzles and connect-the-dot drawings that yielded shamrocks for St. Patrick's Day. Sometimes I complied. I found holiday puzzles and jokes on homeschooling websites, or made them up on my own. But those were rare occasions. More often, I tried to wean my daughter from her childish tastes. I offered her chess when she wanted tic-tac-toe. I gave her acrylics and watercolors and kits of Chinese calligraphy when all she really desired was a new pack of crayons.

If I had the year to do again, I would try to let my ten-year-old act her age.

I would also try to craft assignments better tuned to the habits of Julia's visually oriented brain. Just last month, when I complimented her on how well she knew the stages of osmosis, she shrugged and replied: "Our teacher made us draw it. When I draw things, I learn them."

At that, a tiny light bulb flickered in my dimly lit mind. I always knew that Julia liked to draw, but I never understood how much she learned from drawing. My own language-oriented brain easily absorbs information from a printed page, and from listening to speakers. Julia, however, has a hard time concentrating on other people's nonfiction words, whether printed or spoken. When a teacher begins to lecture, Julia's mind begins to roam.

Drawing helps to keep her thoughts focused. Somehow the

transfer of information from her brain into her fingers and down to her pencil manages to inscribe data within Julia's memory. Had I fathomed that concept earlier, I would have doubled the amount of drawing that she did during our year.

"Draw Africa," I would have said, "and indicate all the major lakes and rivers and national borders. . . . Draw the solar system; draw the human skeleton; draw timelines with small pictures for the major events in the development of the Mayan, Aztec, and Incan civilizations."

Homeschooling could have been Julia's chance to try a year of sketchbook learning.

Ah well—regret is a mother's perennial fate. There is always something that we should have done better, sooner, more lovingly. Especially when it comes to homeschooling, the learning curve is slow and endless. It takes a year of practice, most experts will explain, to understand how to teach one's children. The trouble with short-term efforts is that you quit just when you are starting to get the hang of things.

Professors often feel the same way about sabbaticals. One year barely suffices to get a research project under way, let alone complete it. They return to the classroom temporarily rejuvenated, but with thoughts of everything that waits to be done. And yet, what a wonderful gift sabbaticals are. Adults and children alike need respites from their institutionalized routines, chances to learn and think and grow in new ways, in new settings, with new teachers. Despite its ups and downs, short-term homeschooling strikes me as a wonderful opportunity for any family that has the desire, the academic impulse, and the financial resources to take time off from work to concentrate on their children. It offers a rare chance for parents and kids to gain control of their educations, in a manner that might inspire them to read and write and learn together for years to come. For some families, once they have stepped away from traditional schools, they will never go back.

*

Julia went back. That had always been a nonnegotiable part of our deal. But what was it like for her to return to a public classroom? Was the transition hard, and would she have preferred to stay at home? My friends often asked those questions throughout Julia's sixth-grade year, and the answers were never quick and easy.

Although children who enter the public system after many years at home can find the transition a shock to the system, for Julia, public school was the norm, and homeschooling the anomaly. We took for granted that middle school waited at the end of our road, and my biggest surprise, as we prepared for the new school year, was to learn that not all short-termers expect their child to advance to the next grade. In August, when Julia was busy buying notebooks and pencils and felt-tipped markers, one homeschooling mom explained to me that although her daughter was eligible to enter middle school with Julia, that child was going back to repeat the fifth grade.

"But why?" I asked, taken aback. "Won't she be bored and miss her friends?"

No, this girl had friends in both the fifth and sixth grades; socially, she would be comfortable in either class. She and her mom liked the concept of completing the elementary school experience, and getting more practice in basic skills before reaching middle school. For them, the decision made sense.

For Julia, it would have been torture. Our year had been designed to accomplish more, academically, than could be achieved in a normal classroom. Julia was well prepared for sixth-grade schoolwork. Still, the idea of hanging back was an interesting prospect. Had we embarked on homeschooling with the expectation that Julia would repeat the fifth grade, there might have been advantages.

Above all, our year would have been a lot more relaxed. Removing the assumption that a child will progress to the next grade takes the pressure out of short-term homeschooling. The experience becomes a luxury, an educational bonus with no academic schedule to uphold and no essential skills that must be mastered.

A few days after my conversation with that homeschooling mom, another friend explained that she had long contemplated just such a "bonus year." She dreamed of giving her son nine months of what she called "enrichment," to focus on English, art, and foreign travel. This woman had no interest in keeping up with the usual school curriculum, and if she carried out her scheme, she expected her boy to repeat the grade. That's where her plan hit a brick wall. The child absolutely loathed the stigma of being held back. As John remembered from his own close calls in elementary school, "Being held back is one step above wearing a helmet."

"So long as you keep up with math," I assured that boy's mother, "you could carry out your plan and still move him on to the next grade. All the other subjects get repeated year after year."

The woman smiled and sighed. To her, math was anathema. Homeschooling appealed only if she could avoid all equations. Eventually, she compromised by taking her son abroad for six weeks during the school year, and came back shaking her head.

"I don't know how you did it," she said when we met again in the library. "It was exhausting, trying to require him to read or write, or just settle down. I could never homeschool for a whole year."

"Julia and I sometimes drove each other crazy," I confessed. "It really helped to know that we had a deadline in mind."

Although that deadline had first arrived back in June, with the official start of summer break, I felt it even more tangibly in August, as Julia prepared to enter middle school. A big part of her education was moving out of my hands, and the prospect made me nervous.

My first year of middle school had been rough. I had attended Raleigh's Carnage Junior High, named after Fred J. Carnage, a lawyer who, in 1949, was the first African American appointed to the local school board. The irony of the name was lost on 90 percent of Carnage's students, whose vocabularies were too limited to appreciate the humor.

Carnage enjoyed a decent academic reputation; the problem was getting there. Each morning and afternoon involved a seventy-minute bus ride, which constituted the adolescent equivalent of Lucifer's descent into hell. In the height of some budget-strapped lunacy, Raleigh's school administrators had decided to let high-school students drive the buses, with predictable results. Our sixteen-year-old driver, armed with her newly laminated license, was an avid smoker who bummed cigarettes from the "cool kids" and allowed the bus to become a foggy den of iniquity. On cold winter days, drivers in adjacent lanes were surprised to see billows of smoke plume from our windows whenever we opened them. Meanwhile, the backseat devolved into a notorious brothel, where girls remained perpetually horizontal.

One morning, in her eagerness to please the oldest ninth-grade boys, our driver stopped at a dilapidated corner grocery two blocks from Carnage and let the boys run in and buy several six-packs. (Those were the days before serious ID checks.) The bus roamed the neighborhood for ten extra minutes while the boys held a chugging contest. Every day at Carnage, first period was disrupted by intercom announcements of all the buses arriving fifteen or twenty minutes late, and I often wondered how many of those children had gone on an early morning beer run.

Compared with Carnage, Julia's new school seemed childishly innocent. At Lylburn Downing Middle School there were no buses, and no apparent problems with alcohol, drugs, or tobacco. No girls were visibly pregnant, and in his seven years on the job, the principal had broken up only one fight. "The school is so small," he explained, "I can stand at the door in the morning and look into every kid's face, and know who might be headed for a bad day."

The sixth-grade class that Julia was scheduled to join contained about sixty children—mostly the same kids she had known at Waddell. Her English class would be limited to fifteen, a wonderful student-teacher ratio for any public school, and the teachers seemed smart, friendly, and funny.

As for the building, it was an old 1940s and '50s one-story brick affair, with a tiny library, a primitive cafeteria, and no real auditorium, just a gym with a leaky roof and a small curtained stage. The facilities were so limited that whenever the band teacher wanted a child to practice alone or be videotaped for a solo quiz, she had to set the young musician up in the only space available—a tiny handicapped bathroom. There, children took turns sitting on the toilet, the bell of a French horn pressed into the sink, the slide of a trombone hitting the door.

Nevertheless, LDMS seemed like a good place for Julia.

"I think you'll like it," I said when I dropped her off on the first day. Watching her pale, fragile figure in denim shorts and flip-flops disappear behind the school's heavy doors, I felt the same anxiety as on her first morning of kindergarten—that almost desperate longing for a child to be happy.

Julia entered those doors with a small modicum of confidence.

Over the summer, she had asserted that one year of homeschooling was enough. It was time to rejoin the other kids.

What little enthusiasm she mustered, however, was short-lived. At the end of her first day, Julia collapsed into the backseat of our car and moaned: "There was *no* recess." For seven hours she had remained confined indoors, spending most of her time slumped in a plastic chair, filling out pieces of paper and signing her name in thick, heavy textbooks. In other words, she hated it as much as she had initially hated kindergarten.

"Can you eat lunch outside?" I asked. The school had a small interior courtyard with a few picnic tables.

"Nobody did."

"Didn't you go outside for PE?" Her sixth-grade schedule included PE twice each week.

"We played kickball inside the gym, but we might go outside next week."

For the vast majority of the next nine months, Julia would get no fresh air between 8:15 and 3:00. Although a public park extended to the left of the school, with trees and grass and a covered pavilion perfect for hosting a class of twenty, the teachers rarely used it.

All of this indoor work might have been less irksome if Julia could have spent plenty of time playing outdoors after school. Unfortunately, on the second day she brought home assignments in five subjects, which took all afternoon to complete. In less than forty-eight hours, she had descended back into homework hell.

I suspected that Julia's wandering mind might be dragging out the homework, causing her to spend way too much time, but after polling several parents, I learned that my daughter was not alone. Although some children were breezing through their assignments in ninety minutes, many others shared Julia's plight and were slogging away for twice that long. "Shockwaves of homework," Julia would describe it in later years, when she and Rachel were both struggling with hours of afterschool assignments.

Julia had increased her burden by signing up for Latin, a strong class taught by a quirky veteran teacher who made the students sing their declensions. (Imagine a child warbling "*A . . . A-E . . . A-E . . . A-M*" to the tune of "Tea for Two.") Mrs. Riley's Latin instruction was far superior to anything I could have mustered—one example of the benefits that this school could offer. But Latin involved homework on every school day, weekend, and holiday.

"I have to build a model of the Roman Coliseum," Julia remarked one Friday afternoon in October.

"When it is due?" I asked.

"Monday morning."

My heart sank. Another ruined weekend. One by one our free hours filled with school projects, while family excursions dropped to a minimum.

As for the standard sixth-grade curriculum, it wasn't very hard. Much of it came from old texts that the children followed chapter by chapter, covering Virginia's SOL guidelines. Despite the clear intelligence of Julia's teachers, who engaged their classes in lively conversation, multiple choice still reigned as the most prevalent measure of knowledge, and Julia quickly mastered strategies that had little to do with learning.

"What major strike in 1894 challenged the concept of welfare capitalism?" I asked her one afternoon, reading from one of her quizzes in preparation for a big test.

"It's the answer with a *p* in it," she replied.

"What does the *p* stand for?"

She shrugged.

"The Pullman strike?" I suggested.

"Yeah, that's it." She nodded.

"But what was the Pullman strike about?" I asked. "And what is welfare capitalism?"

"Oh Mom," Julia rolled her eyes. "All I need to know is which word to circle."

All of my gripes from Julia's elementary school days returned with added vigor in middle school: too much multiple choice, too much homework, too much time prepping for standardized tests, and not enough time writing and thinking. Although the English teachers emphasized writing skills, Lylburn Downing as a whole offered minimal writing across the curriculum, and even when papers were assigned, they often were graded but not critiqued. The total quantity of writing instruction was not nearly enough to hone the children's skills.

Not that Julia cared. She was happy to have a break from all the writing I had required in the fifth grade. Multiple-choice quizzes and tests were fine with her, and most of the time she had little problem mastering basic materials. In terms of grades, her chief stumbling block came on her first math test.

"D?" I gawked when she mentioned the results. "Why did you get a D?"

She shrugged, utterly unconcerned. "I got stuck on a problem halfway through the test, so I stopped to think about it, and before I knew it, the class was over."

I could envision Julia at her desk, getting lost in the world of a word problem, unmindful of the clock and her classmates carrying their tests up to the teacher. The previous spring we had reviewed test-taking skills, devoting extra attention to time management. Now I repeated the same advice, and over the next few weeks Julia grew accustomed to the norms of middle-school work and began to make excellent grades. Still, she displayed no pride in the accomplishment, no particular concern about whether her quarterly report card contained As or Cs. Good grades were her concession to me and my academic mind-set; they were signposts from an adult's world of paperwork that she abhorred.

"Would you study for this test if I didn't require you to do it?" I asked her on one occasion.

She shrugged. "Probably not."

"Would you write the papers for your English class?"

"Maybe," she said. "It depends on whether I liked the topic."

I might have called her lazy, except for the pages of unfinished short stories that lay around her bedroom, and for the hours she spent reading and composing tunes on the piano. Julia was not averse to intellectual activity; she was just allergic to school.

Take her out! I can hear the homeschoolers cry. Why subject a child to a traditional school if its academic deficiencies are apparent, and the child is not thriving? Many times I felt the urge to yank Julia out of Lylburn Downing, but I was well aware of the failures in my own teaching, and Julia needed daily exposure to social situations even more than she needed practice writing paragraphs.

Unfortunately, middle school is a miserable place to learn social skills. Especially for girls, early adolescence is at best a difficult journey, at worst, a painful crucible.

"These girls are scary," one mom of an eleven-year-old boy remarked to me after his second day in the sixth grade. "Have you seen what they are wearing?"

Yes, I had noticed. While some of Julia's peers still preferred their elementary fashions—loose blue jeans and T-shirts and dirty-white sneakers—others seemed to have leaped from fifth grade straight to high school, donning tight high-cut shorts and tighter low-cut shirts. Here were cosmetics in endless variety: lipstick and gloss, eye shadow and liner, rouged cheeks and pedicured toes, all accompanied by high-priced accessories, seventy-dollar flip-flops, designer purses, and manicured nails thumbing text messages into cell phones.

Julia stood staunchly in the anti-fashion camp. On the days when she chose to exert some effort . . . behold, the duckling was a swan! But most mornings, when I looked at her wrinkled shirts, unbrushed hair, and dirty fingernails, I felt that I was raising a young Janis Joplin.

For many of Julia's peers, decisions about hair care and clothing seemed calculated to catch the eyes of boys. During the first week of middle school, Julia walked into the bathroom and encountered a couple of girls chatting about which boys were cute, which boys they liked, and, more important, which boys might like *them*.

"Who do you like, Julia?" they asked.

My eleven-year-old replied with absolute honesty, "I'm too young for that."

"Good for you," I said when she described the incident later that night, but I dreaded the social minefield that lay ahead. It startled me, in the coming weeks, to overhear sixth-grade girls flirting diligently with boys and dreaming aloud about Saturday night dates.

"How prevalent is dating in the sixth grade?" I asked one of Julia's peers.

"Oh, *everyone* dates," she asserted, although I had my doubts. From what I could tell, a "date" usually meant a group gathering at the movies. Still, many of the middle-school girls seemed obsessed with the idea that if they weren't dating, they should be, and Lylburn Downing contributed to the carnival of prepubescent hormones by holding monthly dances.

"A dance every *month*?" I gasped when a friend first told me about the middle-school social calendar. I couldn't recall my junior high ever holding a dance, and my high school managed it only three times each year, thank God.

"Isn't that a lot of social pressure for the kids?"

"Oh, the dances are tame," this mom assured me. "The kids enjoy them."

She was right that the dances offered nothing fancy—just social gatherings in the gymnasium, sponsored by athletic teams and afterschool clubs that reaped the two-dollar admission charge and profits from snack sales and raffles. Mostly the kids stood clustered in circles talking, watched by handfuls of parent chaperones and one burly policeman, who stood with arms crossed at the front stage, eyeing groups of boys gathered at the bleachers.

When the time came for a group dance, a large crowd of girls gathered on the floor and shuffled around in rows, with a few brave boys joining in. But the excitement of each evening centered on the slow dances, when the girls watched eagerly to see which couples would assemble with bodies pressed together. The principal occasionally walked over to separate male and female flesh, trying to establish a three-inch rule, but the teenagers merged together again as soon as he walked away.

It's clear why some conservative Christian homeschoolers have fled the public schools, with sex education introduced by age nine and slow-dancing by age eleven. Whenever I pondered Lylburn Downing's world of dancing and dating, I was reminded of the Beardsley School for Girls in Nabokov's *Lolita*. There the curriculum focused on "Dramatics, Dance, Debating, and Dating," much to the consternation of Humbert Humbert. As headmistress Pratt explained, "Dr. Hummer, do you realize that for the modern pre-adolescent child, medieval dates are of less vital value than weekend ones [twinkle]?"

✦

Middle-school rites of passage are an education unto themselves, and for Julia, there has been value in muddling through the rituals of the preadolescent world. But now, as I write these pages, she is finishing the eighth grade, preparing for high school in the fall, and whenever I ask her to look back and ponder the pros and cons of homeschooling versus traditional schools, her response is emphatic:

"Homeschooling is better, because you get to feel that you are remotely in control of your own education. And the scenery changes: in school, I'm stuck in the same building for seven hours every day.

"The only problem with homeschooling," she adds, "is the socialization, because let's face it, Mom, you and I mostly hung out with a lot of *old* people."

At Lylburn Downing, Julia could hang out on the girls' tennis team. She could play in a band filled with kids her own age, and work on group projects with very bright classmates who wrote mini-plays and stories and shared her love of drawing. But all the social interaction didn't compensate for the hours of mind-numbing boredom.

"Being in school," Julia remarked, "feels like sitting in a chair and having someone with a power tool drill holes into your head." Her only escape, she explained, was to get lost in her thoughts, just as she had done in elementary school. "There is a space between being consciously present and being asleep, and in most classes I try to get my mind into that halfway zone. It helps to make the time go by faster, and that's key, because school is a lot like sitting in an airport. The one thing I've learned is how to pass the time."

Those might sound like the words of a child aching for another homeschooling sabbatical, but they are also the sentiments of a thirteen-year-old, and teenage girls don't want more time at home with Mom. In the past year, when faced with my daughter's dreary assessment of school, the one alternative I've been tempted to try is an odd variation on the usual home-ed model: part-time homeschooling.

Two years ago one of my friends thought to remove her rising eighth-grade son from Lylburn Downing, citing concerns that ranged from bullying to a desire to enjoy more time with her child. Her boy still wanted to play with the school's jazz band, but when she asked the principal if that was okay, he said that the student could continue with the band only if he took at least two other classes—the minimum required for the school to receive state funding for a child. The principal's suggestion turned out well for the boy; he took algebra, band, and geography at middle school, and stayed home for English, science, and foreign languages, taught primarily by private tutors. It was a well-timed break for the kid, who entered high school on a full-time basis the following year.

That mixture of public schooling and home education strikes me as an intriguing compromise. I would be happy to have someone else teach my daughters algebra, Latin, and science, and Julia would cheerfully stick with her school's tennis team and art classes. But when it comes to English and all forms of history, ideally my girls would follow a curriculum freed from state mandates and multiple choice, and filled with constant writing.

I once asked the principal if any parent could remove a child for a third, or even half, of each school day, to pursue their own homeschooling. "Yes, that's possible," he said, nodding. "In our system, parents can pretty much do whatever they want. I'd discourage it if a family were just trying to avoid a certain teacher, but if they had a special opportunity planned for a child, that would be okay."

One afternoon I asked Julia what she would think of leaving school after two thirds of each day, to audit my freshman literature and composition class at Washington and Lee. She would read the same texts as the college students, ranging from Chaucer's "Wife of Bath's Tale" to short stories by Alice Walker and Flannery O'Connor, and between listening to the undergraduates' discussion and writing papers that I would critique, she could get a sense of what a college English class involved. But Julia didn't jump at the chance. She balked at the idea of sitting in a room with eighteen-year-olds; the world of young adults was too intimidating.

And now that high school is approaching, the chances of more homeschooling for Julia are fast slipping away. Home education at the senior-high level has never appealed to me, because the stakes are so much greater than in elementary school, with college admission on the line. I couldn't teach most high-school subjects, and I've never been tempted to juggle tutors and community college classes—the usual plan for my homeschooling friends with high-school-age children. For now, it seems that Julia's homeschooling will occur in orchestra rehearsals and trips abroad, in dinner table conversations and in books and films that our family shares. Freed from all assignments and pressures, I hope that she and I will indulge together in the pleasures of learning for years to come.

As for her sisters, I sometimes wonder if Rachel would enjoy a semester of part-time homeschooling. This child who has already begun to read the classics, and whose memory is keen as a sharpened blade, would benefit from greater challenges and fewer hours of homework. But Rachel remains fascinated with the ins and outs of social behavior, enjoying her friends at school and attending every dance. For both Rachel and Julia, "homeschooling" is likely to mean "afterschooling": reading together, sharing concerts, and planting a garden.

Finally, there's Kathryn, currently in the third grade, advancing through Waddell with social and academic ease, but with limited interest in reading and writing. There, perhaps, lies an opportunity—a child happy to spend time with Mom who could benefit from a year of individually tailored learning.

Perhaps I could design a special fifth-grade experience for her, something that would spark a lasting passion for words. Perhaps I could learn from the mistakes and triumphs of my year with Julia, beginning from day one with more patience, more humor, and more openness to outrageous fun.

I recently asked Kathryn, "How do you spell Wednesday?"

She looked into my eyes and replied with absolute certainty, "W-E-N-D-S-D-A-Y," and I thought I heard, in those jumbled letters, the tones of an invitation.

Thinking About Homeschooling?
Ten Great Resources for Getting Started

Books

The First Year of Homeschooling Your Child: Your Complete Guide to Getting Off to the Right Start. Linda Dobson. Three Rivers Press, 2001, 360 pp.

Linda Dobson is America's most prolific author of home-schooling guides, and parents often find her work invaluable. *The First Year of Homeschooling* outlines nine different home education styles, describing curriculums, resources, and common mistakes to avoid. Popular and accessible.

The Well-Trained Mind. Susan Wise Bauer and Jessie Wise. 3rd edition, Norton, 2009, 864 pp.

A homeschooling classic for those who want an intensive academic experience centered on language. This mother-and-daughter homeschooling team outlines an ambitious classical education based on the trivium, with emphasis on grammar, rhetoric, and logic. Art and music receive short shrift, and there is little attention to friends, family bonds, and fun. At 864 pages this is a somewhat intimidating, but very inspiring reference book not only for homeschoolers, but for parents of public and private schoolers who want to supplement their children's education.

Home Learning Year by Year: How to Design a Homeschool Curriculum from Preschool Through High School. Rebecca Rupp. Three Rivers Press, 2000, 432 pp.

Rupp's comprehensive book can help parents keep a curriculum on track from pre-K through twelfth grade. She suggests what should be covered in each grade, how to prioritize, and recommends books for each subject. Parents can supplement with their own interests.

Family Matters: Why Homeschooling Makes Sense. David Guterson, Harvest Books, 1993, 264 pp.

Before becoming the award-winning author of *Snow Falling on Cedars*, Guterson lived the paradox of teaching English in a Washington State public high school, while joining with his wife to homeschool three sons. This lyrical book, set against a beautiful Pacific Northwest background, focuses more on why to homeschool than how, discussing the pros and cons, and ultimately coming down in favor of choices for all families.

Homeschooling for Excellence. David and Micki Colfax. Grand Central Publishing, 1988, 172 pp.

An "oldie but goodie." Throughout the 1970s and '80s, these teachers-turned-ranchers homeschooled four sons on their forty-acres in California, eventually sending three to Harvard. Believing that children learn best by doing, the Colfaxes offered their boys lessons in biology and geometry derived from tending animals and building a homestead. But they also delved into plenty of books, from math to literature. The Colfaxes' manifesto helped to inspire the first generation of homeschoolers, while stressing that homeschooling was for parents who had the financial freedom to avoid full-time jobs.

Internet

A to Z Home's Cool

Ann Zeise provides news, analysis, homeschooling facts, and plenty of links to homeschooling products and information on the web, all in a friendly, colorful layout. (homeschooling .gomilpitas.com) Check out her new blog at a2zhomeschool.com.

Homeschool.com

If you are ready to spend money, this site showcases home-schooling products, and gives away plenty of freebies. You can purchase a "Getting Started eKit," or download complimentary homeschooling reports. Homeschooling information abounds, so it can get a little overwhelming. (www.homeschool.com)

The Homeschool Lounge

This online community offers a lively place to chat, watch videos, and connect with thousands of homeschooling moms. (www .thehomeschoollounge.com) But what about homeschooling dads? They might want to know about Henry Cate, a friendly and knowledgeable resource who maintains the low-key Why Homeschool blog with Janine and Derek Cate. (whyhomeschool .blogspot.com)

About.com: Homeschooling

If you prefer the About.com layout, Beverly Hernandez is their Homeschooling Guide, maintaining a wealth of informa-tion, loads of printable worksheets, a blog, and an active forum for discussion. (www.homeschooling.about.com)

Home Education Magazine

In print or online, *Home Education Magazine* has articles, interviews, book reviews, and a mass of useful information. Around for twenty-six years, HEM is the most established homeschooling magazine in the country. (www.homeedmag.com)

Acknowledgments

MANY PEOPLE HAVE HELPED TO BRING THIS STORY TO life. Above all I want to thank my family for their patience and openness in sharing their experiences with the larger world. I am also grateful for the kindness of all the people of Lexington and Rockbridge County, Virginia, who appear (with names changed) in these pages—especially all the teachers who have influenced my daughters' lives. Special thanks go to Donna Pagnam, for her knowledge of French; Stephanie Wilkinson and Jennifer Niesslein, editors of *Brain, Child* magazine, for publishing my first article on homeschooling; and to Jeanette Coleman and Katherine Tomlin, for the hours of free childcare that have enabled me to write all my books.

Finally, this memoir would never have reached the public without the vision and hard work of my agent, Laurie Abkemeier, who saw its potential and has guided every step, and my editor, Gail Winston, who helped to shape my fledgling manuscript into a much stronger narrative.

About the Author

L AURA BRODIE RECEIVED HER B.A. FROM HARVARD AND her Ph.D. from the University of Virginia. The author of two previous books, *Breaking Out: VMI and the Coming of Women*, and *The Widow's Season*, a novel, she teaches English at Washington and Lee University, and lives in Lexington, Virginia, with her husband and three daughters.